sheet metal
metal
shop practice

Leo A. Meyer

American Technical Publishers, Inc.
Alsip, Illinois 60658

preface

Sheet metal plays an essential role in all aspects of our everyday lives. Its many applications include agriculture; building construction; household, office, laboratory and shop equipment; heating and air conditioning; and all kinds of transportation.

This new Fourth Edition of SHEET METAL SHOP PRACTICE is designed to present the basic skills and knowledge necessary for developing competent and professional workers in all aspects of the sheet metal industry. It provides a useful, thorough training tool for the vocational student or apprentice, as well as an invaluable work for the professional tradesman.

The new Fourth Edition of SHEET METAL SHOP PRACTICE has been updated and revised throughout. Terminology has been updated and many new illustrations provided. New chapters have been added to discuss in detail the materials and fasteners used in the sheet metal trade. A section on job opportunities, training and apprenticeship has also been included in Chapter 1. Chapter 3, "Safety in the Sheet Metal Shop," has been expanded to include welding, power tools, noise control and housekeeping. A glossary has been added which contains trade terms that will be useful to the student.

Chapter 18, "Plastics," has been extensively researched and rewritten by Mr. Alfred del'Etoile, associated with the firm of Delbrook Engineering since 1958 in various capacities from Purchasing Agent to President. Mr. del'Etoile has been invited to a number of conventions to speak on the subject of plastic fabrication. In addition he served on the committee that wrote Chapter 56 "Welding of Plastics" for the American Welding Society, *Welding Handbook*, Sixth Edition. He also served as chairman of the Plastics Application Committee of the Sheet Metal and Air Conditioning Contractors' National Association, Inc. that published the *Thermoplastic Duct Construction Manual*.

Mr. Robert E. Powell, Supervisor of Vocational Education of San Jose Unified School District, carefully read over the revised text and made invaluable suggestions. Mr. Powell has been actively engaged in teaching and supervising sheet metal programs for over 29 years. He has also been actively engaged in preparing and writing sheet metal apprenticeship instructional material for the California State Department of Education.

Mr. Clifford Burnett, Assistant Sales Manager of the Peck, Stowe & Wilcox Co., also made many suggestions for updating the material and adding the newest techniques.

The Publisher

contents

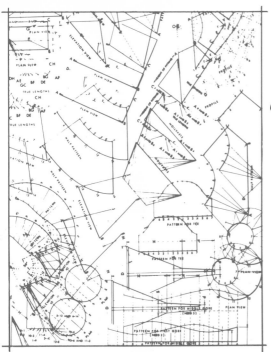

opportunities unlimited

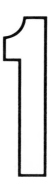

When you finish this chapter, you should be able to:
1. List at least five different jobs in the sheet metal industry, and describe the basic duties of each.
2. List and explain at least five uses of sheet metal in the trades and in industry.
3. List the areas of shop work in which the skilled sheet metal worker must be proficient.

What are the potentials awaiting you as a qualified sheet metal worker in the United States today? The range of opportunities are as wide as your abilities and they will carry you as far as the amount of time and work you are willing to invest in your future. Sheet metal workers are vital to expanding American industry. As the possessor of a much needed and wanted vocational skill, the sheet metal worker is assured of employment and good wages anywhere in the United States.

Job Categories

The jobs in the sheet metal industry are unlimited in variety and opportunity. The one you fill depends a great deal upon your interests and inclinations. However there are definite categories of jobs within the industry. Some of these are as follows.

Sheet Metal Worker

A sheet metal worker may perform

all of the jobs listed below or he may specialize in one area only. The skilled sheet metal worker who is able to do all of these jobs well is the all-around journeyman who draws the highest pay and who is always in demand.

Other sheet metal workers may be able to work efficiently in only a few of these areas and others may work only in one. Naturally, the fewer areas in which a worker can perform skillfully, the less job opportunities there are, and the less the wages.

Sheet Metal Layout Man. Lays out patterns in the sheet metal shop for any type of object that is to be made from sheet metal. Works in the sheet metal shop.

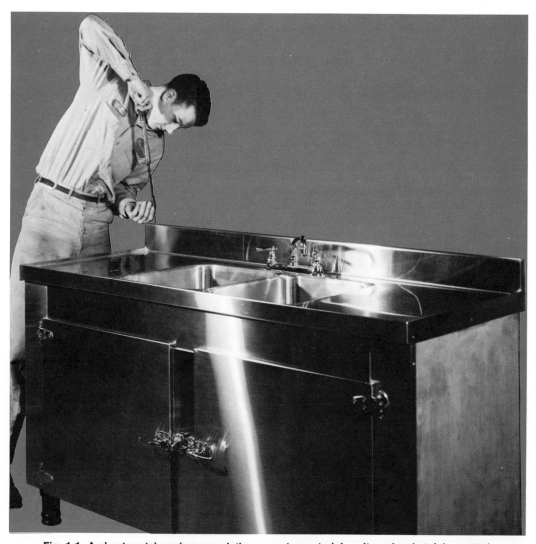

Fig. 1-1. A sheet metal worker completing a restaurant sink unit made of stainless steel.

Sheet Metal Fabricator. Often is the same person who does the pattern layout. Shears, forms, bends, and sometimes assembles all types of sheet metal objects. Works in the sheet metal shop.

Air Conditioning and Ventilation Installation. Installs air conditioning and ventilation ducts and equipment in new and old buildings. Works on the construction site. Work is usually in an unfinished building.

Outside Sheet Metal Worker. Installs all types of sheet metal objects and equipment, including air conditioning systems and ventilation ducts, gutters, furnaces, ventilating hoods, restaurant equipment, sheet metal roofs, flashing, vents, louvers and ornamental sheet metal such as copper hoods. Works inside and outside of buildings. Work is usually on new buildings.

Stainless Steel Worker. Lays out, fabricates, and installs all types of objects made from stainless steel, especially restaurant sinks, tables, hoods and other food preparation equipment. Works inside of buildings. See Fig. 1-1.

Ventilation Man. Lays out, fabricates, and installs duct work for air conditioning, ventilating and exhaust fumes. Works both in the shop and on the job.

Welder. Sets up and welds heavy gage sheet metal items which have been fabricated by the sheet metal worker. See Fig. 1-2.

Architectural Sheet Metal Worker. Lays out, fabricates, and installs sheet metal items such as louvers, skylights, gutters, hoods, roofs and cornices on new and old buildings.

Precision Sheet Metal Worker. Constructs all types of sheet metal objects for the electronics industry, working

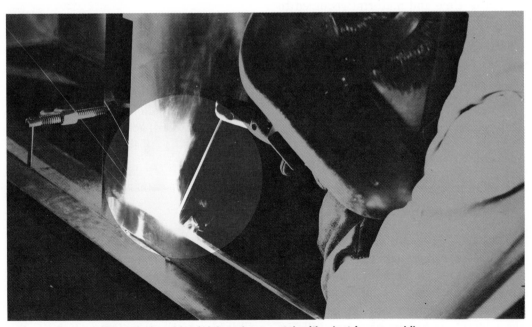

Fig. 1-2. A welder joining sheet metal with electric arc welding.

within extremely accurate dimensional tolerances.

Production Sheet Metal Worker. Works in assembly-line operations that produce large numbers of a particular sheet metal object. Generally a semi-skilled worker that performs only one or two operations of a process.

Power Machine Operator. Operates heavy duty power machinery such as a ten foot press brake or a ten foot shear. Generally operates one particular machine. See Fig. 1-3.

Air Conditioning Man. Installs, services and repairs all types of air conditioning equipment and controls connected with air conditioning systems. Works on the job in new and old buildings.

Fig. 1-3. A high production press operator making an electronic setting. (Niagara Machine & Tool Works)

Sheet Metal Estimator

Picks off material from blueprints or makes measurements in buildings and estimates time and material required to do a particular job. Works mostly in an office.

Sheet Metal Contractor

Owns and supervises a sheet metal shop which contracts for fabricating and installing air conditioning systems and other sheet metal items in new and old buildings.

Salesman

The salesman sells air conditioning equipment and sheet metal objects. He visits potential clients in the field on a regular basis, soliciting fabrication and installation contracts.

Job Training and Apprenticeship

The choice of your particular job in the sheet metal industry is something that need not be made immediately. Your first step is to acquire some understanding of what can be done with sheet metal, and to build some skills in processing sheet metal. Then you will be better equipped for deciding where your eventual career in sheet metal lays. Generally this first step in determining your career in sheet metal is to attend a class which gives instruction in the knowledge and skills needed in the trade.

After completing such a class, the next step is a training job such as helper, trainee or apprentice. In many cases, this first entry job is a formal apprenticeship. A formal apprenticeship is an organized on-the-job training procedure through which the novice can gradually advance to journeyman sheet metal worker. Apprenticeship programs are strongest where there is a strong labor union. The apprenticeship program is governed locally by a Joint Apprenticeship Committee which is composed of sheet metal workers and employers of sheet metal workers. This committee works under the general rules of the particular state concerning apprenticeship programs, but operates the local program by approving shops for training apprentices, approving applicants for apprentice jobs programs, and governing the number of apprentices in the local program so that there is always work for each apprentice. If you become an apprentice you will sign an *Apprenticeship Agreement*. This is an agreement between the Joint Apprenticeship Committee and you which sets forth the conditions of the apprenticeship. Fig. 1-4 shows a typical Apprenticeship Agreement from the State of California. Generally the following things are covered.

Length of Apprenticeship

For sheet metal workers the length of apprenticeship is usually four years, but this can be shortened by the Joint Apprenticeship Committee if they feel that an individual merits more rapid

advancement. Some Committees advance new apprentices that have completed a sheet metal training program prior to apprenticeship.

Related Education

In most states an apprentice is required to attend evening school for Related Training Classes for the term of the apprenticeship. These are classes which instruct in the related knowledge of the occupation such as pattern drafting, related mathematics and sheet metal tools and equipment. In most cases, the Joint Apprenticeship Committee has the power to invoke disciplinary procedures against apprentices who are not attending class or who are not doing well in class. This is usually in the form of suspension from the job, either temporarily or permanently.

Rate of Pay

The apprentice's pay is determined as a percentage of the journeyman's pay scale. The percentages vary, but in general the apprentice begins the first six month period at 40 to 50 percent of journeyman's wages. For instance, if a journeyman's pay scale is $8.00 per hour and the apprentice's scale is 50 percent, then the apprentice is paid $4.00 per hour. In general, the apprentice pay scale provides for a 5 or 10 percent increase every six month period. At the end of 3½ years (the start of the eighth period) the apprentice generally receives 80 to 90 percent of journeyman's wages. At the end of the eighth period, the apprentice becomes

Dis.	Co.	DAS File #	DOT Code	Cons.	Cor.	Type	Start		Complete		Hours	Age	Vet.	Stat.
2	2	5	9	3	1	1	1	2	1	2	2	2	1	1

APPRENTICE AGREEMENT

STATE OF CALIFORNIA

DEPARTMENT OF INDUSTRIAL RELATIONS
Division of Apprenticeship Standards

Apprentice name

Social Security Number

Address (Number and street, city and zip code)

County of residence

Occupation

Term of apprenticeship

Straight time

In agreement with

hours within _____ years   Hours per day   Hours per week

AGREEMENT:

The undersigned parties mutually agree that they will use their best endeavors to secure employment and training for the apprentice. The apprentice agrees to perform satisfactorily all work and learning assignments. The provisions of the Apprenticeship Standards for the above occupation adopted by the employer and/or the union and/or the apprenticeship committee and approved by the Administrator of Apprenticeship, are hereby made a part of this agreement. An official copy of said standards is on file in the headquarters of the Division of Apprenticeship Standards. This apprentice agreement will continue in effect until the training is completed or otherwise terminated in accordance with the standards.

EVALUATION:

The apprentice commenced training under these standards on _____, 19_____. He is accredited with having

_____ months toward completion of his apprenticeship work experience and training prior to the above date. He is

expected to complete his apprenticeship on _____, 19_____.

SIGNATURES:

_____   _____
Apprentice   Employer

_____   _____
Birthday   Address

Veteran: Yes_____   No_____   By _____

C No._____   _____
                                                    Title

_____
Parent or Guardian

AGREED AND APPROVED

_____
Apprenticeship Committee

_____   _____
Secretary/Chairman   Date

_____
Apprenticeship Consultant

DAS 1-A (6-71)

Fig. 1-4. A typical apprentice agreement. (State of California Division of Apprenticeship Standards)

a journeyman and receives 100 percent of journeyman's pay.

In thinking of apprenticeship, you must remember that its main purpose is to provide adequate education and training for young men who wish to learn the sheet metal trade thoroughly. Also remember that it provides a rigorous four-year training program that qualifies the apprentice for a responsible position, earning an extremely good income. Therefore the Joint Apprenticeship Committees are extremely selective in choosing new apprentices from the applicants and choose only the best students who appear very likely to succeed. The Joint Apprenticeship Committee also limits the number of apprentices that can be employed by a particular shop. This is for two reasons. One is that the apprentice is supposed to be taught the trade. Too many apprentices in a shop will mean that the apprentices will be used for cheap labor instead of being taught the basic skills of the trade. Too many apprentices in one shop can also mean that some apprentices may be unemployed during slow seasons. This is something the Committees try to avoid.

Career Advancement in Sheet Metal Work

During your apprenticeship or other training period, you can earn good wages while you plan for the next step of your career. By the completion of your training you will have a good idea of what parts of the trade appeal to you most. Then you can work towards developing the additional special skills required for these areas.

It may be that you decide that you get the greatest satisfaction from general sheet metal work and from being the best sheet metal journeyman possible. If so, you will continue your education in related areas such as welding, drafting and mathematics. You will also develop more skills to work expertly in all aspects of the occupation.

Or perhaps you will find the greatest satisfaction in the business aspects of the occupation. If so, you will pursue some business education courses to add to your sheet metal skills, so that you can become a successful contractor.

On the other hand maybe you will find the most satisfaction in dealing with people. In this case, you may attend courses in salesmanship to become a salesman of sheet metal products. You may take courses in drafting and mathematics with the goal of becoming a sheet metal estimator. Or you may take courses in supervision if your eventual aim is to become a shop foreman, general manager, or supervisor.

The main point is that learning the sheet metal trade is not a dead end job, but instead is an open door to almost any type of career you wish. Acquiring skills at sheet metal work will provide you with immense satisfaction and will also provide you with a way to earn an excellent income and independence while you prepare for the next step of your career.

As you can see, the breadth of activities possible for you within the sheet metal field is very great. Though the uses of sheet metal are too numerous to list here, some of the major industries in which it is obvious that sheet metal plays an important part are heating and air conditioning, roofing, aircraft and shipbuilding, freight cars, refrigeration, steel furniture, cabinets and restaurant and cafeteria installations.

Federal government buildings, including the White House are roofed with sheet metal which adds beauty as well as fire resistance. The most modern of America's new office buildings employ sheet metal extensively in their complex heating and air conditioning systems. Sheet metal applications exist in nearly every building, automobile, plane, ship and train built in the United States.

Fundamentals of Sheet Metal Work

The term sheet metal generally applies to metals and alloys in sheets rolled to thicknesses ranging from ten gage and thinner, according to union agreements. (Chapter 4 will acquaint you with the various metals used in sheet metal work and their properties along with the gage system of measurement.)

Whatever area of sheet metal work you eventually specialize in, a thorough knowledge of sheet metal fundamentals is indispensable. These essentials in the trade will be presented to you in succeeding chapters.

Sheet metal work can be roughly divided into five phases:
1. Planning and layout
2. Fabrication
3. Assembly
4. Installation
5. Repair and Maintenance

Planning and Layout

Planning and layout work is concerned with the steps by which a flat piece of sheet metal is formed into the finished article. Specifically, through the use of tools and methods explained in Chapters 5, 11, 12, 13, 14, and 15, patterns are traced or drawn on the flat sheet of metal in order to serve as a guide for the operations to follow. Drafting, layout, and pattern development must be done with care and accuracy.

Fabrication

The flat sheet metal with the layout on it is fabricated through a number of different operations. These steps vary from job to job. Some of the more common ones are cutting, explained in Chapter 7, turning, burring, and raising, explained in Chapter 10, folding, edging, and making seams, explained in Chapter 9, forming, grooving, crimping, and beading, explained in Chapter 11, and notching patterns explained in Chapter 14. Figs. 1-5, 1-6 and 1-7 show some of these operations being performed by a sheet metal worker. Fig. 1-8 shows a student in a school shop.

Fig. 1-5. Trimming sheet metal with squaring shears.

Fig. 1-6. The adjustable bar folder is used to make seams in sheet metal.

Assembly

Next, individual articles or parts, now shaped and formed, are connected as specified. Such connections may be made in a number of ways. For example, they may be punched, drilled or riveted, as explained in Chapter 8; or they may be soldered, which is explained in Chapter 12.

Installation, Repair and Maintenance

Installation, and repair and maintenance require a good working knowledge of the product, and often involve connecting skills such as drilling, etc., hoisting and scaffolding work, finishing skills (using both hand and power tools such as chisels and buffers). They also require some understanding of basic construction practices. Fig. 1-9 shows a typical sheet metal air-conditioning-heating ductwork installation.

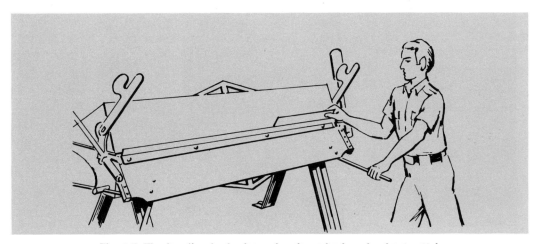

Fig. 1-7. The bending brake forms bends and edges in sheet metal.

Fig. 1-8. A student in a school shop learning the sheet metal trade. (Photo by Rombough)

Fig. 1-9. Sheet metal worker installing a filter in an air conditioning system.

Class Activities

1. Do you think that plastics will entirely replace sheet metal? Be prepared to discuss this in class.

2. In class, list as many jobs as possible that are connected and related to the sheet metal occupation. Check the ones in which a knowledge of the sheet metal trade would be helpful.

3. Should you make the decision now on what your career will be—or should it be postponed until later? Be prepared to defend your position.

4. Invite a sheet metal contractor and a sheet metal labor union official to meet with the class to answer questions about the occupation and about wages and job opportunities.

Ask them to describe their career in sheet metal. How did they reach the position they are now in?

5. Locate at least five completed projects in the shop and identify what they are used for.

STUDENT QUESTIONS AND ACTIVITIES

1. List at least five different jobs in the sheet metal industry and describe the basic duties of each.

2. List at least two jobs in the sheet metal industry that you think you would like. Give your reasons why you think you would like them, in terms of your likes, dislikes, personality, and hobbies.

3. For one day, write a list of all the items you see that are made of sheet metal. Try to separate them into items made by hand and items made on a production line.

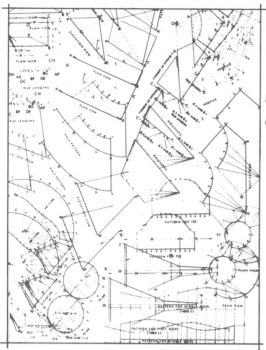

sheet metal working tools and machinery

2

When you complete this chapter, you should be able to:
1. List and describe the use of at least 10 sheet metal working hand tools.
2. Identify by their proper name, all the hand tools shown in this chapter.
3. Identify by their proper name all of the snips shown in this chapter.
4. Identify all the sheet metal working machines shown in this chapter, by their proper name and describe their basic purpose.
5. With a drawing, be able to explain the difference between a single cut file and a double cut file, and explain the advantages of each.
6. Explain the difference between a hand brake, a bar folder, and a press brake.
7. Draw a sectional view of the wheels on the burring machine, the turning machine, and the elbow machine.
8. Explain the difference between *crimping* and *bending*.
9. Identify by name, at least 3 out of 5 stakes when shown the stake or a picture of it.

One of the characteristics of the skilled worker is the way in which he selects and uses the tools of his trade. For this reason, it is essential that you know how to select and properly use both the hand and machine tools of the sheet metal trade. You will find that when you do this, the quality of your work will improve, you will save valuable time and your work will be easier. When you have completed reading this chapter and can associate the proper tool with the proper operation, you have taken the first step toward becoming a successful sheet metal craftsman.

Hand Tools

Sheet metal hand tools are used to scribe or measure lines, perform layout operations and shape or cut metal. Some of the hand tools described in the following pages actually perform these operations, while others, such as stakes and some punches, serve as aids in performing them.

Scratch Awls

There are three common types of scratch awls (also called scribers) as shown in Fig. 2-1. All three awls perform the same function of marking lines on metals. Lines are marked on metal for a variety of purposes in laying out patterns.

Ring Scratch Awl. The ring scratch awl is made of one solid piece of steel approximately eight inches long with a tapered point on one end and a ring on the other.

Socket Scratch Awl. The socket scratch awl has a steel blade approximately five inches long and is made with a replaceable wooden handle.

Shank Type Scratch Awl. For general purposes, this shank type of scratch awl is preferred by most sheet metal mechanics since the steel blade passes through the handle, reinforcing the top.

Dividers

Dividers, such as the wing dividers, shown in Fig. 2-2, are made with each straight leg tapered to a needle point. These wing type dividers may be adjusted to any position by loosening the knurled screw, changing the distance between points and then tightening the screw to retain the desired distance between points. Dividers are manufactured in a number of sizes and types and are used to space off equal distances, to divide lines into equal parts and to scribe arcs and circles.

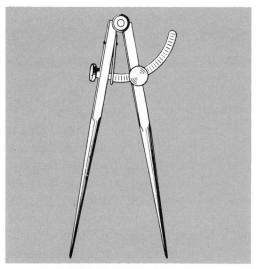

Fig. 2-2. Wing dividers transfer dimensions and scribe arcs and circles.

RING   SOCKET   SHANK TYPE

Fig. 2-1. Typical scratch awls.

Steel Square

The steel square shown in Fig. 2-3 is invaluable for accurate layout work in pattern drafting since all layout must start from a square corner. The long arm of the square is known as the *body* (also called *blade*), and the short arm is called the *tongue*. Squares are manufactured in a number of sizes.

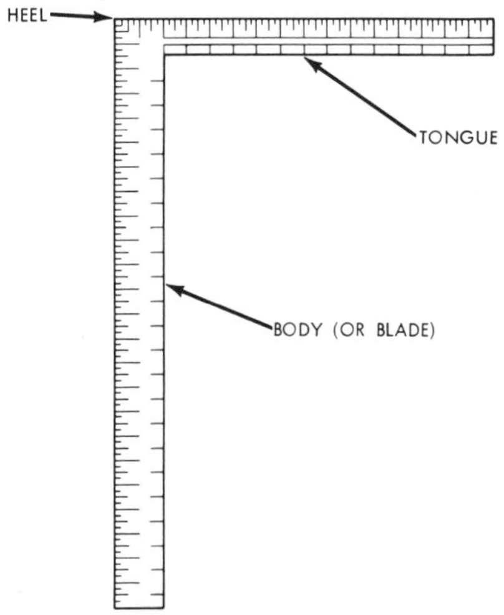

of the points can be moved and often one point has a fine adjustment for more accurate setting. A special clamp for a pencil can be attached to one of the points.

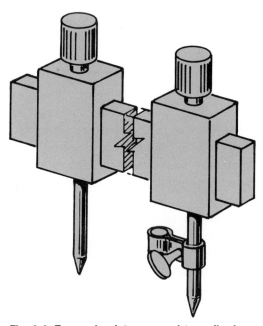

Fig. 2-3. The steel square is used for accuracy in transferring layouts.

Fig. 2-4. Trammel points are used to scribe large circles and arcs.

Trammel Points

Trammel points (sometimes called a beam compass), shown in Fig. 2-4, are instruments used for drawing large circles, arcs, etc. They are manufactured in various types with two straight, removable legs tapered to needle points and attached to separate heads or holders. These heads or holders slide on wood or steel bars or beams, and are held in place by thumbscrews. Either

Rules

Rule instruments are manufactured in a variety of lengths and types; each of which is designed for measuring or laying out different work.

Folding Rule. The six-foot-length folding rule is commonly used for taking job measurements in sheet metal work.

Steel Circumference Rule. The steel circumference rule, used much like the common rule, is invaluable for laying out patterns. Its length is 36 inches or 48 inches; the upper edge having a standard graduation of $\frac{1}{16}$ inch. The lower edge is designed for finding the circumference of a cylinder. The reverse side of the rule contains information to aid the sheet metal worker including: the sizes of 60 objects such as pails, measures, cans, etc., with straight or flaring sides, flat or pitched top; liquid and dry measure in quarts, gallons and bushels.

Tape Rule. The tape rule, either in 6 foot or 12 foot lengths is becoming popular for taking measurements of a job. The various types of rules are shown in Fig. 2-5.

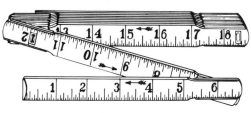

FOLDING RULE

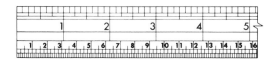

CIRCUMFERENCE RULE

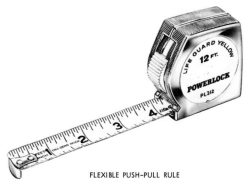

FLEXIBLE PUSH-PULL RULE

Fig. 2-5. Folding, circumference and tape rules used by the sheet metal worker.

Punches

Great care should be used in order to select the proper punch for each operation. The common hand punches are shown in Fig. 2-6.

Prick Punch. Prick punches are made of tool steel and have a tapered point ground to approximately a 30 degree included angle. These punches are used for making small dents or indentations, and/or establishing points for dividers and trammel points.

Center Punch. Center punches are similar in design to the prick punch, except that the tapered point is ground to an angle of approximately 90 degrees. They are used primarily for marking the location of points and the centers of holes to be drilled. Such punches are manufactured in various sizes and may be purchased in sets.

Neither prick punches nor center punches should be used to punch holes. These are both intended for establishing points only.

Solid Punch. Solid punches are used to punch small holes in light gage metal; these punches may also be purchased in sets of various sizes.

Hollow Punch. Hollow punches, shown in Fig. 2-6, are used for cutting circular holes, $\frac{1}{4}$ inch or larger from sheet metal. However, with the development of the modern turret punch described in Chapter 8, the hollow punch is used infrequently in the sheet metal shop. To avoid chipping the edges of the hollow punch, the sheet metal should be placed over a block of lead.

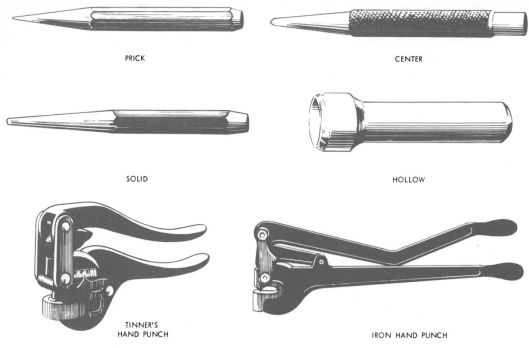

PRICK

CENTER

SOLID

HOLLOW

TINNER'S
HAND PUNCH

IRON HAND PUNCH

Fig. 2-6. Common types of punches used in sheet metal work.

Hand Lever Punches. This type of punch, shown in Fig. 2-6, is equipped with a die and a punch moved by levers. They are made in several different types, but the principle of operation is the same. The tinner's hand punch, used for punching small holes in light and medium weight metal, is furnished with punches and corresponding dies ranging in size from $\frac{1}{16}$ to $\frac{9}{32}$ inch. Each punch is $\frac{1}{64}$ inch larger than the next smaller punch; the size is marked on the punch to aid in punching holes of different sizes. The iron hand punch is used on heavier material, and is equipped with punches ranging from $\frac{3}{32}$ to $\frac{1}{2}$ inch. The punches and dies of both types are easily changed.

Hand Groover

The hand groover shown in Fig. 2-7 is used when grooving a seam by hand, as shown in Fig. 9-42, page 153. The end of the tool is recessed to fit over the lock, making the grooved seam. It is available in various sizes.

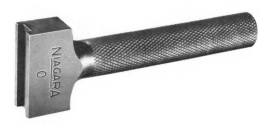

Fig. 2-7. Hand groover.

Rivet Set

The rivet set, shown in Fig. 2-8, is made of tool steel. The deep hole in the bottom is used to draw a rivet through metal. The cup-shaped hole is used to form the finished head of a rivet. The hole in the side is to release the burrs that are punched through the metal with the rivet. Rivet sets are manufactured in a variety of sizes.

Fig. 2-8. Rivet set.

Chisels

The various types of chisels shown in Fig. 2-9 are used for cutting metal.

Flat Cold Chisel. Sheet metal workers generally use this chisel more than the other types since it is used for cutting sheet metal, rivets, bolts, and in chipping operations.

Cape Chisel. Cape chisels are used for cutting grooves and keyways.

Diamond Point Chisel. These chisels are used for cutting V shaped grooves, for chipping corners, and sometimes for removing bolts whose heads have broken off.

Round Nose Chisel. Round nose chisels are used for roughing out the concave surfaces of corners and also for cutting grooves.

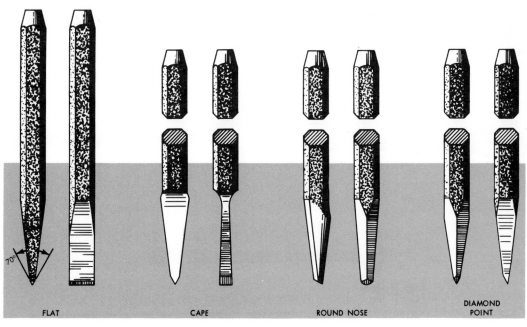

FLAT   CAPE   ROUND NOSE   DIAMOND POINT

Fig. 2-9. Types of chisels used in cutting and shaping sheet metal.

Hammers

It is essential that sheet metal workers have a variety of hammers. These should include the following: riveting hammers, raising hammers, setting hammers, ball peen or machinist's hammers, nail hammers, and mallets. All are shown in Fig. 2-10. These hammers are manufactured in a variety of weights.

Riveting Hammer. The riveting hammer has a square, slightly curved face with beveled edges to prevent the head of the hammer from marking the metal. The peen side is double tapered and has a slightly rounded end.

Setting Hammer. The setting hammer has a square, flat face for flattening seams without damage to the metal. The single-tapered peen with a beveled end is used for peening operations.

Ball Peen Hammer. The ball peen or machinist's hammer has a round, slightly curved face and round head. It is a general purpose hammer.

Raising Hammer. The raising hammer is seldom used in modern sheet metal work and is supplied by the shop rather than by the sheet metal worker. It is one of a set of four hammers used in raising circular disks and ornaments for cornice work and many other raising and bumping operations.

Common Nail Hammer. The com-

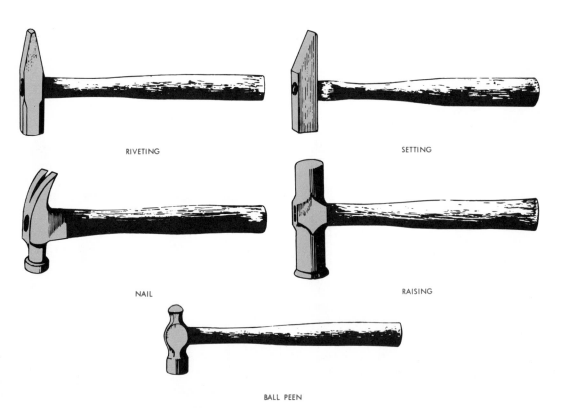

RIVETING

SETTING

NAIL

RAISING

BALL PEEN

Fig. 2-10. Types of hammers used by sheet metal workers.

mon nail hammer is not generally considered a sheet metal worker's tool, though it is very useful in this work and is employed for a variety of operations around the shop.

Mallet. The mallet is one of the most abused tools because it is often used to perform operations for which it is not designed. Mallets are properly used where steel hammers would deface the work. A good grade of hickory or hard fiber mallet, as shown in Fig. 2-11, will last a long time if used in the correct manner on proper materials.

Fig. 2-11. Mallet. (Niagara Machine & Tool Works)

Snips

Snips of various types, as shown in Fig. 2-12 are indispensable to the sheet metal worker. A brief description of blade types and the snips in most common use is given below so that the student can select the best snips for a particular job.

Blade Type. No matter what the purpose of the snips is, the blades are of two basic types—either *straight blade* or *combination blade*. Fig. 2-13 shows the difference between the

straight and the combination blade. The cross sectional view of the two types shows that the straight blade has the face of the blade running straight up from the cutting edge, while the combination blade is curved back from the cutting edge. In use, the difference between the two is that the combination blade allows the metal to slide over the top blade when cutting curves, as shown in Fig. 2-14. The straight blade snips does not allow the metal to curve over the top blade in this manner and is therefore best for cutting straight lines. Also, straight blades, because of their design, have a greater amount of metal to strengthen them and therefore the blades can be made in a greater length than is possible with the combination blade.

General Purpose Snips. General purpose snips may be either combination or straight blade snips, though the combination blade is the most commonly used by sheet metal workers. The snips are used for all routine cutting. General purpose snips are usually used on 26 gage or lighter.

Bulldog Snips. Bulldog snips also are obtainable with either the straight or combination blade. These are heavy duty snips for cutting thicker metals. They are characterized by long handles with comparatively short blades for better leverage. Bulldogs are used for all general cutting on thicker metals.

Aviation Snips. Fig. 2-12 also shows airplane or aviation snips. Though they are only 8 inches long, these snips have a compound leverage that enables them to cut heavier metal than even the large bulldog snips. The design on the blade of the airplane snips is such that they

HAWK BILL

COMPOUND LEVER

BENCH

DOUBLE CUTTING

AVIATION SNIPS

BULLDOG

RIGHT HAND

STRAIGHT

CIRCULAR

LEFT HAND

Fig. 2-12. Sheet metal snips. (J. Wiss & Sons Co., Niagara Machine & Tool Works)

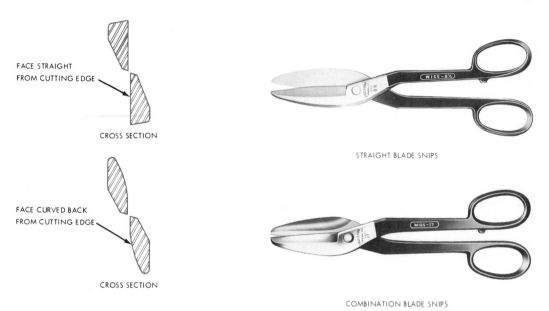

FACE STRAIGHT
FROM CUTTING EDGE

CROSS SECTION

FACE CURVED BACK
FROM CUTTING EDGE

CROSS SECTION

STRAIGHT BLADE SNIPS

COMBINATION BLADE SNIPS

Fig. 2-13. Straight and combination blade snips. (J. Wiss & Sons Co.)

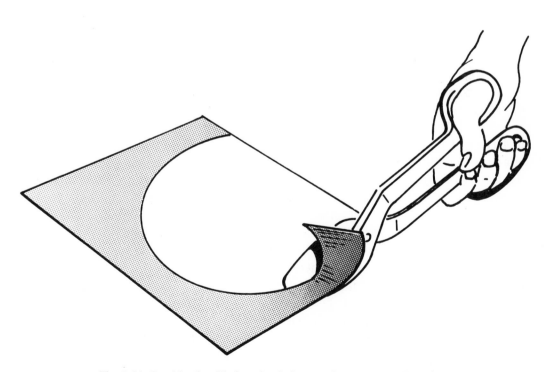

Fig. 2-14. Combination blade snips being used to cut curved sections.

can cut very small irregular curves and can even cut inside corners of 90°.

Aviation snips are available in right-hand, left-hand, or straight-cutting models as shown in Fig. 2-12. In the straight-cutting models, the blades are rolled over rather flat to allow for cutting in either direction. Sheet metal workers sometimes carry the straight aviation snips, but they *always* carry the right-hand and the left-hand snips.

The right-hand and left-hand snips can be distinguished by the position of the upper blade. When the snips are held in a position to cut the metal, if the upper blade is on the operator's right, then they are right-hand snips. If, in this position, the upper blade is on the left, they are left-hand snips. A frequent question concerning this explanation is, "What if the snips are held upside down?" Observe the illustration of the aviation snips in Fig. 2-12. Here you can see that even if a right-hand snips is held upside down, the upper blade is on the operator's right.

It is necessary that the sheet metal worker carry both right and lefts in order to do all jobs. The use of rights and lefts will be explained later in the chapter on notching and cutting.

Hawk Bill Snips. Before the development of the aviation snips, the hawk bill and some of the other special-purpose snips were in wide use to cut curves and scrolls. Now, however, they are seldom used by the sheet metal worker since the aviation snips can cut as intricate a curve, and in heavier metal. The hawk bill snips are shown in Fig. 2-12. They will cut lighter weight metals.

Circular Snips. Circular snips have blades that curve sideways. They are designed for cutting inside circles and also for cutting metal close to an obstacle, such as when trimming off a metal duct flush to a wall. Like the hawk bill snips, the circular snips have largely been replaced by the aviation snips. Many sheet metal workers, however, still carry the circular snips for trimming off sheet metal which is flush with the wall.

Bench Shears. Both the compound lever shears and the bench shears shown in Fig. 2-12 are designed to fasten onto the bench for heavy cutting. The bottom handle is bent at a right angle and is square in shape to fit into a square hole on a metal bench plate shown in Figs. 2-26 and 2-27, pages 29 and 30. These shears are two to three feet long and are used for cutting sheet metal which is $\frac{1}{16}$ inch thick, or more. With the development of the modern squaring shears and electric shears, these bench shears are no longer in common use.

Double Cutting Snips. Double cutting snips are so called because they make two cuts at once to cut out a slit of metal $\frac{1}{8}$ inch wide from the sheet. Double cuts are designed in this manner so that the right-hand and the left-hand pieces of metal being cut can lay flat. This makes these snips especially valuable in cutting off lengths of sheet metal pipe since neither side of the metal has to slide over the bottom blade as with conventional snips.

Pliers

Various types of pliers, as shown in Fig. 2-15, are used in sheet metal work for holding, cutting and bending work.

Fig. 2-15. Types of pliers used by the sheet metal worker.

Flat-Nose Pliers. Flat-nose pliers have flat jaws with small grooves and are used for forming and holding work.

Round-Nose Pliers. Round-nose pliers have long jaws rounded on the outside and are used in holding and forming the various shapes and patterns.

Slip-Joint Combination Pliers. Slip-joint combination pliers are constructed with an adjustable jaw. A screwdriver is sometimes formed at the end of one handle. These pliers are a general-purpose tool.

Fig. 2-16. Handy seamer.

Handy Seamer or Tongs

The handy seamer or *tongs* shown in Fig. 2-16 is made of drop-forged steel with 3½ inch blades and an adjustable gage. This tool is used in seaming operations, and bending in situations where it is impossible or inconvenient to bend metal on the brake.

Soldering Coppers

The soldering coppers, shown in Fig. 2-17, are commonly called *soldering irons* and are made of a forged copper

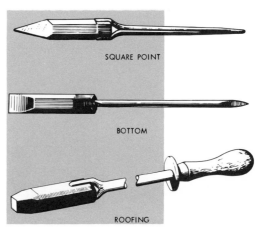

SQUARE POINT

BOTTOM

ROOFING

Fig. 2-17. Soldering Coppers.

bar. The metal is fastened to a wooden handle by an iron rod or heavy twisted wires.

Square Pointed Soldering Copper. The square pointed soldering copper is the ordinary soldering copper used for general soldering. The points of soldering copper are often forged to a particular shape to meet the requirements of different varieties of work.

Bottom Soldering Copper. The bottom soldering iron is used for soldering bottoms of objects such as pails, tanks, etc.

Roofing Soldering Copper. The roofing soldering copper with shield and handle is used for soldering metal roofing.

Soldering Copper Handles. A soldering copper handle is shown in Fig. 2-18. Both wood and fiber handles are available. The most popular handle is the screw-on type. This handle has a coarse thread in a steel insert inside the wood so that it will screw onto the tapered end of the iron rod. Screw-on handles are generally more solid than the pound-on type and are less apt to work loose.

Fig. 2-18. Soldering copper handle.

Hacksaws

There are two styles of hacksaw frames used by the sheet metal worker. These are shown in Fig. 2-19. The straight handle is usually preferred for fine work. Either type of frame is adjustable for various lengths of blades, eight to twelve inches in length. Tension is applied to the blade to make it taut by means of a wing nut on the pistol-grip type frame or by turning a threaded handle on the straight handle type.

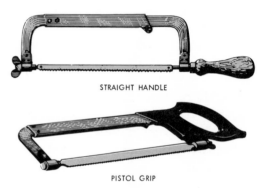

STRAIGHT HANDLE

PISTOL GRIP

Fig. 2-19. Types of hacksaws.

Files

There are many files of various kinds and shapes. However, only the files generally used in the sheet metal trade will be described. (See Fig. 2-20). Files are used to remove burrs from sheets of metal, to square the ends of band iron, to straighten uneven edges, and for various other operations that require a small amount of metal to be removed.

Parts of Files. The parts of a file are the point, the edge, the face, the heel, and the tang, as shown in Fig. 2-21.

Cuts of Files. The single-cut files shown in Fig. 2-22, top, have a single set of teeth cut at an angle of 65 to 85 degrees. The double-cut files have two

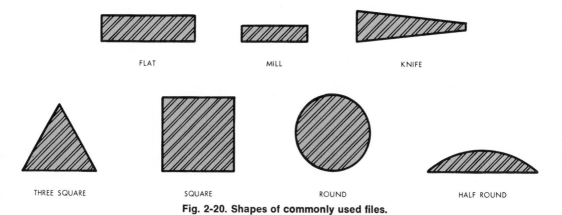

FLAT   MILL   KNIFE

THREE SQUARE   SQUARE   ROUND   HALF ROUND

Fig. 2-20. Shapes of commonly used files.

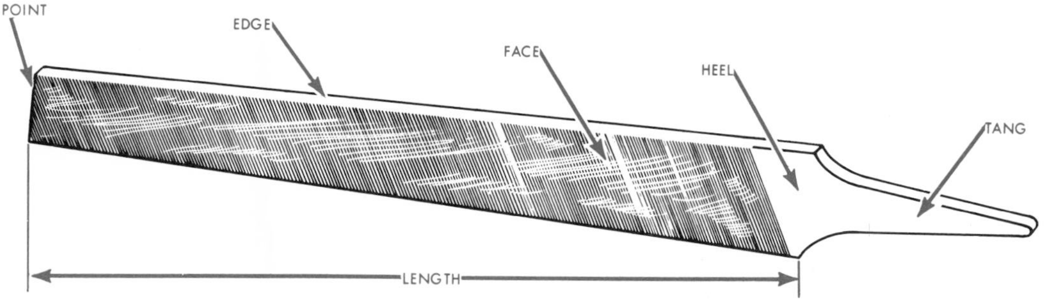

POINT   EDGE   FACE   HEEL   TANG

LENGTH

Fig. 2-21. Parts of a file.

sets of teeth crossing each other, as shown in Fig. 2-22, bottom. Double-cut files are used for rough filing, since they remove material faster than do the single-cut files.

File Handles. File handles are usually made of wood and are designed to fit the hollow of the hand. A metal ferrule on the end of the handle prevents it from splitting.

Flat File. This file is used to file flat surfaces as well as for other operations that require a fast cutting file.

Mill File. The mill file is an all-purpose, single cut file especially adapted for finish filing.

Knife File. This file is suited for finishing the sharp corners of grooves and slots where other files would not fit.

Three Square File. The three square file (commonly called *three cornered file*) has angles of 60° and is used for

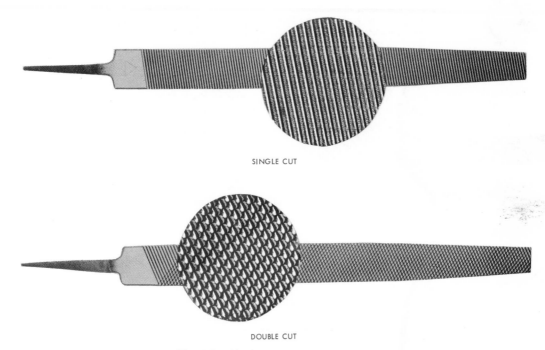

SINGLE CUT

DOUBLE CUT

Fig. 2-22. Single and double cut files.

filing internal angles, clearing out corners, etc.

A file card or brush with a scorer is used to remove particles which clog the file.

Bench Stakes

The metal worker often finds it necessary, when suitable machines are not available, to rivet, seam, form, or bend sheet metal objects over various types of steel anvils. The anvils are referred to as *stakes* and are designed to perform many operations for which machines are not available or readily adaptable.

The shank of each stake has a tapered point which fits the holes in the bench plate, shown in Fig. 2-26, page 29. These stakes are available in a variety of shapes and sizes.

Parts of a Stake. The parts of a stake, shown in Fig. 2-23, are the

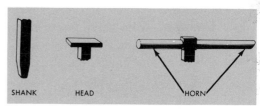

SHANK   HEAD   HORN

Fig. 2-23. Parts of a stake.

HAND DOLLIES CAN BE USED
AS BUCKING BARS, p. 29

shank, the head, and the horn. The shanks of the stakes are generally standard; head and horns are available in various shapes and sizes.

Description of and Use of Stakes. It would be impossible to describe all of the stakes and the operations that are performed on each one. However, the more common stakes as shown in Fig. 2-24 will be described along with some of the uses.

Blowhorn Stake. The blowhorn stake was originally designed to form fish peddler's horns. It has a short, tapered horn at one end, and a long, tapered horn at the other. This stake is now used in forming, riveting, or seaming tapered objects such as funnels, pitched covers, etc.

Beakhorn Stake. This stake was originally designed to form powder beakers. It has a thick tapered horn at one end and rectangularly shaped horn at the other. It is now used in forming, riveting, and seaming articles not suitable for the blowhorn stake.

Candlemold Stake. The candlemold stake was originally designed for forming molds used in making candles. It has two horns of different tapers, and is now used in forming, riveting, and seaming long, flaring articles.

Needlecase Stake. The needlecase stake has a small, tapered horn at one end, and a small, rectangular horn with a rounded beveled edge at the other. This stake is used for very fine hand work.

Creasing Stake. This stake is available in two patterns. One has a double, rectangularly shaped horn and contains a number of grooved slots for creasing metal and bending wire; the other pattern has a round and tapered horn at one end and a rectangularly shaped horn on the other, and is used for forming, riveting, or seaming small, tapering objects.

Hollow Mandrel Stake. This stake is in almost every sheet metal shop. It has a slot running through its length in which a bolt slides, permitting the stake to be fastened to the bench at any angle or length. The rounded end is used for riveting and seaming pipes. The rectangularly shaped end is used for forming laps, riveting, and double seaming corners of pans, boxes, etc.

Solid Mandrel Stake. This stake has a double shank so that either the rounded or flat side can be used to perform operations similar to those of the hollow mandrel stake.

Double-Seaming Stake. The double-seaming stake, with four heads, has a double shank so arranged that the stake may be used either horizontally or vertically. It is used for double seaming large work.

Another type of double-seaming stake consists of two elliptically shaped horns with two enlarged knobs at the ends. This stake is generally used for double seaming small cylindrically shaped articles.

Conductor Stake. The conductor stake has two cylindrical horns of different diameters and is used when forming, riveting, and seaming tubes and small-sized pipes.

Hatchet Stake. The hatchet stake has a sharp, straight edge, beveled along one side. It is used for making sharp bends, bending edges, and forming pans and boxes by hand.

Teakettle Stake. The teakettle stake

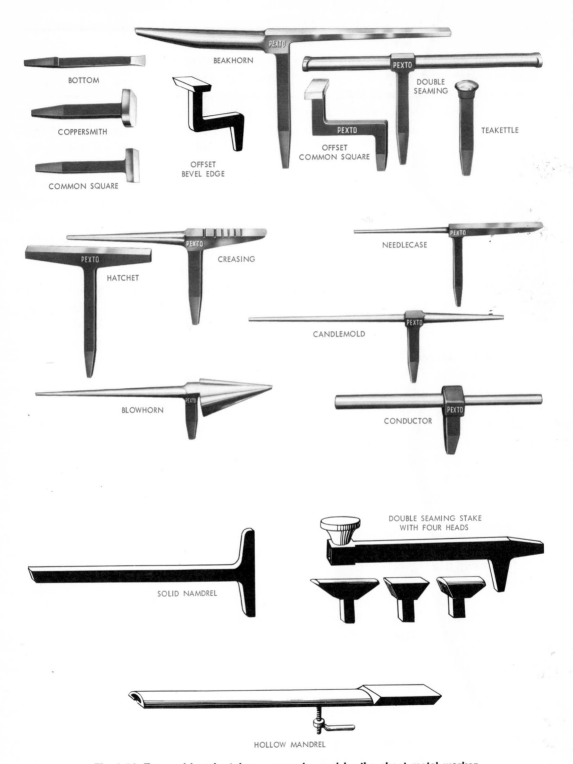

BEAKHORN

DOUBLE
SEAMING

BOTTOM

COPPERSMITH

OFFSET
BEVEL EDGE

OFFSET
COMMON SQUARE

TEAKETTLE

COMMON SQUARE

CREASING

NEEDLECASE

HATCHET

CANDLEMOLD

BLOWHORN

CONDUCTOR

DOUBLE SEAMING STAKE
WITH FOUR HEADS

SOLID NAMDREL

HOLLOW MANDREL

Fig. 2-24. Types of bench stakes commonly used by the sheet metal worker.

has four differently shaped heads and is useful in many operations for which other stakes are not adapted.

Bevel-Edge Stake. This stake has a flat, square head with a bevel edge on the outside of the head for double seaming. It also has an offset shank which permits the work to clear the bench.

Common Square Stake. The common, square stake has a flat square-shaped head with a long shank, and is used for general operations.

Coppersmith Stake. The coppersmith stake has a rounded edge on one side of the head and a sharp rectangular edge on the other. The stake is used for general operations.

Bottom Stake. This stake has a fan-shaped, beveled edge, slightly rounded. It is used for dressing burred edges on a disk, for special double seaming, and for turning small flanges.

Hand Dolly Stake. The hand dolly stake, shown in Fig. 2-25 is designed with a flat face, two straight edges, one convex edge, and one concave edge. It is a handy stake for all general purposes such as bucking rivets and double seaming. Hand dolly stakes come in various shapes and sizes.

Care of Stakes. The condition of the stake has much to do with the workmanship of the finished job. If a stake has been roughened by punch marks or is chisel marked, the completed job will look rough and lacking in craftsmanship. Therefore, a stake should not be used to back up the work directly when prick punching or cutting with a cold chisel. A mallet should be used whenever possible when forming sheet metal on stakes.

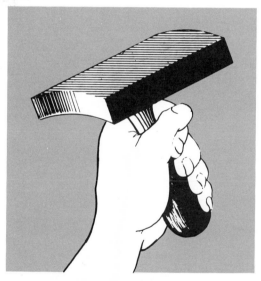

Fig. 2-25. Hand dolly.

Stakeholders

The most common holder used is the rectangularly shaped cast iron bench plate, shown in Fig. 2-26, which is fas-

Fig. 2-26. Bench plate.

tened to the bench with bolts. The tapered holes are conveniently arranged so the stakes may be used in different positions. (The smaller holes are used to support the bench shears.)

Another type of stakeholder consists of a revolving plate with tapered holes to support the stakes. This plate is held in any desired position by being clamped to the bench. See Fig. 2-27.

Many mechanics prefer to use the stakeholder with a complete set of anvils as illustrated in Fig. 2-28. This is referred to as the universal holder and stake set. Such a stakeholder does not require a bench plate. One stake may be substituted for another very quickly by simply turning a swivel handle and replacing the stake. The holder is clamped to any desired position on the bench.

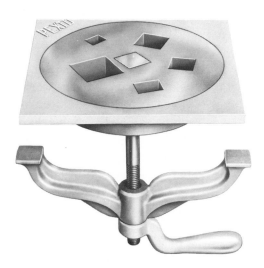

Fig. 2-27. Revolving bench plate.

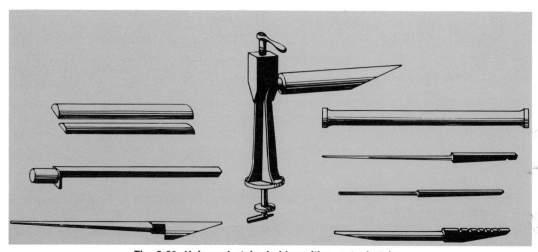

Fig. 2-28. Universal stake holder with a set of stakes.

Machines

Machines for working sheet metal are designed to perform a variety of operations on straight and circular outlines, namely, forming, folding, bending, creasing, edging, grooving, double seaming, setting down, turning, burring, slitting, crimping, swedging, cutting, beading, wiring, punching, drilling, grinding, corrugating and cutting metal disks.

Machines that are adapted for specific operations are available as either bench or floor models. However, to make it more convenient to discuss machines, the smaller ones are usually referred to as bench machines and the others as floor machines.

Machine Supports

There are five methods of supporting machines in the proper position:

1. Frames made in one piece, with the gears enclosed, resting on or fastened directly to the floor. See Fig. 2-29.

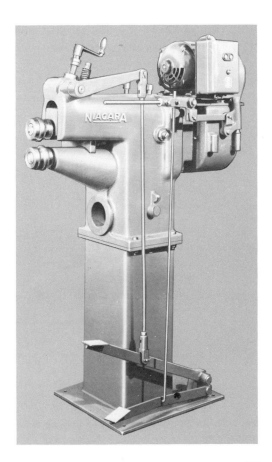

Fig. 2-29. Machine housing with floor mounted base. (Niagara Machine and Tool Works)

2. Machines such as small forming machines, bar folders, such as the one shown in Fig. 2-30, etc., bolted directly to the bench.

3. Small rotary machines are held in position by bench standards. Fig. 2-31*A* shows the regular standard that may be fastened securely to the bench by a screw hand lever. The adjustable bench standard in Fig. 2-31*B* is the type usually used for supporting the larger machines.

4. The floor standards shown in Fig. 2-31*C* and *D* are used where bench space is limited. The standard at *C* is for light work, the one at *D* for heavy.

5. The revolving machine standard, Fig. 2-32, is one of the most efficient. It has many features, such as the revolving turret which permits four different operations without changing the machine. This eliminates the necessity of taking down or putting up machines many times a day, thereby saving time and wear and tear.

6. Fig. 2-33 shows a mobile table equipped to provide electric driving power to up to four otherwise hand-operated machines. The hand cranks are removed and the machines are mounted on the table and connected to the power take-off by means of coupling shafts and universal joints. This system allows for any four hand machines involved in a single project to be connected to a single power source and moved to any location in the shop.

Fig. 2-30. An adjustable bar folder may be fastened directly to the bench. (Niagara Machine and Tool Works)

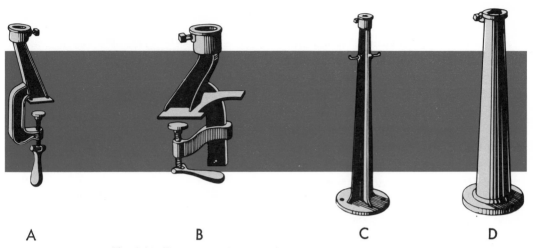

A   B   C   D

Fig. 2-31. Four types of standards used to support machines.

Fig. 2-32. Revolving machine stand. (Niagara Machine and Tool Works)

Fig. 2-33. Mobile power table. (Niagara Machine and Tool Works)

Bench Machines

The following so-called bench machines, which include the burring, turning, wiring, and edging machines, are somewhat similar. Each one is designed to perform a special operation and should be used according to the recommendation of the manufacturer. Operating these machines is not difficult; with a little practice each machine can be mastered. The variety of operations of each machine will be described later.

Burring Machine. The burring machine shown in Fig. 2-34 is used to turn burrs (edges) on circular disks such as bottoms and covers and also for preparing edges for double seaming cylindrically shaped articles.

Turning Machine. The turning machine as seen in Fig. 2-35, while somewhat similar to the burring machine, differs in the sharpness of the edge it makes. A burring machine produces a sharp edge, while the turning machine makes a rounded edge for wiring operations, for bodies of cylinders, and for double seaming.

Wiring Machine. The wiring machine has special rolls, Fig. 2-36, to complete the wired edge after the seat to receive the wire has been prepared on the turning machine.

Crimping and Beading Machine. The crimping and beading machine shown in Fig. 2-37 is designed for crimping and beading in one pass, or, by changing the rolls the machine may be used for beading or crimping only. This machine is used also for crimping the small ends of pipes, flanges, etc.

Setting-Down Machine. This ma-

Fig. 2-34. Burring machine. (Niagara Machine and Tool Works)

Fig. 2-35. Turning machine. (Niagara Machine and Tool Works)

Fig. 2-36. Wiring machine. (Niagara Machine and Tool Works)

Fig. 2-38. Setting-down machine. (Peck, Stow & Wilcox Co.)

Fig. 2-37. Crimping and beading machine. (Niagara Machine and Tool Works)

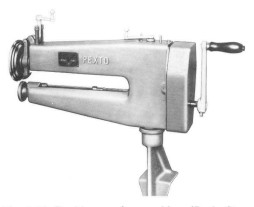

Fig. 2-39. Double-seaming machine. (Peck, Stow & Wilcox Co.)

chine, shown in Fig. 2-38, is used for setting down seams on containers of various shapes, thereby facilitating the operation in double seaming to do a better seaming job.

Double-Seaming Machine. The double-seaming machine, Fig. 2-39, is used for double-seaming flat bottoms on straight or flared cylindrical pieces. It is recommended as a labor-saving device in cases where a number of double-seaming operations are required on projects such as waste cans, etc. and for production work.

Grooving Machine. The grooving machine, as seen in Fig. 2-40, is used for grooving longitudinal seams in cylinders. This is a specialized machine which completes the seam by grooving and flattening in one operation of the carriage.

Elbow Edging Machine. The elbow edging machine (Fig. 2-41) is designed for turning the edges of elbows for tight or adjustable joints. The apron gage shown is generally used on the power machine. This machine is used for light gage elbows which are creased on the ends to allow the section to enter the next corresponding section. Small, power elbow edging machines are used where large quantities are required, and are available with rolls of three types.

Beading Machine. The beading machine shown in Fig. 2-42 is furnished with single and ogee rolls for all beading operations. Special rolls are obtain-

able when necessary and are easily interchangeable.

Forming Machine. Roll forming machines are used to form cylindrically

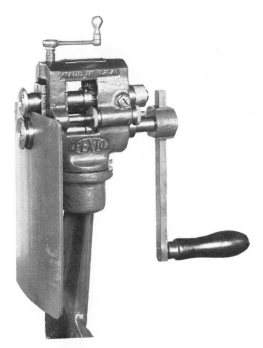

Fig. 2-41. Elbow edging machine. (Peck, Stow & Wilcox Co.)

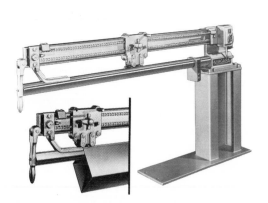

Fig. 2-40. Grooving machine. (Niagara Machine and Tool Works)

Fig. 2-42. Beading machine. (Niagara Machine and Tool Works)

Fig. 2-43. Slip roll forming machine. (Peck, Stow & Wilcox Co.)

shaped articles and are indispensable when making pipe. The slip roll forming machine, Fig. 2-43, is the type most generally used by the sheet metal worker, since the forming machine with solid housings is more difficult to operate.

Rotary Circular Shears. The rotary circular shears, Fig. 2-44 is used for cutting sheet metal disks for bottoms and tops of cans. These shears are also designed for slitting sheets of metal into pieces of any desired width.

Combination Machines. Machines such as those shown in Figs. 2-34 and 2-35 are designed so the rolls are interchangeable. Thus an operator may be able to construct a complete project on one machine simply by installing the proper rolls for each step in the operation.

Floor Machines

The following machines are generally classed as floor machines since the ma-

Fig. 2-44. Rotary circular shears. (Peck, Stow & Wilcox Co.)

jority are made in floor models.

Squaring Shears. There are many kinds of squaring shears used for squaring, trimming, slitting, and cutting sheet metals into various shapes and sizes. The foot-power squaring shears generally has a 36 inch cutting blade.

Hand Brake. The hand brake, Fig. 2-45 is a floor machine used for bending and folding the edges of metal. Its various operations will be described in later chapters.

Quality hand brakes are designed to give many years of service. For this reason, shops may have brakes of different ages and models. Fig. 2-45 shows a modern hand brake.

Fig. 2-46. Pan brake. (Peck, Stow & Wilcox Co.)

Fig. 2-45. Hand brake. (Dreis & Krump Co.)

Pan Brake. The pan brake, shown in Fig. 2-46 is similar to the hand brake. It is used for bending edges in the same way as the hand brake. The difference between the two brakes is that the pan brake has the upper blade in sections that can be easily removed. In this way the pan brake can reach in between the sides of a box or pan to bend the last side.

Power Shears. The power shears are similar to the squaring shears, and are shown in Fig. 2-47. Power shears

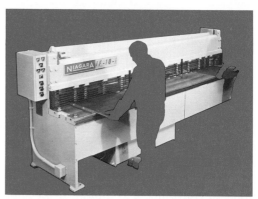

Fig. 2-47. Power shears. (Niagara Machine and Tool Works)

are motor operated and are run either by a mechanical or a hydraulic arrangement. Though power shears are available in the smaller sizes, they are gen-

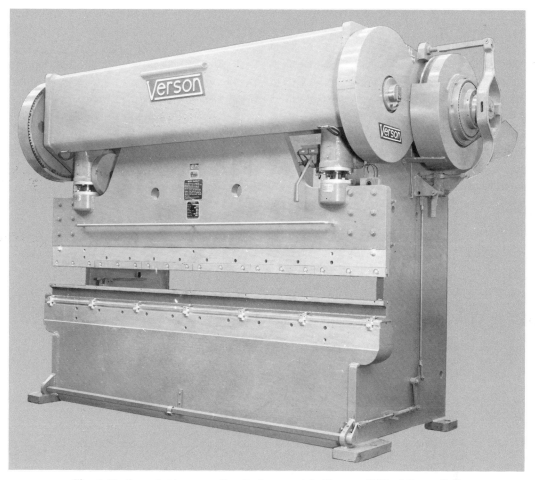

Fig. 2-48. Press brakes use dies to form metal. (Verson AllSteel Press Co.)

erally used in larger sizes. The ten-foot power shear is a very common size.

Press Brake. This brake, Fig. 2-48, is another machine for bending metal. This machine is quite different from the hand or the pan brake because it bends or forms the metal by pressing it into special dies. The dies of the press brake are changed to fit the operation being done. The press brake is more of a production tool than the hand brake. That is, it is better suited to doing a large number of the same operations rather than doing many different operations. Press brakes are available in all sizes from four-feet long up to thirty-five feet long. The most common size is the ten-foot brake.

Class Activities

1. The instructor will give you a sheet metal object made with shop tools. List the sheet metal tools—both hand and machine—that you think were used to make it.

2. Re-arrange the list of tools from Item 1 into the order that you think they were used.

3. Meet with students who have the same object as you and compare your lists. Discuss the differences and arrive at one list in the proper order of use that the whole group agrees on.

4. Assign one person of the group to write the list on the chalkboard and report to the class.

STUDENT QUESTIONS AND ACTIVITIES

1. Name three different types of scratch awls.
2. Name the major parts of a file.
3. Name two general cuts on files.
4. What tool is used for drawing large circles and arcs?
5. What rule instrument is used for finding the circumference of a circle?
6. What tool is used to remove particles from a file?
7. Name four shapes of files.
8. What type of shears is used in cutting pipes?
9. Name five tools used in cutting sheet metal.
10. What type of shears is used in cutting inside circles?
11. Describe a riveting hammer, a setting hammer, a ball-peen hammer, and a raising hammer.
12. Name and describe ten different types of bench stakes.
13. **Tell the uses of the hand brake, the bar folder, and the press brake.**
14. **What is the difference between the burring and turning machines?**
15. Distinguish between a turning machine and a regular elbow edging machine.
16. Name as many machines used in sheet metal work as possible. (You should be able to name at least twelve machines.)
17. What machine is used for turning small burrs on metal disks?
18. Name the machine used for turning burrs on bottoms of cans, pails, etc.
19. Describe the use of a groover and a rivet set.
20. Explain with the aid of sketches the difference between straight-blade and combination-blade snips.
21. Explain how to tell a right-hand from a left-hand snips.

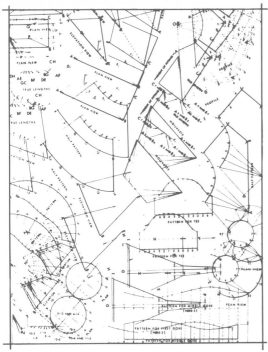

safety in the sheet metal shop

When you complete this chapter, you should be able to:
1. Work safely in the sheet metal shop and on the job.
2. Recognize and correct safety hazards in the sheet metal shop.
3. Correct unsafe actions in other workers.
4. Explain how electric shocks occur and what can be done to prevent them.
5. Explain what the safety hazards are when soldering, and explain how to avoid them.

One of the most valuable skills you can acquire in your sheet metal work, or any other work, is the formation of a positive safety attitude. The development of your knowledge and skills in sheet metal shop practices is not separate from your knowledge of and attitude toward safety, but is an integral part of it. The worker with an informed attitude towards safety will have increased value to his employer because of a minimum of time lost from on-the-job injury. In addition, he will carry the importance of such attitudes into his off-the-job hours as well. Since the National Safety Council reports that nearly seven out of ten workers' deaths and more than half of the injuries occur off the job, safety is just as important off the job.

Safety education today has become an important phase of every training program. Under the 1970 Federal *Occupational Safety and Health Act* (OSHA), the employer is required to furnish a place of employment free of known hazards likely to cause death or injury. The *employer* has the specific duty of complying with safety and health standards as set forth under the 1970 act. At the same time, *employees* also have the duty to comply with these standards.

This chapter will deal specifically with some of the more common hazards in the sheet metal shop and will outline some of the generally accepted safe practices which are employed to avoid them. More safety instruction will also be given in subsequent chapters dealing with specific processes.

Positive Attitude

It is logical to be constantly aware of the great importance of safety when you know how vital it is to cultivate a positive attitude toward safe work habits. Did you know, for example, that the time lost due to on-the-job injuries equals the loss of one full year's employment for one worker in every ten in American industry every year?

The need for a sound attitude toward safety becomes immediately apparent when you consider the consequences of neglect in only one area of safe practice; that of putting on a pair of protective goggles or a face shield when required as in Fig. 3-1. Industrial eye injuries account for up to 5 percent of the total workmen's compensation cases and have proved to be the most costly and permanent of all disabilities. Since we all value the sight of both eyes, the conclusion here is obvious.

In fact, this aspect of safety is considered so important that many states

Fig. 3-1. Always wear a face shield or goggles when grinding.

have passed laws requiring that persons in school shops must wear eye protection devices *at all times* when working in a shop where any possible eye hazard exists.

Safe practices in the sheet metal shop make good sense! Why? First, because the most efficient way to use a tool or machine in the shop is the safe way. Second, by engaging in unsafe practices you risk injury to yourself and damage to your tools and machinery. Industry has recognized the importance of safe practices by the safety programs they conduct and by the safety regulations which have been established. All safety rules should receive 100 percent enforcement in the sheet metal shop. There must never be any exception to the enforcement of safe practices for any reason.

In the field of traffic safety, evidence shows that where traffic enforcement is increased, traffic accidents decrease. The implications here for the enforcement of sheet metal shop safety rules are clear.

General Safety

The following rules for safety as applied to the sheet metal shop have been established for three very good reasons: (1) to protect you and your co-workers from bodily harm, (2) to minimize damage to the facilities, machinery and tools with which you must work, and (3) to provide you with experience in safety concepts as they apply not only to sheet metal work but to all vocational fields. Remember, however, that the keystone to your personal safety and that of your co-workers rests just as much with your own positive safety attitude and awareness as with any set of safety rules.

1. Keep your mind on your job!
2. The sheet metal shop is no place to play! Careless or thoughtless acts such as playing, running, tripping, or pushing may cause accidents resulting in serious injury. Whether you are in the sheet metal school shop, classroom or place of business, remember why you are there and conduct yourself accordingly.
3. Lift by crouching as close to the load as possible, keeping your back muscles locked so that the back is held rigid, and with your leg muscles in tension ready to do the work (see Fig. 3-2). If the load is not within your lifting capacity, always secure help in lifting the load. It is a sign of good judgment to ask for such help. Remember that the after effects of a back strain, arm or leg strain or hernia could plague and possibly restrict your activity for the rest of your life.
4. Report any injury immediately! Failure to do so can have serious consequences for you in unnecessary infections and resulting time lost.
5. Never carry tools in your pockets. Should you fall, sharp ends might be driven into your body or you may injure another worker.
6. Wear snug fitting clothing. Loose garments are easily caught in machinery. Never wear wrist watches, rings, or neckties when working around machinery.
7. Don't use dull tools. Using dull tools may damage them permanently and may cause serious injury to yourself.
8. Report damaged tools and machinery. The possibility of someone being injured or the tool or

Fig. 3-2. Lift with your legs, not your back. (National Safety Council)

machine being damaged beyond repair increases when such damage goes unreported.

9. Always put a handle on a file before using it as shown in Fig. 3-3. Using a file without a proper handle may lead to skin abrasions or puncture wounds.

10. Avoid hand cuts by using a brush rather than your hand to remove chips from machine areas.

11. Oily rags and other material subject to spontaneous combustion should be kept in self-closing metal receptacles.

12. Never remove guards from machines!

13. When you enter a new shop, learn immediately where the fire extinguishers and exits are located.

14. Do not hold small work in your hand when working with a screwdriver or chisel. It may slip and injure your hand.

Fig. 3-3. Always use a handle when filing.

15. Gas fumes, mist from paint spray and fine dust can cause explosions. Always report any such concentrations immediately.

16. Chisels, punches, and similar tools often burr over the top after continual pounding. These are called "mushroomed" heads. See Fig. 3-4. These mushroom heads will splinter off when hit and cause cuts and steel slivers

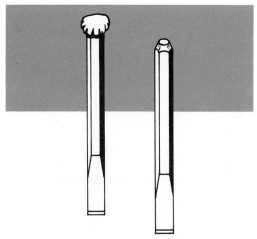

Fig. 3-4. Grind off mushroom heads on chisels.

in the arms and face. Grind off all mushroomed heads whenever they start to form.

17. Never use a hard hammer on machined, tempered, or hardened surfaces. Use a soft-faced hammer such as brass, lead, or rawhide. Using a hard hammer on hardened work will cause either the hammer or the work to splinter which may cause serious injury.

18. When using a wrench, always pull—never push. This gives you greater control and leverages and will avoid skinned knuckles if the wrench slips.

19. Whenever you are in doubt about the correct safety procedure, ask your foreman (instructor).

Squaring Shears

1. Do not remove any guards on squaring shears.

2. Learn the capacity of the squaring shears you are using and do not try to cut metal heavier than the capacity of the shears.

3. The greatest danger with the squaring shears is cutting off the ends of the fingers. This is one of the most common of all accidents in the sheet metal shop and has happened countless times. *Never put your fingers under the blades of the squaring shears.* See Fig. 3-5.

4. Do not reach behind the shear blade to hold small pieces being cut off. The danger in this is that the tips of the fingers cannot be seen and can easily be placed under the blade.

5. Keep your fingers clear of the hold-down on the shears or they may be crushed when the metal is cut.

6. Do not try to hold small pieces of metal while they are being cut. They are liable to tip up and tip your fingers into the blades.

7. Avoid getting the foot caught under the foot treadle. Two or more persons attempting to operate a machine is an unsafe act which is often the cause of this kind of accident.

Brakes

1. Do not place your hand in the hand brake when someone else is operating the handle.

2. Never place your hand in the dies of the press brake unless the main switch is off and locked.

3. Always when operating the hand

Fig. 3-5. Keep fingers clear of the blades on squaring shears. (Niagara Machine and Tool Works)

brake, see that no one else is near enough to the counterbalance balls to be hit by them. If you are working near the cornice brake, be careful to stay clear of the counterbalance balls. See Fig. 3-6.

4. If you are standing in front of the hand brake, stand back so that you will not be struck by the handles that project from the leaf when it is swung up.

5. Never bend rod or wire on any sheet metal brake. This will damage the blade and the bending leaf.

6. Steel hammers should never be used around a sheet metal brake. Mallets, as described in Chapter 2, should always be used. If you use a steel hammer to start a bend on sheet metal which is in the brake, you may miss the metal and hit the brake, causing damage beyond repair.

Soldering

1. Be extremely careful when using soldering acid. The most common acid for soldering in the sheet metal shop is hydrochloric acid (commonly called raw acid). This acid is not concentrated, but is still dangerous if used carelessly. It will ruin your clothes and will burn your skin. However, its greatest danger is to your eyes. If you get even a drop in your eye,

Fig. 3-6. Be sure that no one is near the counterbalance balls when operating a brake.

you could easily be blinded. Treat the acid with extreme caution. If you do get any acid on your skin or in your eyes, *it is absolutely essential to wash it off with plenty of cold water as quickly as possible.* Medical aid should then be secured immediately.

2. The safest and most efficient method of testing a soldering copper for the correct heat is to apply the copper to the solder. When the solder begins to flow, the correct temperature has been achieved. Other old fashioned methods for testing the soldering copper's heat are both dangerous and amateurish.

3. Fumes from soldering flux and from tinning a soldering copper are harmful when breathed in quantity and should be avoided.

4. Molten solder (or other metals) often spatter if dropped on a cold or moist surface because molten metals sometimes trap a pocket of moisture under them. This moisture then turns to steam and, when enough pressure builds up, the molten metal may be blown back into your face. You can avoid this situation by placing the soldering copper into the acid flux and permitting the solder to run down the iron.

5. Be careful of explosions from gas firepots. Stand to one side when lighting the pot. If the gas does not ignite immediately, turn off the valves before investigating the reason for the failure. Be sure that all valves are in the off position before attempting to light any gas appliance.

47

Sheet Metal

1. Do not let sheet metal slip through your hands. Most cuts from sheet metal result from allowing it to slide through the hands. Almost always, cuts from metal are a consequence of a slicing motion. If you grip the work firmly you will minimize such cuts from metal.

2. When cutting out a pattern, the scrap metal remaining often comes to a sharp point. Snip these points off to avoid later possible injury.

3. When the beginner cuts sheet metal with snips, he usually leaves small, needlelike, curved slivers of metal on the cut edge. Sheet metal workers call these *fish hooks* because they are curled and are as difficult as a fish hook to remove when they are run into a finger. Whenever you cut sheet metal, examine the edge and trim off any fish hooks to prevent possible injuries.

Welding

1. Adequate ventilation is necessary for any type of welding operation. Sheet metals containing zinc, brass, bronze, cadmium or beryllium give off toxic fumes when heated for welding or cutting. If these metals are to be welded or cut in confined quarters, mechanical exhaust systems should be used. If for some reason adequate ventilation cannot be provided, the operator must wear a respirator.

2. Protective clothing is most important in welding. Fire resistant gauntlet gloves should be worn for most welding operations. Woolen clothing is preferable to cotton because it does not ignite as readily and insulates better against temperature changes. Rolled-up sleeves, cuffs in trousers and pockets in front of clothing should be avoided because sparks may become lodged in them. High-topped shoes should be worn for work where sparks or slag are present around the feet. Clothing should be clean and free from grease or other combustible substances.

3. Proper eye protection is the singly most important safety practice in all types of welding and cutting. For oxy-acetylene welding and cutting, goggles with suitable filter lenses are required. For arc welding, a shield or helmet which protects the face as well as the eyes is necessary for protection from ultra-violet and infra-red rays produced by the arc. These rays are dangerous at distances up to 50 feet.

4. When setting up and operating welding equipment, the manufacturer's specifications and recommendations should be complied with at all times. Only thoroughly trained personnel should be allowed to operate equipment. As with any type of electrical equipment, arc welders should be prop-

erly grounded and never used in wet or damp areas. Gas welding equipment should be constantly checked for leaks and defective valves. Gas cylinders and hoses should not be exposed to sparks or excessive heat. Any defective equipment should be reported promptly, labeled as unsafe and removed from the job site.

5. During a welding operation a work piece should never be placed on the concrete floor. Heat may explode a piece of concrete with sufficient force to injure the welder.

Power Tools

In addition to the other hazards of using power tools, there is also danger of electric shock. A shock occurs if electric current finds a path through the body. The intensity of the shock depends upon how much current passes through the body. The amount of current depends not only upon the voltage of the electrical system but also upon how well the body acts as a conductor to carry the current into the ground.

Electricity will follow the easiest path into the ground. Therefore, if an electrical tool has a short circuit the current will try to pass through the body into the ground. If the body is in contact with moisture or with metal attached to the ground, the amount of current will be extremely heavy and the 110-120 volt current ordinarily used in the shop can cause death. On safely designed electrical tools a third wire is provided which provides a safe path for the current to flow into the ground if there is a short circuit. This third wire should never be disconnected and power tools should always be used in a grounded outlet as shown in Fig. 3-7.

When using power tools, all safety regulations should be carefully observed since accidents are likely to occur more often because of the speed at which the tool works and the great amount of energy that must be kept under control. In addition to the usual safety rules, also watch especially for the following:

1. Be sure that the power cord is properly grounded. This will eliminate the chance of shock. Fig. 3-7 shows the recommended type of grounded plug and receptacle that should be used for 110-120 volt power tools.

2. Always wear goggles when using power tools.

3. When using grinding or sanding tools, be careful that the sparks are thrown in a safe direction. Do not allow the sparks to be thrown in a direction where other persons are working.

4. Sanders, grinders, twist drills and other power tools may get caught on the work if used carelessly. They can be jerked out of the operator's hands, or they can throw the operator off balance. Always be ready for such an occurrence.

5. Never use power tools when they are wet or in wet locations. The dampness will provide a perfect ground and lead to a heavy shock. In this circumstance, a 115 volt power tool can cause a shock that kills.

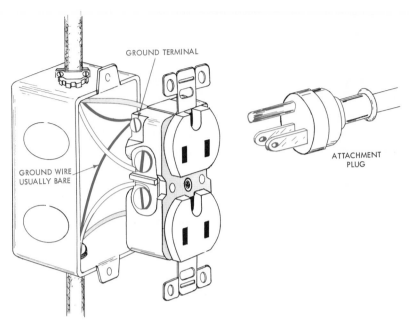

GROUND TERMINAL

GROUND WIRE
USUALLY BARE

ATTACHMENT
PLUG

Fig. 3-7. Typical plug and receptacle with terminals for grounding as required by the National Electrical Code.

6. Never change tools or make adjustments until the power line is disconnected. This is especially true on such things as disc sanders where the operator must hold the disc in order to change it.

7. Take care that the power cords are completely clear of the work so that they can not become entangled with the working parts of the tool. Also be sure that they are not exposed to oils or chemicals, and that they are not going to be run over by moving vehicles.

8. Never wear loose clothing, neckties, etc., around power tools. Long hair must be tied back or tucked into a cap to prevent catching in the power tool.

Noise Control

Exposure to excessive noise is perhaps the most insidious hazard in the shop. Permanent damage to hearing usually occurs before definite symptoms emerge. In order to control conditions where dangerous noise levels exist, the Occupational Safety and Health Administration (OSHA) has set forth directives on methods to detect and measure danger areas and on corrective action to be taken. OSHA now requires that employees be exposed to no more than 95 decibels of steady-state or interrupted noise levels during their eight hour working day, and that exposure to extreme noise be rigidly limited. If noise exceeds these levels, then ear protection must be worn.

Housekeeping

Good housekeeping is not just another extra chore for the workman. It is an important element in accident prevention and efficiency on the job. Good housekeeping begins with planning ahead. Storage areas should be planned for ease of access to materials but not in the way of traffic and construction.

Materials should be neatly stockpiled. Access areas and walkways should be kept clear of loose materials and tools. Containers for trash and bins for waste materials should be provided and conscientiously used.

It is the responsibility of each and every man on the job to maintain his area in good working order. A neat and orderly work area is a reflection of a proper attitude toward safety by all concerned.

Class Activities

1. *Inspect your school shop for safety hazards, and list all those that you observe. Compare your list with those of other students and decide which hazards should be corrected immediately.*

2. *For one week, write down every safety violation you observe in the school shop. Compare your list with those of other students.*

3. *Suggest at least one thing that could be done to make the school shop a safer place to work.*

4. *Assume that you are the instructor. How would you teach your students to work safely in the school shop and on their future jobs?*

STUDENT QUESTIONS AND ACTIVITIES

1. Why is it important to study safety rules?
2. What are the reasons for having safety rules in the sheet metal shop?
3. What are the most common causes of cuts from sheet metal?
4. What are the greatest dangers near the soldering bench? What are the proper methods of avoiding these dangers?
5. Explain what "fish hooks" are in sheet metal work.
6. What are the dangers involved in putting your fingers in the brake?
7. What are the safety hazards concerning the counterbalance balls on the brake?
8. Why must you never bend rods or wires on the brake?
9. Since you are not hitting the brake itself, why it is wrong to pound on sheet metal with a steel hammer while the sheet metal is in the brake?

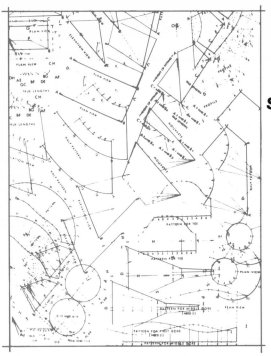

sheet metal types

When you complete this chapter you should be able to:
1. Give the thickness of a piece of sheet metal taken from a gage table.
2. Tell the type of gage or measuring system used on any of the common sheet metals.
3. Read the thickness of sheet metal by using a micrometer caliper.
4. Explain the difference between steel and non-ferrous metals.
5. Describe the characteristics of any of the common sheet metals.

Not only is it essential for the sheet metal worker to know the tools and machines of his trade and how to use them safely, but it is also important to know the materials of the trade. A finished job may be a masterpiece of fine workmanship but it would also be virtually useless if the wrong material were used. It is therefore extremely important to know what the correct materials are for a given job.

In this chapter you will learn about the various types of sheet metal—their sizes and characteristics and where they are used. The two main groups of sheet metal are *steel* and *non-ferrous*, each group including several types of metal for different uses.

52

Steel Sheet Metals

Steel is the most commonly used material in the sheet metal shop. This is because it is inexpensive and available in alloys and with special coatings for a great variety of uses. The most commonly used types of sheet steel are galvanized, stainless and tin plate.

Coated and Solid Sheets

Sheet steel may be either coated or uncoated (solid). The most commonly used coated sheets are galvanized and tin plate. Stainless steel is the most widely used solid sheet. Plain steel sheets are seldom used because of their susceptability to rust and corrosion. The non-ferrous metals discussed later are also considered to be solid sheets. The student or apprentice should learn to identify solid and coated sheets both by sight and by the manufacturer's markings to be sure that he is using the right material for the job. For example, the coatings on galvanized sheets and tin plate are for corrosion resistance. If these metals were used on a job which required welded seams, the product would fail because the welding process would burn off the protective coating. On the other hand, stainless steel may be safely welded because it is resistant to corrosion and has no coating.

Sheet Steel Gages

The thickness of steel sheet metal is designated by a series of numbers called *gages*. Each gage number designates definite thickness. While there are several gage systems in use, the most commonly used is the *Manufacturers' Standard for Sheet Steel* which is based on ounces or pounds per square foot. The gage thickness is given in decimals of an inch. See Table 4-1.

As you work with sheet metal, you will eventually learn to distinguish between the various gages merely by feeling the sheet with your fingers. This, however, requires much practice and experience.

A general rule for remembering the approximate thickness of the various gages is that when the gage number is increased by 6, the thickness is decreased by approximately $\frac{1}{2}$. For instance, note in Table 4-1 that the thickness of 16 gage is 0.0598″, or about 0.06 (about $\frac{1}{16}$″). Now, note that 22 gage (16 + 6) is 0.0299″ or about 0.03 which is $\frac{1}{2}$ of 0.06 (about $\frac{1}{32}$″).

Measuring Tools

Sheet Metal Gage. The term *sheet metal gage* also refers to a tool used for measuring and determining the thickness of the metal if it has not been marked on the sheet. One face of the gage as shown in Fig. 4-1 is marked with the standard gage numbers as shown in Table 4-1. Each number is opposite a slot which corresponds to the gage number. The thickness of the gage in decimal parts of an inch is marked

TABLE 4-1 U.S. MANUFACTURERS' STANDARD GAGE FOR UNCOATED SHEET AND STAINLESS STEEL

Standard Gage Number	Ounces per Square Foot	Pounds per Square Foot	Thickness in Inches
10	90	5.6250	0.1345
11	80	5.0000	0.1196
12	70	4.3750	0.1046
13	60	3.7500	0.0897
14	50	3.1250	0.0747
15	45	2.8125	0.0673
16	40	2.5000	0.0598
17	36	2.2500	0.0538
18	32	2.0000	0.0478
19	28	1.7500	0.0418
20	24	1.5000	0.0359
21	22	1.3750	0.0329
22	20	1.2500	0.0299
23	18	1.1250	0.0269
24	16	1.0000	0.0239
25	14	0.87500	0.0209
26	12	0.75000	0.0179
27	11	0.68750	0.0164
28	10	0.62500	0.0149
29	9	0.56250	0.0135
30	8	0.50000	0.0120
31	7	0.43750	0.0105
32	6.5	0.40625	0.0097
33	6	0.37500	0.0090
34	5.5	0.34375	0.0082
35	5	0.31250	0.0075
36	4.5	0.28125	0.0067
37	4.25	0.26562	0.0064
38	4	0.25000	0.0060

on the other face. The measurement is made by sliding the slots over the edge of the sheet as shown in Fig. 4-1. The slot that makes a snug fit denotes the gage of the metal. Note: the sheet metal gage applies only to solid steel sheets. Other metals have different systems of measuring thickness which will be described along with the discussions of the individual metals.

Micrometers. To determine gages of metal and wire, it is important that the worker knows how to read and use the *micrometer*. Since the micrometer is a delicate tool, it must be handled care-fully. Avoid dropping the micrometer and sliding or forcing the work to be measured between the spindle and the anvil. Open the spindle to insert the work. Learn how to tighten the spindle sufficiently to get an accurate reading. If the spindle is repeatedly tightened too much, the frame will be sprung and the micrometer made useless.

Reading the micrometer is quite simple once you become familiar with the parts and markings. Fig. 4-2 shows a standard 1 inch micrometer. Study the working parts and then carefully read the following instructions.

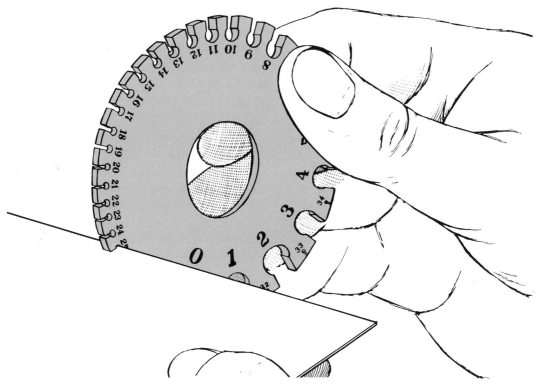

Fig. 4-1. Sheet metal and wire gage.

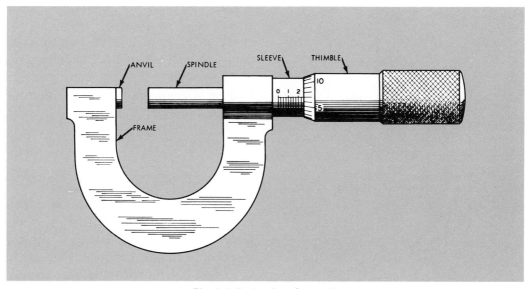

Fig. 4-2. Parts of a micrometer.

1. Hold the micrometer in the right hand (provided the user is right-handed) across the palm and fingers as shown in Fig. 4-3. The little finger is curled around the *frame*. Revolve the *thimble* by using the thumb and forefinger. The *spindle* revolves with the thimble.

2. Place the article to be measured between the *anvil* and the spindle. Then carefully tighten the spindle, using only a light pressure between the thumb and forefinger.

3. The measurement of the opening between the spindle and the anvil is shown by lines and figures on the barrel and the thimble. For example, one complete turn of the thimble changes the opening between the spindle and the anvil 0.025″. Also, each line on the barrel represents 0.025″. Four complete turns of the thimble change the opening

between the spindle and the anvil 0.100″. The thimble has also moved from 0 to 1 on the barrel. Each number on the barrel, therefore, represents 0.100″, giving readings of 0.100″, 0.200″, up to 1.000″. The beveled edge of the thimble is divided into twenty-five equal parts, each division representing 0.001″. These divisions are marked every five spaces by 0, 5, 10, 15, and 20. When 25 of these divisions have passed the horizontal line on the barrel, the spindle has moved 0.025″, and the first line of the barrel is visible, denoting 0.025″. The final reading is obtained by adding the three figures mentioned above as shown by the examples in (A), (B), (C), and (D) of Fig. 4-4.

Fig. 4-5 illustrates four different micrometer readings. Study them carefully and, using the method outlined above, determine the readings. You should get the following readings: (A) 0.200″; (B) 0.166″; (C) 0.280″; (D) 0.025″.

As well as the standard micrometer just described, there are several other shapes and sizes for special purposes. One that is particularly useful in the sheet metal shop is the deep-throated model shown in Fig. 4-6. The advantage of this design is that thickness readings may be taken much further in from the edge of the sheet than is possible with standard micrometers.

Galvanized Sheet Metal

Galvanized sheet metal is soft steel sheets coated with zinc. There are two methods of applying the zinc. In the most common one, the steel is dipped in an acid bath for cleaning and then is dipped in molten zinc. In the other, the

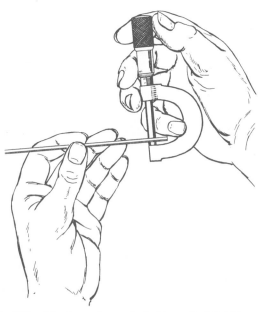

Fig. 4-3. Correct way to hold a micrometer.

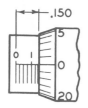

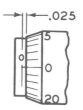

```
NUMBER OF 10THS ON SLEEVE, LAST VISIBLE FIGURE (ONE).. .100"
NUMBER OF .025 SPACES ON SLEEVE (TWO) ................. .050"
NUMBER OF DIVISIONS ON THIMBLE (NONE)............... .000"
                                        TOTAL   .150"
```

```
NUMBER OF 10THS ON SLEEVE, LAST VISIBLE FIGURE (NONE). .000"
NUMBER OF .025 SPACES ON SLEEVE (ONE) ................. .025"
NUMBER OF DIVISIONS ON THIMBLE (NONE)................ .000"
                                        TOTAL   .025"
```

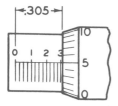

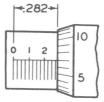

```
NUMBER OF 10THS ON SLEEVE, LAST VISIBLE FIGURE (THREE). .300"
NUMBER OF .025 SPACES ON SLEEVE (NONE)................. .000"
NUMBER OF DIVISIONS ON THIMBLE (FIVE)................. .005"
                                        TOTAL   .305"
```

```
NUMBER OF 10THS ON SLEEVE, LAST VISIBLE FIGURE (TWO).. .200"
NUMBER OF .025 SPACES ON SLEEVE (THREE)............... .075"
NUMBER OF DIVISIONS ON THIMBLE (SEVEN)............... .007"
                                        TOTAL   .282"
```

Fig. 4-4. Examples of micrometer readings.

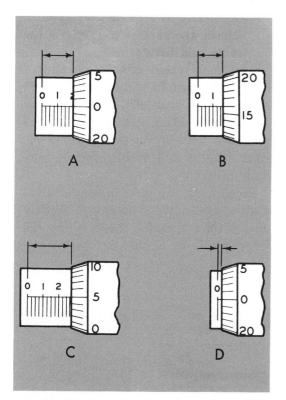

Fig. 4-5. Sample problems in micrometer reading.

Fig. 4-6. Special sheet metal micrometer. (The L. S. Starret Co.)

coating is done by an electroplating process. Electroplated sheets are distinguished by their even gray color, and are used mainly for their ability to hold a painted surface.

Galvanized sheet metal can be easily recognized by its typical spangled appearance, as shown in Fig. 4-7. These spangles are from the molten zinc as it cools on the sheet. Since galvanized is a coated sheet, its corrosion resistance is dependent upon the condition of the zinc coating. Zinc is highly resistant to corrosion and, as long as it remains intact on the sheet, galvanized steel will have high corrosion resistance. A good quality galvanized sheet should last from 5 to 10 years under constant contact with water. However, if the zinc is damaged through welding, grinding, or any other process, then the steel will be exposed and this portion of the sheet will rust through very quickly.

Of all the sheet metals, galvanized is one of the least expensive. Its cost is in the same general range as plain steel sheets, and steel bar. It is probably the most commonly used of all types of sheets in the general sheet metal shop. Air conditioning ductwork is made almost entirely of galvanized sheet metal. All types of roof flashing and gutters are made principally from galvanized sheet metal also. In addition to this, all general sheet metal objects such as tanks, signs, and boxes are usually made from galvanized because of its low cost and good corrosion resistance.

Good quality galvanized sheet metal can be bent and straightened out several times without the zinc peeling from the sheet. All galvanized sheets bend well, with no problems in breaking when they are bent severely. It solders well, but welding is complicated by the fact that the zinc gives off toxic fumes and a residue which makes the weld itself more difficult. In addition, welding destroys the coating on the sheet, and for this reason galvanized sheet metal is seldom used in applications requiring welded joints. Galvanized sheet metal can be painted. It is good practice to wash the sheets with a dilute solution of acid before the primer is applied. This etches the sheet which allows the primer to hold better.

Like most sheet metals, galvanized can be obtained in widths of 24″, 30″, 36″, and 48″, with 36″ being the most commonly stocked size. Sheet lengths generally are 96″ or 120″. However, other lengths and widths can be specially ordered.

Because of the zinc coating, galvanized sheets will measure slightly thicker than uncoated sheets. Since the difference is so slight, the gage num-

Fig. 4-7. Galvanized sheet metal has many applications.

TABLE 4-2 GALVANIZED SHEET GAGES

Gage Number	Thickness in Inches
10	0.1382
11	0.1233
12	0.1084
13	0.0934
14	0.0785
15	0.0710
16	0.0635
17	0.0575
18	0.0516
19	0.0456
20	0.0396
21	0.0366
22	0.0336
23	0.0306
24	0.0276
25	0.0247
26	0.0217
27	0.0202
28	0.0187
29	0.0172
30	0.0157
31	0.0142
32	0.0134

bers for galvanized sheets remain the same as those for solid steel sheets. Table 4-2 gives the Manufacturers' Standard Gage thicknesses for galvanized sheets.

Stainless Steel

Stainless steel is one of the most important materials in the sheet metal trade. As the name indicates, stainless steel has high resistance to foreign or corrosive elements. It is also very easily cleaned. For these reasons, it is widely used in residential, institutional and restaurant kitchens for hoods, sinks, spatter guards, etc. These items are usually fabricated in the shop.

Stainless steel is a high grade steel to which has been added such elements such as manganese, silicon, phosphorous, chromium, nickel, and molybdenum. Of these elements, chromium and nickel are in the largest quantity. According to the particular type of stainless, it will contain from 10 to 30 percent chromium and from 10 to 25 percent nickel.

Stainless steel is classed by type number such as type 302. There are over forty types of stainless steel available. These are distributed through three series of numbers: the 200 series, the 300 series, and the 400 series. Stainless steel is classified according to the heat treating properties of the steel and also its alloy content. The type number is of great importance because handbooks list by type number the characteristics of each, the recommended uses, and the degree of resistance to various types of chemicals.

The common type of stainless used in the sheet metal shop is type 302. This is the type that is used for architectural work, containers of all sorts, and for sinks and counters in restaurant work. However, for special applications such as photography labs where special chemicals are used, the sheet metal worker must look in a handbook showing the type of stainless recommended for a specific use.

Another designation is the finish number. Every type of stainless steel can be ordered in several different classes of finish from a number 1, which is unpolished, up to a number 7 which is virtually a mirror finish. The finish that is usually used on standard stainless steel jobs in the sheet metal shop is the number 3 finish.

Stainless steel has a silver-chrome appearance and generally can be easily recognized by its "grained" appearance. The grain in stainless steel is caused by the minute polishing scratches generally found on most finishes. These all run in the same direction just as the grain in wood. Just as in wood, it is easier to cut the metal with the grain than across it. Unpolished stainless has no grain and has a dull gray finish very similar in appearance to unpolished aluminum. The student may confuse these two metals; however, stainless can be easily identified by its greater weight and by its greater resistance to bending.

Stainless steel is gaged by the Manufacturers' Standard Gage in the same manner as other steel sheets. The only difference is that stainless sheets are rolled more accurately and are therefore closer to exact gage dimensions.

Though some stainless sheet is available in a hardened state, almost all of the types used in the sheet metal shop are in the unhardened state and can be bent in the brake as severely as can galvanized steel sheet. The principle difference between stainless and other sheet metals is its extreme toughness. Though it can be bent as severely as galvanized, its toughness makes it more difficult to bend. It is also more difficult to cut and requires more pressure to shear. The general rule is to add four gages to the capacity of any shear or brake when using them on stainless, since capacity ratings are based upon mild steel. This means that a shear rated for cutting 16 gage, has only a capacity of 20 gage for stainless steel.

Stainless steel is a solid sheet, not coated. This, along with its beauty and corrosion resistance, is its great advantage. It can be welded and the welded joints ground off and polished until the weld is not visible, yet its corrosion resistance is not affected.

Though stainless is tough, it can be readily worked in the sheet metal shop. Any skilled welder can weld it, and when special flux and solder are used it can be easily soldered.

The cost of stainless is high, running about seven times the cost of galvanized steel. However, in applications where galvanized may last only five years, stainless will last indefinitely. Because of its almost complete resistance to corrosion, the high cost of stainless does not necessarily mean it is the most expensive metal to use, since its long life often makes it the cheapest material to use in the long run. Stainless was developed in 1918, so it is one of the newest metals in common use. Its beauty and long life have made it one of the most popular of all the sheet metals. Canneries, dairies, food processing plants, restaurants, and any other industries that process foods, use stainless almost exclusively since it is not only long lasting but also easy to keep clean and always keeps its neat and clean appearance. Wherever corrosion conditions are high, as in chemical plants, stainless is necessary since it is the only metal that will last for any length of time. In addition, stainless is used extensively for architectural work—many of the largest buildings in New York City used stainless steel exclusively for their outside covering.

Tin Plate

Tin plate is sheet steel coated with

pure tin. It was once widely used in roofing, dairy equipment, food canning and other large-scale applications but has been largely replaced by stainless steel, aluminum and other materials. However, one type of tin plate still commonly used is *terne plate*. Terne plate is sheet steel coated with an alloy of tin and lead. Terne plate usually comes in 36 × 96 inch sheets and is gaged by the Manufacturers' Standard Gage.

Non-Ferrous Sheet Metals

Non-ferrous metals are those which have no iron or steel content. The most common non-ferrous metals used in the sheet metal shop are copper, aluminum, lead and zinc.

Copper

Copper is a solid sheet, easily recognized by its typical reddish color. Until the mid 1800's, copper, along with tin plate was the principal metal of the sheet metal worker. In fact, Paul Revere, immediately after the American Revolution, pioneered one of the first copper rolling mills in America.

The great advantage of copper is its high corrosion resistance. There are many examples of copper roofs on cathedrals in Europe that were installed in the Middle Ages and are still in good condition. Another desirable feature of copper is its beauty. For many types of architecture—especially to supplement brickwork—copper adds warmth and color that cannot be duplicated by any other type of metal. Copper sheet is comparatively high in cost, running about three times the cost of galvanized steel.

In the sheet metal trade today, the greatest use for copper is in architectural sheet metal. It is used extensively for high quality roofing on public buildings. A properly installed copper roof will require no additional care for the life of the building, which makes it a cheap roofing material when compared to the maintenance costs of other roofs over a fifty year period. Gutters, downspouts, roof flashings, and hoods are some of the common applications for copper. Many restaurants use copper hoods where appearance is a factor, especially in installations against dark wood panelling where copper complements the color of the panels.

Copper sheets are available in either cold rolled or hot rolled sheets. Cold rolled sheets are sheets that have been through a final process of running through finishing rolls. This gives the metal a smooth finish and work-hardens it to a half-hard condition. Cold rolled copper is still softer than galvanized steel and is bent and formed easily. Though cold rolled copper is much stiffer than the hot rolled, it is not as rigid as steel sheets, and usually a thicker sheet of copper is used than would be used of steel under the same conditions. Cold rolled copper is the type commonly used in the sheet metal shop.

Hot rolled copper is copper that has had only the hot rolling process and has not been rolled while cold. It does not have the shiny appearance of cold rolled copper and is much softer. Hot rolled copper is used when the metal will be subjected to stretching when it is formed, since it is soft enough to take severe forming. As it is formed, the hot rolled copper work-hardens and approaches the hardness of cold rolled copper. Copper that work-hardens can be annealed (softened) by heating it up to a cherry red and then cooling either by quenching in water or allowing to cool in air.

In the sheet metal trade, copper sheets are specified by ounces per square foot. For example, *18 ounce copper* means copper sheet that weighs 18 ounces per square foot. In other trades, copper sheet is sometimes designated by decimals of an inch thickness or by the *American Wire or Brown and Sharpe Gage*. See Table 4-3.

TABLE 4-3   GAGE NUMBERS AND THICKNESSES FOR SHEET COPPER AND ALUMINUM

American Wire or Brown & Sharpe Gage Number	Thickness in Inches
10	0.1019
11	0.0907
12	0.0808
13	0.0720
14	0.0641
15	0.0571
16	0.0508
17	0.0453
18	0.0403
19	0.0359
20	0.0320
21	0.0285
22	0.0253
23	0.0226
24	0.0201
25	0.0179
26	0.0159
27	0.0142
28	0.0126
29	0.0113
30	0.0100
31	0.0089
32	0.0080
33	0.0071
34	0.0063
35	0.0056
36	0.0050
37	0.0045
38	0.0040
39	0.0035
40	0.0031

Aluminum

The main properties of aluminum are its light weight, corrosion resistance and appearance. Sheet aluminum weighs approximately ⅓ as much as sheet steels and is just about as strong. For these reasons, aluminum is sometimes used instead of galvanized steel for such items as exposed ductwork, gutters and downspouts, etc., where appearance, corrosion resistance and case of handling are more important factors than economy.

Pure aluminum is too soft to hold a permanent shape in sheet form so the sheets are always manufactured as *alloys*. Alloying means that one or more metals are added to the pure aluminum to increase its strength and hardness. Some of the more common alloying metals are manganese, copper, chromium, silicon and magnesium. Very small quantities of these metals are required to give the desired properties. In fact, most alloys for sheet metal work are almost 99 percent pure aluminum.

There are several combinations of

materials and processing methods used in manufacturing aluminum alloys. However, only a few apply to sheet metal work. The standard alloy for sheet metal work is designated by the number 3003. It contains 1.2 percent manganese as the alloying agent. After the alloy number, a letter and number combination are given. These designate the hardening process used in manufacture and the relative hardness or *temper* of the finished product. The letter O denotes that the material has been *annealed* (softened by heat). The letter H means *strain-hardened*. That is, material has been subjected to stress to increase its strength and hardness. The letter T means that the material has been *thermal tempered* (alternately heated and cooled to achieve a high and stable degree of hardness). Almost all of the aluminum used in sheet metal work will have the H designation. The numbers following the letter H indicate the type of processing and the degree of hardness. The first digit indicates any additional processing after strain-hardening. For sheet metal work, the letter H will be followed the numeral 1 which means that there has been no additional treatment after strain-hardening. The second digit indicates the *degree* of hardening. This is based on a scale of 0 to 7, 0 indicating very soft and 7 approaching maximum hardness. Thus, the designation -H14 means the material has strain-hardened only and is medium hard. The complete designation as it appears on each sheet would read 3003-H14. This is by far the most commonly used designation and is known in the trade as *commercial half-hard*. The thickness of aluminum is usu-ally gaged in decimals of an inch. However, it is also sometimes gaged by the American Wire Or Brown and Sharpe Gage as shown in Table 4-3.

Lead

Lead is one of the oldest of sheet metals. Its high resistance to corrosion and easy workability were recognized early in the middle ages and many architectural applications were found for it. Many medieval churches are still using the same lead roofs, gutters and downspouts that were installed when the churches were built. Although lead has been largely replaced in the sheet metal field by stainless steel and, to some extent, plastics, it still has some important applications. It is used particularly in highly corrosive situations such as tanks for acid baths. It is also impervious to X-rays and is used in installations where there is the possibility of hazardous radiation leaks.

Lead is too soft to be handled in flat sheets so it is marketed in rolls and is gaged in pounds per square foot.

Zinc

Sheet zinc is highly resistant to corrosion and is used in some instances where galvanized steel cannot provide adequate resistance. Compared to other metals, zinc is rather brittle so care must be taken while bending it. Zinc sheets are usually ordered by specifying decimal parts of an inch for thickness.

Oxides of Metal

When considering the characteristics of the different sheet metals, the student should also consider the importance of the oxides of that metal. Though we speak of the characteristics of a metal, what we are actually referring to most of the time are the characteristics of the oxide of the metal.

Whenever a metal is exposed to air, the oxygen in the air combines with metal to form a chemical film over the metal. This chemical is called the *oxide* of the metal. A familiar example of an oxide is the rust that forms on uncoated iron and steel. This is called iron oxide. The green chemical that often forms on copper is an oxide of copper.

The importance of the oxide is that the characteristics of the oxide determine many of the characteristics of the metal. Rust (iron oxide) forms quickly and is porous and flaky. Since iron oxide is porous, it allows moisture to seep through it and form more oxide underneath. Since it is flaky, as soon as a large amount of oxide is formed it flakes off to expose more metal which will form more oxide. This action eventually eats through the metal which is the reason why plain steel is a poor metal to be exposed to corrosive conditions.

Stainless steel, on the other hand, forms an oxide that is transparent, tough, and impervious to air and almost every chemical. This transparency is the reason stainless steel keeps its lasting beauty. The toughness of the oxide is the reason for the long life of stainless, since actually, nothing ever contacts the metal itself.

Copper and lead also have oxides which are impervious to air and most chemicals and this is why they are so long lasting.

Aluminum oxide is hard to dissolve and reforms immediately if removed. For this reason, aluminum is difficult to solder. In soldering, the oxide must be removed so that the solder contacts the metal directly.

Class Activities

1. *Make a chart of the sheet metals listed below describing appearance, composition, gage system and two typical uses.*

    A. *Galvanized steel*
    B. *Tin plate*
    C. *Copper*
    D. *Aluminum*
    E. *Stainless steel*

2. *Obtain samples of as many different types of sheet metal as possible. Number the samples and have each class member identify the samples.*

3. *Using the samples from Item 2 above, have each class member determine the decimal thicknesses of the samples by using a micrometer.*

4. *Take the micrometer readings from*

Item 3 and make a chart showing the type of sheet metal for each sample, the micrometer reading for each and, where applicable, the corresponding gage number according to appropriate tables.

STUDENT QUESTIONS AND ACTIVITIES

1. Explain the difference between steel and non-ferrous metals.
2. Explain what is meant by *alloy* and list the metals most commonly used in alloying.
3. Give the approximate thickness in fractions of an inch for the following Manufacturers' Standard Gages:
    A. 10 gage
    B. 16 gage
    C. 22 gage
    D. 28 gage
4. Explain two methods of galvanizing.
5. What is the difference between hot-rolled and cold-rolled copper? Explain in terms of processing, characteristics and uses.
6. Explain the meaning of the designation 3003-H14 for sheet aluminum. What is this designation commonly called?
7. What is the *oxide* of a metal?
8. What is the importance of oxides?
9. Why is uncoated steel unsuited for corrosive conditions?

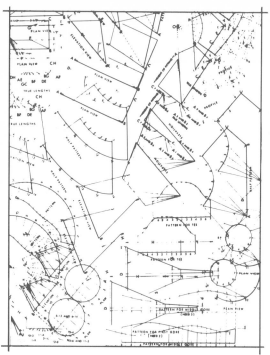

materials of the sheet metal trade

When you finish this chapter, you should be able to:
1. Sketch sectional views of at least five different mild steel shapes and show on each how the size is designated.
2. Explain the difference between wire cloth, expanded metal, and cane metal.
3. Describe wire cloth products that the sheet metal worker uses.
4. Define *hot-rolled* and *cold-rolled* steel.

In addition to the sheet metals covered in Chapter 4, the sheet metal worker must be familiar with a variety of other materials. This chapter will acquaint you with the many other materials used in the sheet metal trade.

Mild Steel Shapes

Rods, bars, and other forms of steel used in the sheet metal trade are called *mild steel shapes*. Sectional views of the steel shapes commonly used in the sheet metal trade are shown in Fig. 5-1.

Round Bar

The steel shape that is round in shape is called round bar or rod. In general the term *rod* is used when speaking of $\frac{1}{2}$ inch diameter or less. *Rod* is also

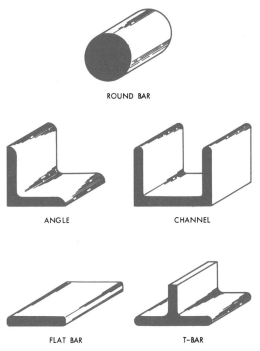

ROUND BAR

ANGLE   CHANNEL

FLAT BAR   T-BAR

Fig. 5-1. Typical mild steel shapes.

up to $6 \times 6 \times \frac{3}{8}$. Angle steel is used for stiffeners around the tops of sheet metal objects such as boxes. It is riveted on large pieces of sheet metal to reinforce the sheet metal. It is used for legs, braces, hangers and stiffeners on a variety of things such as air conditioning ducts, fans, blowers and hoods.

Flat Bar

Flat bar can be obtained in almost any size. Its size is designated by width and thickness. Thus $1 \times \frac{1}{8}$ flat bar means that the flat bar is one inch wide and $\frac{1}{8}$ inch thick. By far the most common size used in the sheet metal trade is $1 \times \frac{1}{8}$ bar, though other sizes are used if the need arises. Flat bar is commonly called *strap* in the sheet metal trade. Strap does not refer to any particular size, but generally is used in connection with $1 \times \frac{1}{8}$ flat bar or smaller. Flat bar, especially strap, is most commonly used in the sheet metal trade for hangers to suspend air conditioning duct or equipment such as fans and heaters. Because it can be easily rolled into circular shapes it is often used as stiffeners on the tops of round cans or tanks.

used when speaking of short lengths such as *welding rod*. Usually the round bar used in the sheet metal trade is $\frac{1}{2}$ inch in diameter or less. It is used for stiffeners on the edges of sheet metal, for control rods on air conditioning dampers, and for damper shafts.

Angle Steel

Angle steel is designated by the width of each side and the thickness of the metal. Thus a $2 \times 2 \times \frac{1}{4}$ means each side of the angle measures 2 inches and that the angle is $\frac{1}{4}$ inch thick. The most common sizes used in the sheet metal trade are $1 \times 1 \times \frac{1}{8}$, $1\frac{1}{2} \times 1\frac{1}{2} \times \frac{1}{8}$, and $2 \times 2 \times \frac{3}{16}$. However other thicknesses are available from $\frac{1}{2} \times \frac{1}{2} \times \frac{1}{8}$

Channel

Channel steel, often called *channel*, is used much in the same way as angles, and generally is used in place of angles where additional stiffness is needed. A typical application would be fastening channels across two rough beams to provide a base for a platform for an air conditioning unit or a fan. Channel steel can be obtained in almost any size. It is designated by width, depth, and thickness. Thus, $3 \times 1\frac{1}{2} \times \frac{3}{8}$ means the channel steel is 3 inches wide, $1\frac{1}{2}$ inches deep and is $\frac{3}{8}$ inch thick.

Tee Bar

Tee bar is obtainable in a variety of sizes, and is used in the sheet metal trade interchangeably with channels and angles, depending upon availability or the particular requirements of the job. Tee bar is designated by width, height, and thickness, thus a $2 \times 2 \times \frac{1}{4}$ tee bar means that it is 2 inches wide, 2 inches high, and $\frac{1}{4}$ inch thick.

Manufacturing Processes of Steel Shapes

Mild steel shapes can be obtained either *black* or *galvanized*. It is also either *hot-rolled* or *cold-rolled*. The designation of black simply means that it is the same as black steel sheet. The designation of galvanized means that the black steel shapes have been pickled in acid and dipped in zinc in a manner similar to galvanized steel sheets.

Hot-rolled and cold-rolled are the same type of steel and this designation refers merely to the processing. Hot-rolled means only that the steel is shaped while hot by running it through specially formed rollers. Cold-rolled steel is hot-rolled steel that has been given an additional rolling process. After the hot-rolled forming, the steel is run through an additional set of forming rolls while cold.

Hot-rolled steel is softer than cold-rolled and has a comparatively rough surface. Cold-rolled is harder because the cold-rolling process work-hardens the steel. It has a smoother, denser finish, and its edges are more sharply shaped than hot-rolled.

Materials for Openings

The sheet metal worker uses a variety of different materials to cover openings such as a rough vent, an air conditioning outlet, a ventilating duct or a guard over machinery. In general, the purpose of this material is to allow air to pass through while keeping out foreign objects such as dirt and trash. In some cases such as machinery guards, the purpose is to allow passage of air but to prevent the worker's hands from contact with moving machinery parts.

Wire Cloth

Wire cloth is woven strands of wire with the space between wires regulated to form a specified opening size. Hardware cloth shown in Fig. 5-2, wire screen and plastic screen shown in Fig. 5-3 and wire cloth are all in this category. Hardware cloth is the term used for larger mesh, usually from $\frac{1}{8}$ inch to $\frac{1}{2}$ inch squares, and is almost always made from steel wire which is galvanized after the cloth is woven. Screen

Fig. 5-2. Hardware cloth. (Photo by Joe Van Witsen)

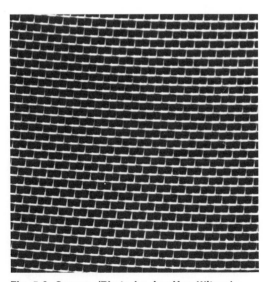

Fig. 5-3. Screen. (Photo by Joe Van Witsen)

(such as the common window screen) is finer mesh wire cloth and generally refers to wire cloth with a mesh from 16 to 20. *Mesh* refers to the number of openings per inch in the screen. Thus *16 mesh* means that there are 16 openings per lineal inch in the screen.

Although all of these materials are wire cloth, the specific name of wire cloth generally refers to a very fine mesh that is finer than screen. Wire cloth can be obtained in brass, copper, or stainless steel wire and can be ordered from stock for as fine as 100 mesh (100 openings per lineal inch) and can be special-ordered for even finer mesh.

Grills and Registers

Other types of coverings for openings are grills and registers such as those shown in Fig. 5-4.

Grills are those with fixed bars that cannot be turned. Registers are those with movable bars to direct the flow of air, and commonly have a damper arrangement on the back so that the amount of air flow can be regulated. Grills are used in duct openings in floors where they will be walked on and strength is needed. They are used principally on duct openings where it is not required to control the direction of the air flow, such as a ventilating duct through a roof or a duct opening that is pulling air from a room to return it to the forced air heater.

Registers are used on heating and air conditioning duct outlets where it is necessary to control the flow of the air. Usually the front bars of a register are movable so that they can be adjusted to regulate the direction of the air flow.

Grills and registers are generally used in place of hardware cloth where strength and appearance are a large factor.

Expanded Metal

Although expanded metal appears to be somewhat like hardware cloth it is made by an entirely different process. Expanded metal has diamond-shaped openings and is not made from woven wire. Expanded metal is made from a solid sheet of metal in which slits have been cut. Then the metal is stretched across its width or *expanded*. This forms the diamond mesh pattern as shown in Fig. 5-5. Expanded metal is generally used in place of hardware cloth where a large opening requires a stiffer material. It is widely used as a security closure over vulnerable openings.

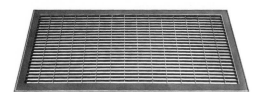

Fig. 5-4. Top: Grill. Bottom: Register. (Lima Register Co.)

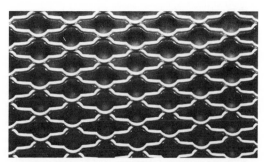

Fig. 5-5. Expanded metal. (Photo by Joe Van Witsen)

Fig. 5-6. Perforated metal patterns. (Diamond Perforated Metals)

Perforated Metal

Perforated metal is made from a solid sheet in which a regular pattern of holes has been punched. It is sometimes called *cane metal* because of its similarity in appearance to the woven cane fiber material used for furniture, screens, etc. Cane or perforated metal is available in a variety of patterns such as are shown in Fig. 5-6.

Cane metal is not used as frequently as expanded metal and hardware cloth because of its extra expense and because it restricts the flow of air more than expanded metal or hardware cloth. It is generally used in a situation where a material more decorative than expanded metal or hardward cloth is desired and the control of air flow is not important.

Pipe and Tubing

Pipe

The sheet metal worker uses both black pipe and galvanized pipe as legs and stiffeners. In general, the actual installation of pipe is the work of a plumber or a steamfitter, but the sheet metal worker may sometimes have to connect a few small fittings to connect his equipment to the installed pipe. Although pipe can be obtained in almost any size, the ones commonly used in the sheet metal trade are from $\frac{3}{8}$ to $1\frac{1}{4}$ inches in diameter. Pipe sizes are specified by the inside diameter of the hole. Thus a $\frac{1}{2}$ inch pipe is $\frac{1}{2}$ inch inside the pipe and approximately $\frac{7}{8}$ inch outside diameter.

Copper Tubing

Installing copper tubing is generally

the work of the plumber or steamfitter, but the sheet metal worker often connects short pieces of tubing when installing equipment. Copper tubing is measured by outside diameter. Thus a ⅜ inch tubing measures ⅜ inch outside diameter. Tubing is connected by brass fittings such as those shown in Fig. 5-7.

Split Pipe

For a smooth, very stiff edge, the sheet metal worker uses special pipe called split pipe, such as shown in Fig. 5-8. Split pipe can be obtained either in galvanized, black, or stainless steel. A typical use for split pipe is shown in Fig. 5-9 as the top edge of a sink.

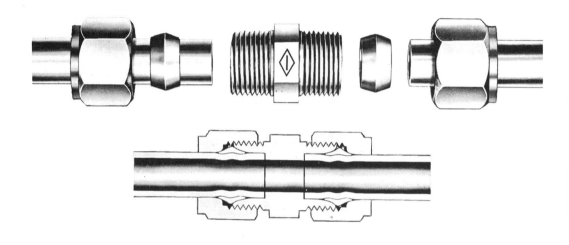

COPPER TUBING WITH BRASS FITTING

Fig. 5-7. Connection fittings for copper tubing.

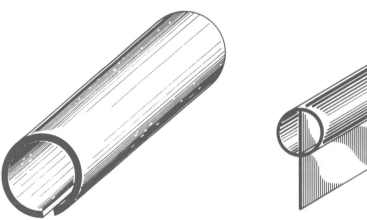

Fig. 5-8. Split pipe.

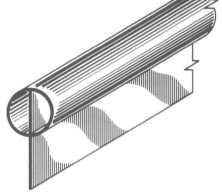

Fig. 5-9. Split pipe installed on a sheet metal sink.

Dampers

This is a general term used to describe any kind of mechanical device that is inserted in a sheet metal duct to regulate the flow of air. They are used to regulate the amount of air that can pass through a duct or they are used to guide the air smoothly around turns in the duct. Some dampers, especially large ones, are purchased from the manufacturer ready to install in the duct. Others are built out of 10 gage or 16 gage galvanized steel when the sheet metal worker is building the duct. Dampers can be adjusted from outside the duct by moving the handle and set screw. In large commercial installations, dampers are controlled automatically by air-operated motors.

Wire

Tinned, copper, or galvanized wire is available in a variety of sizes and is shipped in 100 lb. rolls. Wire is used for handles, for wiring tops of pans and boxes, and for many other uses.

Types of Wire

Though the metal worker may occasionally make projects from the more expensive types of wire such as aluminum, stainless steel, or copper, the more common types of wire such as steel and iron are used for ordinary jobs. Steel wire is stronger, and should be used where strength is needed. To facilitate soldering and to prevent rust and corrosion, these types of wire are coated with zinc, tin, or copper, and are usually referred to as galvanized, tinned, or coppered wire.

Class Activities

1. *In the school shop, list as many different types of materials of the sheet metal trade as you can find. For each one, list how they are used.*

2. *Suggest to the instructor as many additional materials as you can think of that might be used in the sheet metal trade, and discuss with him in class whether they are in fact materials used in the sheet metal trade.*

3. *Assign some members of the class to read and report on the use of plastics in place of sheet metal.*

STUDENT QUESTIONS AND ACTIVITIES

1. Sketch sectional views of at least five different mild steel shapes.
2. For the sectional views shown in Fig. 5-1, tell how the size is designated for each.
3. Explain the difference between wire cloth, expanded metal and perforated metal.
4. Define *hot-rolled* and *cold-rolled* steel.
5. Explain the difference between grills and registers.
6. Give at least two uses for pipe in sheet metal work.

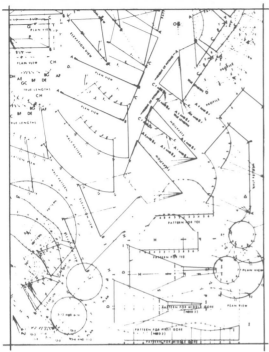

fasteners for sheet metal

When you complete this chapter you should be able to:
1. Describe tinners' rivets and explain how they are designated for size.
2. Explain how machine screws and bolts are designated for size and explain such designations as 1/4-20X 1.
3. Describe sheet metal screws and lag bolts.
4. Describe the following welding processes:

    A. Oxy-acetylene   D. TIG
    B. Arc   E. Spot
    C. MIG

There are several types of fasteners used to join pieces of sheet metal and to attach sheet metal to other materials. This chapter will cover the commonly used types of fasteners, their characteristics and standard designations, and the various types of welding used in sheet metal work.

Rivets

Before modern welding techniques came into common use, riveting was one of the most common methods for joining sheet metal. Since the advent of the new welding techniques and modern machines that form seams on sheet metal, riveted seams are not so common in modern sheet metal work. However, the sheet metal worker will often use rivets on sheet metal too heavy for machine forming and where welding is not practical.

Rivets may be made of steel, copper, brass, aluminum or other materials. Standards for rivet sizes and shapes have been put forth by several agencies. The most commonly used standard in the United States is the *American Standard Small Solid Rivets*.

Tinners' Rivets

Tinners' rivets are small, flat headed rivets with relatively short lengths. The size numbers of tinners' rivets are determined by the approximate weight per thousand rivets. Thus the designation 2lb. rivet means that 1000 of these rivets will weigh 2 pounds. Each weight of rivet has a definite diameter and length. Fig. 6-1 shows the actual size of each rivet.

Standard Rivets

Besides tinners' rivets, there are many other types available in a variety of materials, sizes and head shapes. The more common head shapes are shown in Fig. 6-2. These rivets are specified by the diameter and length of the body. Thus a 1/4 × 1 rivet is 1/4 inch in diameter and 1 inch long. *Note:* Except for countersunk, the length dimension is only the length of the body. It does not include the thickness of the head.

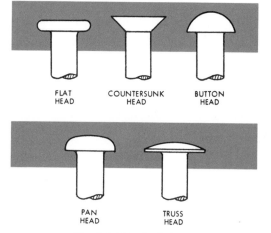

Fig. 6-2. Standard rivets.

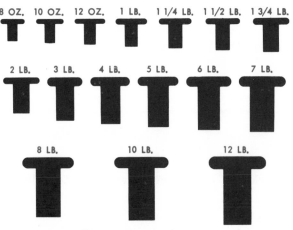

Fig. 6-1. Tinners' rivets.

Blind Rivets

Blind rivets are so called because they may be installed completely from one side of the work. This convenience has caused a wide-spread popularity for blind riveting. One of the most popular types of blind rivets is shown in Fig. 6-3. This is a hollow rivet mounted on a mandrel which is made of harder metal than the rivet. The rivet and mandrel assembly is inserted into the work and a special tool (Fig. 6-4) is placed squarely on the head of the rivet as shown in Fig. 6-3. By squeezing the handles, the mandrel is drawn back, causing the wedge-shaped head to expand the foot of the rivet. The mandrel then snaps off and falls free. For high-speed production riveting and a greater variety of rivet sizes, power riveters are used. They may be powered either by compressed air (pneumatic) or by combination air and fluid (air-hydraulic). Fig. 6-5 shows a pneumatic riveter.

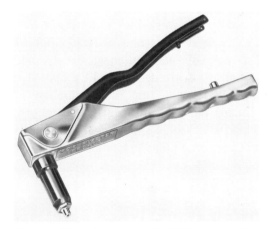

Fig. 6-4. Blind riveter (hand). (USM Corporation)

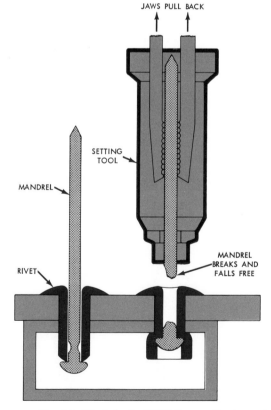

Fig. 6-3. Blind rivets. (USM Corporation)

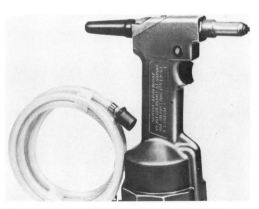

Fig. 6-5. Pneumatic blind riveter. (USM Corporation.)

77

Bolts and Machine Screws

Bolts and machine screws are widely used in the sheet metal trade so it is important that the sheet metal worker be familiar with how bolt and screw sizes are designated.

Bolts

A bolt is generally defined as an externally threaded fastener which is secured to the work by tightening a nut. Fig. 6-6 shows some of the common types of bolts used in sheet metal work.

Bolt sizes are designated by diameter in fractions of an inch, number of threads per inch of length, and length. Thus, a 1/4-20 × 1 bolt means that it is 1/4 inch in diameter, has 20 threads per inch and is one inch long.

Machine Screws

Machine screws are similar to small bolts in that they are threaded to receive nuts. The difference is that the screws have slotted, recessed or hexagonal heads so that they may be driven by the head. Thus, they are commonly used in situations where a bolt and nut assembly is not practical. See Fig. 6-7. Size designations for machine screws are the same as that for bolts except that the diameter dimension is given as a fixed code number. For instance, in Table 6-1, note that a 10-24 screw means that it is size ten (about 3/16 inches in diameter) and has 24 threads per inch of length.

Thread Designations

For both bolts and machine screws, the thread designation is commonly followed by the letters UNC or UNF. These letters stand for *Unified National Coarse* and *Unified National Fine*. These are the two major series of thread designations used in America. For example, note in Table 6-1 that a number 10 UNC bolt or screw has 24 threads per inch while the number 10 UNF has 32 threads per inch. In sheet metal work, the most commonly used bolt is the 1/4-

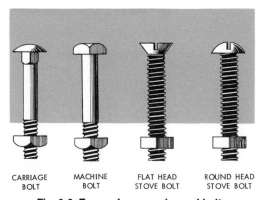

CARRIAGE BOLT   MACHINE BOLT   FLAT HEAD STOVE BOLT   ROUND HEAD STOVE BOLT

Fig. 6-6. Types of commonly used bolts.

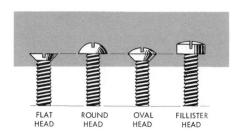

FLAT HEAD   ROUND HEAD   OVAL HEAD   FILLISTER HEAD

Fig. 6-7. Machine screws.

TABLE 6-1 UNIFIED NATIONAL THREAD SERIES

SIZE	THREADS PER INCH UNIFIED NATIONAL COARSE	THREADS PER INCH UNIFIED NATIONAL FINE
4	40	48
6	32	40
8	32	36
10	24	32
12	24	28
1/4	20	28
5/16	18	24
3/8	16	24
7/16	14	20
1/2	13	20
9/16	12	18
5/8	11	18
3/4	10	16

20 UNC bolt. The designation UNEF stands for *Unified National Extra Fine.* This type of bolt or screw is seldom used in sheet metal work. The few sizes that are not in UNC, UNF or UNEF are designated UNS which stands for *Unified National Special.* A commonly used size in this category is the 3/16 inch stove bolt. This is designated as 3/16-24 UNS. Note: On blueprints or specifications, the letter U may in many instances be dropped from the designation, leaving only NC or NF. The measurements remain the same.

As the United States adopts the metric system, it is probable that a new international system for fastener designation will be adopted. However, the Unified series will still be used for many years before the new system can be developed and put in use.

Sheet Metal Screws

Self Tapping Screws

Sheet metal screws are designed especially for sheet metal work. They are also called *self-tapping screws* because they tap their own mating threads as they are driven into the material. See Fig. 6-8. Note in Fig. 6-8 that the screws are threaded the full length of the screw. This causes the two pieces of metal to be fastened tightly together under the head of the screw. Most types of sheet metal screws are available with slotted, phillips and hex type heads.

Sheet metal screws are classified by the type of point and threading. The most common types are shown in Fig. 6-8. Type *A* has a sharp (or *gimlet*) point and coarse threads for ease in assembling. This type is used for fastening thin sections. Type *AB* is a modified form of type *A* and is now recommended in place of type *A*. Type *B* has a blunt point and threading similar to type *A* and is used for joining thicker sections. Type *C* has finer threads than types *A* and *B* and is used to heavier sheets and where greater strength is required. Types *D, F, G, T* and *Z* have blunt points and fine threads. They are used mainly for joining heavy metals, metals of different thicknesses and to fasten sheet metal to structural members or castings. These types are used where great strength is required. Types A through C are *thread forming* screws. That is, as they are driven, the pressure

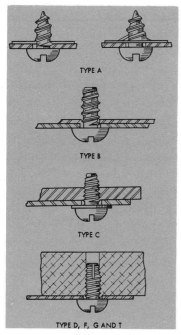

Fig. 6-8. Self tapping sheet metal screws.

cept that they are equipped with special chuck assemblies to receive insert bits for slotted and phillips type screw heads and sockets for hex heads. See Fig. 6-9.

Fig. 6-9. Electric screwdriver. (Milwaukee Electric Tool Corp.)

forms the mating threads in the metal. The other types are *thread cutting* screws. These screws make threads by cutting and removing part of the sheet metal.

In drilling holes for sheet metal screws, it is important to use the proper size bit, especially for types *D, F, G, T* and *Z*. The drill bit size to use is usually indicated on the box containing the screws. If the hole is too large, the screws will not hold. If the hole is too small, the screw will either not start or will be difficult to turn and may break off in the hole.

Sheet metal screws may be driven with hand screwdrivers or with electric drills with special screwdriver bits. Also, there are electric screwdrivers which are similar to electric drills ex-

Self-Drilling Screws

Self-drilling screws are a further refinement of the self-tapping screws previously described. Note in Fig. 6-10 that the tip of the screw is like a drill bit. This eliminates the need for pre-drilling or punching starter holes. Also, because the threads automatically tap the mating threads, the self-drilling screw drills, taps and threads in one operation as shown in Fig. 6-10. The sizes and threading of self-drilling screws are the same as those for self-tapping screws.

Drive Screws

The type U drive screw shown in Fig. 6-11 is considered to be a sheet metal

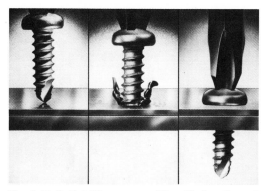

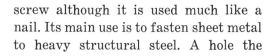

Fig. 6-10. Self drilling screws. (Great Lakes Screw)

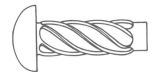

Fig. 6-11. Sheet metal drive screw.

screw although it is used much like a nail. Its main use is to fasten sheet metal to heavy structural steel. A hole the same size as the tip of the screw is drilled through both pieces and the drive screw is driven in with a hammer. The raised threads then form mating threads like the self tapping and self drilling screws.

Installation Fasteners

The sheet metal worker will often be required to install the objects he has fabricated in the shop. Many times, this will involve fastening the sheet metal to other materials such as concrete, masonry, wood, plaster or drywall. There are many types of fasteners available for these purposes. The following examples are the more commonly used types in the sheet metal trade.

Nails. Many types of nails such as copper, zinc and tin coated are used in sheet metal work. Copper nails are used whenever sheet copper is fastened to wood. Tinned nails are used extensively in all kinds of tin roofing. Galvanized nails are used in all applications of gal-

vanized sheet metal. Nails are designated by the symbol "d." This is the English symbol for *penny*. Thus, *10d* means ten penny. The smaller the number, the smaller the nail. The largest size generally used are 16-penny nails.

Lag Screws. Lag screws, as shown in Fig. 6-12 are large wood screws with a square or hex head instead of a slotted head. This is so that they can be turned with a wrench instead of a screwdriver.

Fig. 6-12. Lag screw.

Lag screws can be purchased either black or galvanized and are designated by diameter and length. Thus a 1/4 × 4 lag screw is 1/4 inch in diameter and 4 inches long. Lag screws are available in a variety of diameters and lengths up to 6 inches. They are used to fasten metal to wood.

Toggle Bolts. Toggle bolts are used to fasten sheet metal or other material to hollow surfaces. The wings may be either spring loaded as in Fig. 6-13, left, or the tumble or gravity type as in Fig. 6-13, right. The bolt itself is a machine screw available in sizes from ⅛ to ½ inch diameter. The spring wing type provides constant tension on the machine screw which helps absorb vibration. The tumble type is used mainly where vibration is not a factor.

Hollow Wall Screw Anchors. There is a nut set in the bottom which, when the machine screw is tightened, draws that end up tight to the back of the material in which it is used. See Fig. 6-14. The flange on the face remains on the outside surface of the wall, and once tightened, the screw may be removed without losing the anchor. Sizes range up to that designed for a wall 1-3/4 inches thick.

Star Dryvin Expansion Device. This is furnished complete with either single or double head nail, Fig. 6-15. Lengths range from 7/8 inch to 3-1/2 inches. The shield holds the fixture, while the nail expands the lead wrapper on the bottom end.

Fiberplug Anchor. A fiber anchor that is fitted with a hollow metal core for use with wood screws. It can be used in almost any material, and is not af-

Fig. 6-13. Toggle bolts. (Star Expansion Co.)

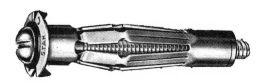

Fig. 6-14. Hollow wall screw anchor. (Star Expansion Co.)

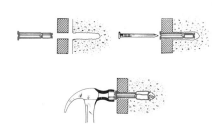

Fig. 6-15. Star Dryvin expansion device. (Star Expansion Co.)

fected by temperature, moisture, shock or vibration. Sizes run 6, 8, 10, 12, and 14. These size numbers refer to the size of screw for which they were designed although they will take one size smaller. Larger sizes are designed for use with lag screws. See Fig. 6-16.

Lead Screw Anchors. These are used in a similar way to fiberplugs and

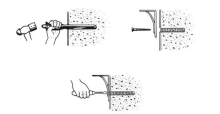

Fig. 6-16. Fiberplug anchor. (Star Expansion Co.)

Fig. 6-18. Lag expansion shield. (Star Expansion Co.)

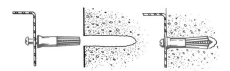

Fig. 6-17. Lead screw anchor. (Star Expansion Co.)

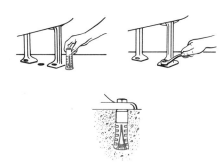

Fig. 6-19. Machine expansion shield. (Star Expansion Co.)

take three different sizes of screw, Fig. 6-17. Lengths range from 3/4 inch to 1-3/4 inches.

Plastic Anchors. Plastic anchors are now being commonly used for light loads. These are similar in appearance to the lead screw anchors. Sheet metal screws are used to expand the anchor.

Expansion Screw Anchors. These may take a machine screw or the larger sizes take a machine bolt. They consist of two parts, the conical member is tapped, and a lead sleeve slides over it. A pilot setting punch which comes with this anchor sets the lead sleeve tight in the hole. Sizes range from 1/8 inch machine screw to 1 inch machine bolt.

Lag Expansion Shields. These take a lag bolt. There is no nut in these anchors. The lag bolt screws itself further in as it is tightened. Used in heavy con-

struction, sizes vary from 1/4 inch to 3/4 inch. See Fig. 6-18.

Machine Expansion Shields. These take a machine bolt, and are used in heavy construction, Fig. 6-19. There is a tapered nut in the bottom which locks when the bolt is tightened, and thereafter will be securely anchored even if the bolt is removed. The smaller sizes are for 1/4 inch bolts and the larger ones for up to 1 inch bolts.

Hammer Fastening Tools. Pins and threaded studs may be set directly into concrete, building block, and light gauge steel by the use of a specially designed hammer and fastener holder. See Fig. 6-20. A solid steel hammer with a rubber encased handle is used for striking. The fastener holding device allows the whole force of the hammer blow to be transmitted directly to the head of the

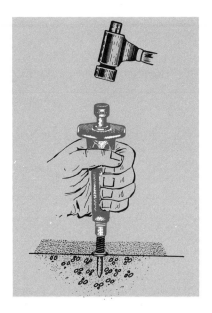

Fig. 6-20. Hammer fastening tool.

fastener. Fasteners may be set into hard materials with a few quick blows. No drilling is necessary.

Self Drilling Snap-Off Anchors. The fastener itself drills the hole and is then snapped off and left in place. The insertion of a screw expands the fastener to give a secure hold.

They may be drilled into place by an impact hammer or by a specially designed manual tool. Fig. 6-21 illustrates the self drilling snap off anchor and the method by which it is installed. Goggles should be worn when installing this anchor.

Powder-Actuated Fasteners. For fastening metal to concrete, powder-actuated fasteners are often used. These are called "powder-actuated" because fasteners such as nails and bolts are shot into the concrete by means of a powder-filled cartridge similar to those used in a rifle. The powder-filled cartridge looks like a blank cartridge. A common size is 22 caliber. The cartridge,

when fired, literally makes the fastener a bullet and fires it into the concrete.

The powder-actuated tool is one of the most potentially dangerous tools on constructions jobs. If used carelessly or without proper instruction, a worker could be shot by it, just as with a gun. There is also danger of shooting completely through a thin partition and hitting someone on the other side. Another hazard is that the fastener, when shot into the concrete, can hit steel and ricochet off. As with all tools when properly used, the powder-actuated tool is safe.

To insure safety, most states have safety regulations that only allow powder-actuated tools to be used by persons who have a license or certificate. Generally this license or certificate is obtained by attending a specified number of hours in the proper and safe use of the tool. These classes are usually conducted by manufacturers and distributors of the tools.

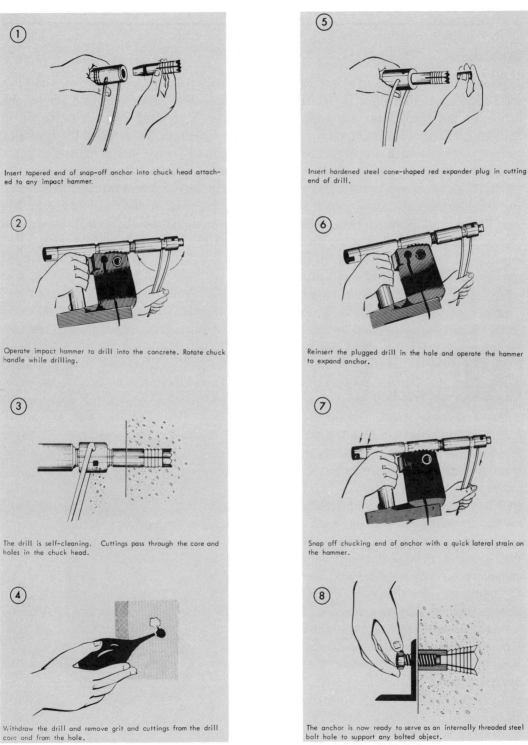

① Insert tapered end of snap-off anchor into chuck head attached to any impact hammer.

② Operate impact hammer to drill into the concrete. Rotate chuck handle while drilling.

③ The drill is self-cleaning. Cuttings pass through the core and holes in the chuck head.

④ Withdraw the drill and remove grit and cuttings from the drill core and from the hole.

⑤ Insert hardened steel cone-shaped red expander plug in cutting end of drill.

⑥ Reinsert the plugged drill in the hole and operate the hammer to expand anchor.

⑦ Snap off chucking end of anchor with a quick lateral strain on the hammer.

⑧ The anchor is now ready to serve as an internally threaded steel bolt hole to support any bolted object.

Fig. 6-21. Installation of snap-off type anchor. (Phillips Drill Co.)

Welding

Welding is one of the most important methods of fastening sheet metal. In addition to the traditional oxy-acetylene and simple arc welding, many newer techniques have been developed which have wide applications in sheet metal work. Some of these are inert gas welding and electric resistance or spot welding. Those sheet metal workers who are skilled in these techniques are in high demand. To develop ability in these areas requires much study and practice which is beyond the scope of this book. The purpose of this section is to describe the most commonly used welding techniques for joining sheet metal.

Oxy-acetylene Welding

Oxy-acetylene welding uses oxygen and acetylene gases which are regulated and fed into the torch to produce an extremely high-temperature flame. A typical oxy-acetylene welding outfit is shown in Fig. 6-22. This type of welding is commonly called *gas welding*. As a welding process, this type of welding is seldom used in the sheet metal shop because arc welding is faster and cheaper. In addition, since gas welding is a slower process than arc welding, it allows more heat to spread throughout the metal thus creating more problems with warping. The greatest use of the oxy-acetylene torch in the sheet metal shop is to heat pieces of heavy steel to bend them and to join metal by brazing.

Brazing is a process of joining metal with a brass rod rather than steel welding rod. Brazing is actually a soldering process since it does not melt the parent metals as welding must, but the brass brazing enters the pores of the pieces of metal and joins them much in the same manner as glue. Brazing is generally used on heavy pieces of metal where the heat required would be extreme and is used on some metals, such as cast iron, which are difficult to weld.

Arc Welding

The basic principle of arc welding is that two cables extend from the arc

Fig. 6-22. Oxy-acetylene welding outfit. (Union Carbide Corp., Linde Div.)

welder with one carrying the positive current and the other carrying the negative current. One cable is connected to the work that is to be welded while the other cable has the holder for the arc welding rod. The current passes through the arc welding rod and jumps across a small gap to the workpiece. This spark creates an intense heat which is enough to melt the metal and the welding rod to create a welded seam. The advantage of arc welding is that it is comparatively fast, and requires no preheating of the metal because the area of the heated metal is extremely small. This means that there is much less warping of the metal with arc welding than there is with gas welding. In addition, arc welding requires no special gases and therefore is a much cheaper process than gas welding.

Arc welding is generally used for all welding applications in the sheet metal shop. It was formerly used for welding stainless steel but has largely been replaced by the inert gas processes.

Inert Gas Welding

Inert gas welding is a general term that describes a number of different welding processes. However, all of them are based upon the idea of electric arc welding with the addition of a cone of inert gas which always covers the arc. This protects the molten metal from the air which can cause oxidation and a weak weld. In regular arc welding, the welding rod is covered with a flux which melts and covers the molten metal of the weld to perform this same function of protecting the weld from oxidation. In inert gas welding, the arc and heat are

much less than in arc welding and the inert gas protection results in a cleaner and stronger weld with less warpage. In most sheet metal shops that do much stainless steel work, the inert gas welding is a common process. See Fig. 6-23. It is particularly good for stainless steel welding and aluminum welding—both of which are difficult to perform with electric arc welding.

The two most common types of inert gas welding are *TIG* and *MIG* welding. TIG stands for *tungsten inert gas*. This means that the welding electrode is a tungsten rod which is not consumed in the weld. In TIG welding the welding rod is fed in by hand, much in the same way as in gas welding. MIG welding stands for *metallic inert gas*. In this type of inert gas welding the electrode, instead of being a tungsten rod, is the actual welding rod. In MIG welding the welding rod is fed automatically by a motorized feeder down through the center of the torch and is consumed in the welding process.

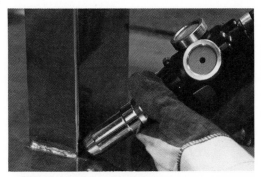

Fig. 6-23. Inert gas welder being used on stainless steel.

Resistance Welding

Resistance welding, commonly called *spot welding* is widely used in the sheet metal industry today. The basic principle of resistance welding is that the two pieces of metal to be joined are clamped between two pointed copper rods or electrodes which are connected to an electric power source. As electric current is passed from one point to the other, the metal acts as a resistor to the current which creates enough heat at the point of contact to melt the metal. Spot welders may be bench mounted or portable.

Fig. 6-24 shows a hand-carried spot welder being used to fabricate air-conditioning ductwork in the shop. Fig. 6-25 shows a heavier model with a bail attachment which is suspended from overhead for easy handling.

Another type of resistance welding is seam welding. This process is similar to spot welding except that the electrodes are disk shaped rollers. As the metal is fed between the rollers, current is released automatically at regular intervals. The spots may overlap or spaced at short intervals, making a continuous weld seam. See Fig. 6-26.

Fig. 6-24. Portable spot welder. (The Lincoln Electric Co.)

Fig. 6-25. Spot welder with bail attachment. (The Lincoln Electric Co.)

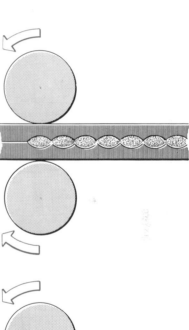

Fig. 6-26. In seam welding the metal pieces pass beween roller type electrodes.

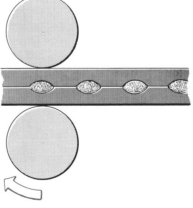

Class Activities

1. *Assign a member of the class to try to arrange it with a distributor of powder-actuated tools to give a demonstration to the class.*

2. *Arrange for a demonstration of blind riveting.*

3. *Assign a group from the class to obtain samples of as many sheet metal screws as possible and arrange them on a demonstration board.*

4. *Assign a group from the class to obtain as many different types of nails as possible and arrange them on a demonstration board.*

5. *Assign a group from the class to obtain as many different types of nuts and bolts as possible and arrange them on a demonstration board.*

STUDENT QUESTIONS AND ACTIVITIES

1. How much will 500 three-pound tinners' rivets weigh?
2. Give the diameter, threads per inch and length of a 1/4-20 × 1 bolt.
3. Define UNC and UNF.
4. What is meant by the term *self-tapping screws?*
5. What is a *self drilling screw?*
6. What is the difference between a wood screw and a lag screw?
7. Define the term *brazing.*
8. Name and describe the two types of inert gas welding.
9. Describe the difference between spot welding and seam welding.

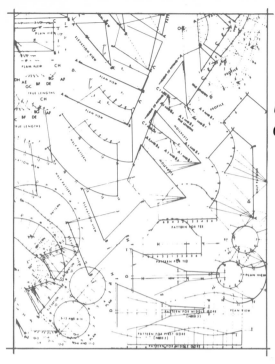

using patterns and cutting metal

7

When you finish this chapter, you should be able to:

1. Define the following terms:
   A. Pattern
   B. Template
   C. Master Pattern
   D. Stretchout
   E. Layout
   F. Pictorial Drawing
   G. Working Drawing
   H. Notching
   I. Elevation View
   J. Plan View
2. Given a series of points on a piece of metal, draw a smooth curve through these points with the use of a flexible rule.
3. Given a circumference rule and the diameter or radius of a circle, give the circumference of the circle within 30 seconds and to the nearest 1/16 of an inch.
4. Given the diameter of a circle, figure the circumference to the nearest 1/16 of an inch by the use of mathematics.
5. Use sheet metal snips to cut out any pattern or any kind of inside hole while observing the seven rules for the proper use and care of snips as given in this chapter.
6. Identify the following tools and machines.
   A. Compound Shears
   B. Bench Lever Shears
   C. Pipe Crimper
   D. Nibbler
   E. Double Cutting Shears
   F. Squaring Shears

In this chapter you will learn how sheet metal patterns are used and about the correct use and care of the various types of tools used in cutting the patterns.

In sheet metal work, a *pattern* is a piece of material which is cut to the exact size and shape that the sheet metal must be cut in order to be formed into the product desired. Original patterns are usually done on paper. In most cases, however, the same pattern will have to be used several times so it is transferred to a piece of metal which becomes a permanent pattern which may be used repeatedly without wear or damage.

Patterns and Drawings

Sheet metal articles are made of flat pieces of metal cut according to outlines that are drawn or traced on the sheets of metal. To obtain the correct size and shape, patterns are used. These patterns may be drawn on paper first, then transferred to the metal, or they may be laid out directly on the metal. It is better for the beginner to draw the patterns on paper first, since the paper pattern can be cut out and fitted together and any corrections made, saving valuable material. Patterns that are used repeatedly are made of metal and are called *templates* or *master patterns*. Paper patterns soon become worn and inaccurate if used repeatedly.

The term *stretchout* refers to the distance across the flat pattern or flat piece of metal before it is formed into shape. The illustration in Fig. 7-1 shows the stretchouts for square and cylindrical jobs. The stretchout is the same as the distance around the object. On a round pipe it would be the circumference of the pipe.

Layout, in general, refers to the method of developing the lines which

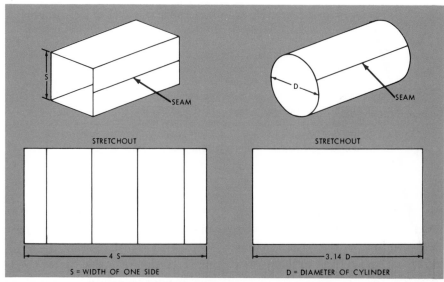

Fig. 7-1 Stretchouts for square and cylindrical objects.

form the pattern. The common methods of layout are: *simple pattern layout, parallel line development, radial line development,* and *triangulation.* These methods are treated in Chapters 14, 15, 16, and 17.

Pictorial Drawings

Pictorial drawings show the object as it actually appears after being formed into shape. This is illustrated in Fig. 7-2. Such a drawing is useful to show the shape of the finished object, and it is sometimes used in the shop to show simple dimensions. However, for many objects, the true shape of each side cannot be shown and it becomes difficult to put on clearly understood dimensions. For more complex items a *working* or *mechanical* drawing is used.

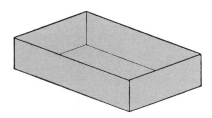

Fig. 7-2 Pictorial drawings show the shape of objects as they appear after forming.

Mechanical Drawing

A working or mechanical drawing shows the exact size and shape of each side. See Fig. 7-3. Notice that each view is just what you see by looking directly at the various sides as in the illustra-

tion. Since some of the views are alike—top and bottom, front and back, right and left end—it is only necessary to make the number of views required to show the size and shape of the object. In most cases this will be three—top, front, and end views.

In sheet metal work, the term *elevation* means any view which shows the height of the job. The term *plan view* refers to the top view, *front elevation* refers to the front view, and *end elevation* refers to the end view. With this information, a pattern, such as shown in Fig. 7-4, is easily developed. The X symbols near the end of the lines indicate the places where the metal is to bent or folded. These lines are called *brake lines.*

The working drawing, which may be a blueprint (blueprints are exact reproductions of working drawings and can be made quickly and inexpensively) should give all the information necessary to complete the job.

Pattern Information

The master pattern should contain all of the allowances and details necessary to fabricate the job. In addition, this information is contained in the specifications, or written description, which include the following information.

Allowance for Edges. Different types of edges are used to stiffen the edges of the sheet metal articles, and to eliminate the sharp sheet metal edge which may cut someone. Edges are made by bending the metal in various ways, or by wrapping the metal around wire, flat bar, or angle. The amount of metal allowed for the edge depends upon

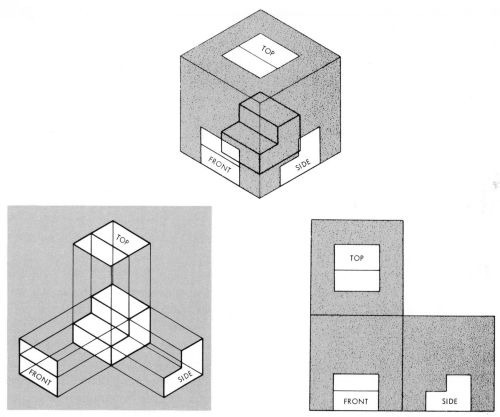

Fig. 7-3. The white areas in the drawing at the right are mechanical or working drawings. The drawings at the left and top show the placement of various views in relation to each other.

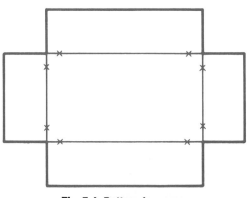

Fig. 7-4. Pattern for a pan.

the type of edge used. The advantages of each type of edge and the amount of metal to allow for each one will be discussed in Chapter 9.

Allowances for Seaming. Sheet metal parts are joined by seams of various kinds. The addition of the seams makes it necessary to add material to the pattern. Allowances for each type of seam will also be given in Chapter 9.

Prick Punching Brake Lines. On metal patterns, the brake lines are prick punched. If the master pattern is being traced from a paper pattern, the brake lines are prick punched through the paper pattern onto the metal.

Every brake line should be prick punched because many of the brake lines must be bent from the other side of the metal. The student often tries to avoid prick marking all the lines, and this invariably means several return trips from the brake to the bench to prick mark a line that is needed. Put a prick mark near the end of each brake line as shown by the *X* marks in Fig. 7-4. These prick marks should be located about ¼″ from the end of the line so they can be easily covered if the job is soldered.

Notching and Clipping. Notching and clipping are used to cut away portions of the metal to prevent overlapping and bulging on seams and edges. The operations are different as illustrated by Fig. 7-5. Detailed information will be given in Chapter 14 about the allowances necessary for notching and clipping.

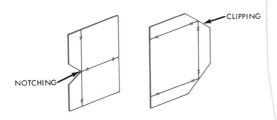

Fig. 7-5. Notching and clipping.

Fig. 7-6. Clamp pliers.

Tracing Around a Metal Pattern. When tracing around a metal pattern, the pattern should be held in place on the metal with weights, C clamps, or other devices to prevent the pattern from slipping.

The vise clamp pliers shown in Fig. 7-6 is a more convenient tool than the C clamp for securing the pattern. It operates simply by pressing the hand grips together. An adjustable screw on one of the handles makes it possible to regulate it for any thickness of work.

A sharp scratch awl is usually used to scribe around the outline of the metal pattern.

Transferring a Paper Pattern to Metal

Trying to trace around a paper pattern is very difficult since the paper will wrinkle at the slightest pressure. The best method of transferring a pattern from paper to metal is not to cut out the paper pattern at all, but leave it intact on the paper. Then lay it over the metal with weights to keep it from moving, and prick mark through the paper at the ends of all lines and at intervals around curves. If possible, prick mark the center points of any arcs that must be swung. Then remove the paper and with a rule and scratch awl, draw lines connecting all prick marks in the proper manner.

Direct Layout on Metal

Many experienced workmen do many of their layouts directly on the metal. However, for the student it is better to make the more difficult layouts on paper, and only those for the simple fittings directly on the metal.

Preparing the Metal. One of the first steps in preparing to lay out a pattern on metal is to square the left end of the metal. Sheet metal is not usually squared before it leaves the factory. The steel square may be used for this purpose, or the sheet may be squared directly by the use of the squaring shears. The next step is to see that the sheet of metal lies perfectly flat on the bench and not on the bench plate.

The measurements for the layout on metal should be taken from the bottom of the sheet and from the squared-up line at the left end of the sheet. Patterns are always located in the lower left hand corner of the sheet. This practice minimizes the waste of metal when cutting out patterns.

Marking Irregular Curves. When laying out a pattern on metal, a series of points along any irregular curve are located and then a smooth curve must be drawn through these points. The most common method of doing this is by means of a flexible rule instrument such as is shown in Fig. 7-7. These instruments are made of spring steel so they can be bent to a curve and still return to their original straightness. Though the one shown is a two-foot folding rule, flexible rules can be obtained in many lengths. In fact, most three-foot circumference rules used in the sheet metal shop are flexible rules. Fig. 7-8 shows how the rule can be bent through several of the points along the curve and a smooth curve drawn in with a scratch awl or a pencil.

Taking Measurements

How to Read the Common Rule. In denoting measurements taken with a rule, the symbol ′ is always used for feet and ″ for inches. If you will examine the section of the rule shown in Fig. 7-9, you will notice that the inch is divided first into two parts, each being one-half inch long. The halves are again equally divided into quarters of an inch and again into eighths and sixteenths of an inch. For sheet metal work, the rules usually are not divided into smaller than $\frac{1}{16}″$. This is as accurate a measurement as needed for most sheet metal work. For precision work, the

Fig. 7-7. One type of flexible rule. (Lufkin Rule Co.)

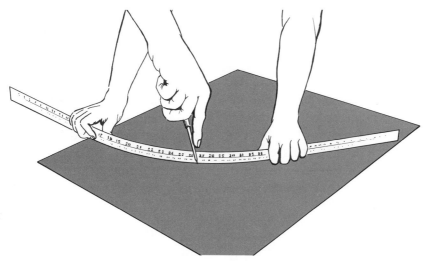

Fig. 7-8. Locating points on a curve using a flexible rule.

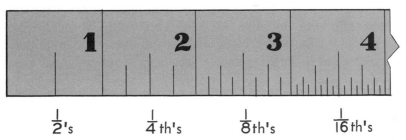

Fig. 7-9. Fractional divisions of an inch on the common rule.

rules may be divided into $\frac{1}{32}''$ and $\frac{1}{64}''$ measurements.

Practice using the rule, making lines $1\frac{1}{16}''$ long, $3\frac{5}{8}''$ long, etc., until you can take measurements quickly and accurately. Remember that a fraction is a part of a whole number, 1, and consists of a numerator and denominator as shown by the following example:

$$\frac{1 \text{ (numerator)}}{4 \text{ (denominator)}}$$

How to Read the Circumference Rule. There are two general methods of finding the circumference of a cylinder: by the circumference rule and by the use of figures.

Finding the accurate circumference of a cylindrical pipe with the circumference rule is both simple and accurate. If you will examine the rule carefully, you will observe that the upper part of the rule is used in a manner similar to the ordinary rule. The lower part is used to find the circumference of pipes. The reverse side of the rule contains useful data and information in table form.

To read the circumference rule, determine the pipe diameter (for purposes of demonstration, assume it to be 3″), and locate this figure (in this case, 3) on the upper part of the rule, as shown in Fig. 7-10. Notice that the divisions on the lower part of the rule represent eighths of an inch. Also notice that figure 3 lines up directly between the third and fourth divisions reading from 9 to 10 on the lower part of the rule. The circumference is then read as $9\frac{7}{16}$″. The circumference rule is usually calibrated down to $\frac{1}{8}$″ and the nearest $\frac{1}{16}$″ is estimated.

Finding Circumference by Use of Figures. Occasionally the sheet metal worker needs to find the distance around a pipe without the use of a circumference rule. The method for doing this is to multiply the diameter of the pipe by 3.14 or $3\frac{1}{7}$. The former is generally preferred. For example, suppose that a pipe 5″ in diameter is to be made. The first step would be to find the circumference in inches. This can be done in the following steps:

1.   Multiply 3.14 by the diameter, 5″.

$$\begin{array}{r} 3.14 \\ \times 5'' \\ \hline 15.70'' \end{array} = \text{circumference of pipe}$$

2.   Change the decimal remainder .70 to a fraction that can be read on the common rule. To do this, multiply the decimal by the denominator of the fraction to be used. The fractions commonly used in sheet metal work are $\frac{1}{8}$, $\frac{1}{16}$ or $\frac{1}{32}$ of an inch, depending upon the degree of accuracy required. For this problem, consider that the accuracy

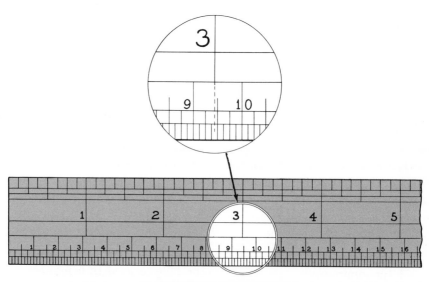

Fig. 7-10. Circumference rule.

should be within the nearest $\frac{1}{16}$ of an inch. Thus:

$$\begin{array}{r} .70 \\ \times 16 \\ \hline 420 \\ 70 \\ \hline 11.20 \text{ or } \frac{11}{16}'' \end{array}$$

3. The decimal .70 is now read as

$\frac{11}{16}''$ so the circumference of the 5 inch pipe would read 15-$\frac{11}{16}''$ on the common rule.

Hence, we see that multiplying the decimal by the denominator of any of the fractional inch graduations on the rule will give the numerator of the desired fraction as shown by the preceding example.

Cutting Metal

Snips

The most commonly used types of snips in the sheet metal shop are the *bulldog, combination* and the left-hand and right-hand *aviation snips.*

Bulldog snips are heavy duty tools and are generally used for cutting metal that is 24 gage or thicker.

Combination snips are used for general cutting on 24 gage metal or thinner. Since a great deal of the sheet metal used in the shop is 24 gage or lighter, the combination snips are probably the most commonly used snips.

Aviation snips are very versatile tools with many applications in the sheet metal shop. For a review of how aviation snips operate, see page 19 in Chapter 2. The advantage of aviation snips is that they can cut very small and complex curves that would be difficult or impossible to cut with bulldog or combination snips. They are also the best snips to cut inside circles and inside corners as shown in Fig. 7-11.

There is more to using snips than merely working the handles. Both practice and knowledge are necessary to be able to make a clean cut on sheet metal in all sorts of circumstances. Too often the student of sheet metal work will at first cut very jagged and rough edges on the metal. Since these edges reflect upon the entire job and in many ways affect the quality of the finished job, it is essential that the student master the snips. It is impossible to do a workmanlike job in sheet metal until you first learn how to cut sheet metal skillfully. As in any other trade, successful sheet metal work depends upon accurate accomplishment of each individual operation for a complete, skilled job. If any given operation is done sloppily, the result will be evident throughout the rest of the operations. Like any skill, the operation of snips depends upon practice. However, much of the mastery of snips also depends upon knowledge. If you study the following rules to learn the proper use and care of snips and practice them, then you will find that mastery of the actual hand processes is relatively simple.

1. *Keep the small piece of metal over the bottom blade of the snips.* In

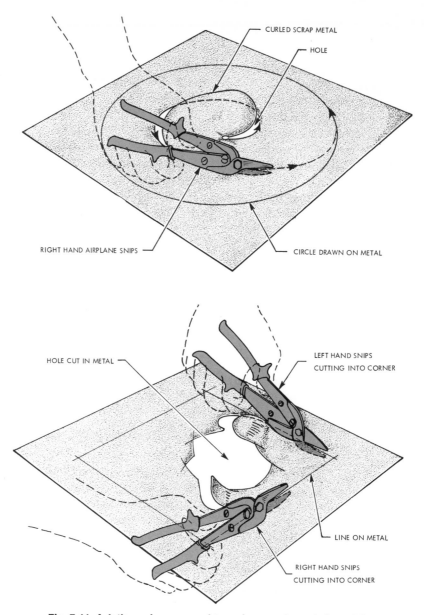

CURLED SCRAP METAL

HOLE

RIGHT HAND AIRPLANE SNIPS

CIRCLE DRAWN ON METAL

HOLE CUT IN METAL

LEFT HAND SNIPS
CUTTING INTO CORNER

LINE ON METAL

RIGHT HAND SNIPS
CUTTING INTO CORNER

Fig. 7-11. Aviation snips are used to make complex cuts in metal.

using snips, the greatest problem is not in making the actual cut, but in getting the snips into the end of the cut. This is because one piece of metal must slide over the bottom blade of the snips and up over the snip handle. If the metal sheet is large, it resists the bending necessary to accomplish that operation and makes it difficult to get the snips into the end of the cut. This in turn makes it difficult to control the snips after they are in the cut. However, if the piece of metal is narrow, it will naturally curl during the cutting operation itself and will curl up over the snips blade with no trouble. Even if the piece is too large to to curl naturally, when it is the smaller of the two pieces it will still be easier to lift it up out of the way.

2. *Trim off excess metal before making the cut on the line.* The reason for this is the same as discussed previously. If the excess metal is trimmed to within a ¼ inch of the line, then when the final cut is made the scrap will curl up out of the way and the cut can be made easily.

3. *Whenever possible, rest the blade and handle of the snips on the workbench.* This rule does not apply to aviation snips, since they are too small to use in this manner. However, all other snips should be rested on the bench rather than held in the air. Doing this allows you to use your arm muscles instead of your wrist muscles for the cutting operation, therefore giving more power and control over the cut. In addition, using your arm muscles means that your arm will not tire as quickly.

4. *When notching, keep the end of the snips blades at the point where the notch will end.* It is common for students to put the blades beyond the end of the notch. This results in having to make a very slow and careful cut to avoid cutting past the notch. And even with care, the cut will very often go slightly past the notch. Since bends are generally made to the corner of notches, this results in the metal breaking at the corners when the bend is made.

5. *Keep oil from the blades of snips.* A drop of oil should occasionally be put on the swivel bolt of snips to keep them moving freely. However, do not allow it to run onto the blades, since this will cause the metal to slip out of the blades.

6. *Cut only sheet metal with snips.* The clearance on snips blades is for sheet metal thicknesses only. If you use them to cut wire, no matter how soft the metal, you are almost sure to nick the blades.

7. *Don't force snips.* Extending the snips handles, placing all your weight on the handles, or pounding on the backs of the blades puts more pressure on the snips blades than they are designed for and will spring the blades making them useless. If snips blades are sprung there is too much clearance between the blades which means that when small edges of sheet metal are trimmed, the blades will bend the edge rather than cut it. Another common result of sprung blades is that the tips of the blades no longer meet, which means that notches cannot be made with the tip of the blade.

Cutting Inside Circles. Many times a hole must be cut in sheet metal. This operation employs the same methods as cutting any type of sheet metal and some additional ones as well. If a large sheet metal punch is handy, the hole can be started by punching a large hole. Many times a punch is not available and the hole is started by making a slit with the peen of the tinner's hammer or with a hammer and chisel. Once the slit is made, then the blade of the airplane snips is inserted and a spiral cut is made gradually increasing the diameter until about ½ inch away from the line. Trim out all the excess metal from the hole,

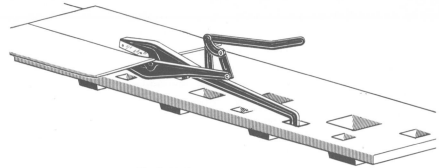

Fig. 7-12. Compound-lever shears.

leaving about ½ inch from the line. Then the second cut on the line is made without interference from the excess metal in the hole and an accurate cut can be made.

If a square hole must be made instead of a round one, the same procedure is followed except that both the right-hand and left-hand airplane snips are used to cut into the square corners, as shown in Fig. 7-11.

Compound-Lever Shears

The compound-lever shears, because of the arrangement of levers, has a mechanical advantage sufficient to allow the cutting of metal up to 12 gage steel. The lower handle is bent to allow the shears to be placed on the bench plate. Fig. 7-12 shows how the metal is placed in the shears when cutting.

Bench Lever Shears

A shears which is used in almost every sheet metal shop is shown in Fig. 7-13. This is a heavy duty shears—models are available to cut ³⁄₁₆″ thick metal

Fig. 7-13. Bench lever shear. (Beverly Shear Manufacturing Corp.)

with ease. The operating principle of these shears is the same as snips except that they are built stronger and have a compound leverage system for greater power. The blades are designed to cut curves and circles as well as straight lines. When using this type of shears, keep the good piece of metal over the lower blade and run the scrap piece under the upper blade since the piece that goes under the upper blade will be curled and distorted by the cutting action.

Cutting Pipe

Cutting pipe requires different methods for pipes of different gages. The double-cutting shears are indispensable to the sheet metal worker when cutting apart light gage pipe. When in good condition, they will not leave burrs or ragged edges. These shears have a center cutting blade that operates between the double jaw when cutting. The center blade is pointed and can be easily inserted in light gage metal to start the cut, as shown in Fig. 7-14. When cutting 24 gage metal pipe, use a sharp cold chisel to make the opening for the blade.

Another important feature of some double-cutting shears is an attachment which is designed for crimping the small ends of pipes after they are cut. Fig. 7-15 illustrates a separate crimper.

Cutting pipes of 22 gage or heavier requires another method, inasmuch as double-cutting shears are designed only to cut light gage metal. The most common method of cutting heavy gage pipe is to use both right hand and left hand airplane snips. Make a cut with the right hand snips until it becomes difficult to insert the snips into the cut. Then take the left hand snips and make a parallel cut. This releases the metal between the two cuts and allows it to flow over the bottom of the blade. By alternating the cuts between the right hand and the left hand snips the metal can be cut much in the same way as with double-cut snips.

Fig. 7-14. Double cutting shears.

Fig. 7-15. Hand pipe crimper.

Power Hand Shears

Many modern sheet metal shops have stepped up production through the use of one or more models of hand power shears. These shears are designed to cut straight and irregular curved lines. With a little practice, anyone can use them to cut out templates with hairline accuracy, without burrs, and without distortion of the metal. The shears shown in Fig. 7-16 have sufficient capacity to cut 18 gage metal. Others are made to cut 16 or 12 gage metal. A great advantage of these portable shears is that they can be taken right to the job and plugged into any electric outlet or light socket.

Fig. 7-16. Power hand shears. (The Black and Decker Manufacturing Co.)

Nibbler

Another common cutting machine in the sheet metal shop is the nibbler, shown in Fig. 7-17. The nibbler is actually a fast acting punch that "nibbles" a small hole out of the metal at every stroke. The strokes on a nibbler are very fast—faster than the eye can follow. The advantages of the nibbler are that it can cut very heavy metal in any intricate form and also that the piece of metal being cut is not distorted since both sides of the cut remain perfectly flat during the cutting action.

Fig. 7-17. Nibbler. (The Black and Decker Manufacturing Co.)

Band Saw

The vertical band saw, also called *contour saw,* is one of the most versatile machines in the sheet metal shop. If a job calls for several pieces of the same size and shape, they may all be cut in one operation on the band saw. This is called *stack sawing.* The sheets are stacked evenly and then clamped or bolted together. The pattern is then transferred to the top piece and all pieces are sawed simultaneously.

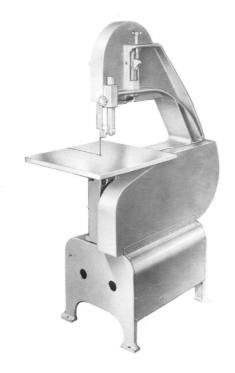

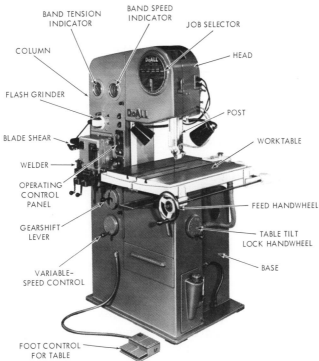

Fig. 7-18. Band saws. Top: Deep throated saw for large pieces. (DiAcro). Bottom: Large saw with blade welder. (DoALL Co.)

The band saw in Fig. 7-18, top, has a deep throat which allows for cutting large patterns. The saw in Fig. 7-18, bottom, is a more complex machine which is designed for extensive production work. This machine is equipped with a built-in blade welder. This is to facilitate internal cutting without the use of hand snips. A hole is drilled in the work piece. The blade is then cut and fed through the hole. The blade ends are then squared and fed into the welder. When the cut is complete, the blade is cut again and the work piece removed. Then the blade may be either replaced or rewelded.

Note the adjustable saw blade guard on both machines in Fig. 7-18. This guard should be lowered to just above the work piece to protect the operator's fingers. Safety glasses or goggles should always be worn when operating the band saw to protect the operator's eyes from flying chips.

Squaring Shears

The principal parts of the squaring shears shown in Fig. 7-19 are as follows:

The bed is the horizontal, rigid, cross-ribbed channel section. The top of the bed has two transverse T slots for the front and bevel gages. It also has graduations for setting the front gage and a large depression in the center of the bed to give clearance for grasping the metal.

The crosshead is the horizontal beam connecting the housings for supporting the upper cutting blade and the hold-down clamp.

The housings are the two vertical standards supporting the crosshead and are of truss construction.

The foot treadle is used to force the cutting blades together when cutting metal.

The hold-down acts as a clamp for holding the metal in place and also serves as a safety guard.

The extension arms or front brackets are for supporting the front gage.

The two graduated scales for setting gages are located conveniently on the top of the bed.

The front gage can be fastened in the T slot on the bed or front brackets for the purpose of making straight or angular cuts.

The side gage is located on each side of the bed and is used for squaring the corners of the sheet metal.

The bevel gage is attached to the bed of the shears for making angular cuts.

The back gage is mounted on the rear of the shears and used to cut large metal pieces.

Fig. 7-19 shows the 36″ foot-operated squaring shear used in every sheet metal shop.

The squaring shear is safe only if operated properly. The following safety precautions must always be followed. Never place your fingers under the blade or hold-down bar. The blade is very sharp and comes down with tremendous pressure so your fingers could be completely severed. When operating the treadle, use only one foot and keep the other well back to keep from crushing your toes. Be sure the gage of the metal is within the rated capacity of the machine. Cut only one thickness of metal at a time The shear should be locked when not in use.

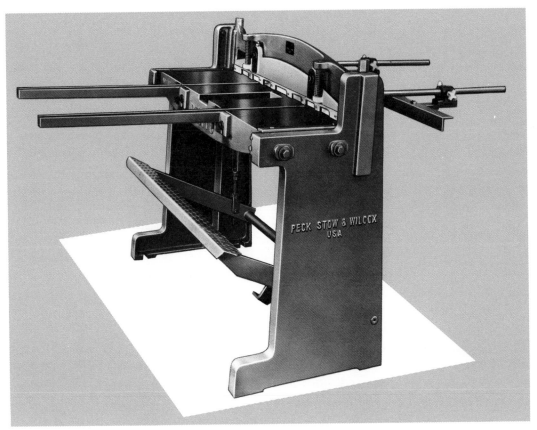

Fig. 7-19. Squaring shears. (The Peck, Stow & Wilcox Co.)

Shop Projects

Transferring Paper and Metal Patterns onto Metal

Aim. To develop the ability to transfer paper and metal patterns to metal.

Operations. (transferring a paper pattern onto metal using a pencil)

1. *Cut around the outline of the paper pattern with a pair of scissors (use any pattern). Stay at least 1″ outside the outline.*
2. *Place the sheet of metal to be used on the wood part of the bench. If the metal rests on the bench plate, the point of the prick punch will become dull if punched on the iron surface.*
3. *Place the paper pattern on the metal in the proper position to avoid waste. See Fig. 7-20.*
4. *Place metal weights on the paper pattern to keep it from creeping, as shown in Fig. 7-21. C clamps should not be used with a paper pattern.*
5. *Make slight indentations with a sharp prick punch on all bend lines and on the outline lines as described in this chapter.*

107

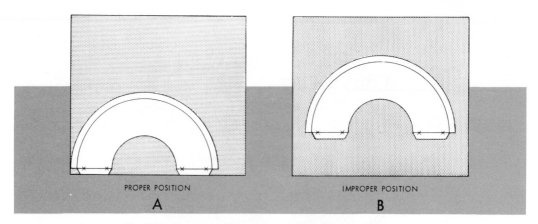

Fig. 7-20. Proper and improper position of pattern on metal.

6. *Remove the weights and cut out the pattern using the proper snips.*

Operations. (transferring a metal or master pattern onto metal)

1. *Place the metal on the bench in the same manner as in previous operations.*

2. *Place the metal pattern on the metal in the proper position.*

3. *Secure the pattern with weights or vise-clamp wrench to keep it from creeping.*

4. *Scribe on the metal the outline of the pattern with a sharp scratch awl, as shown in Fig. 7-22.*

5. *Make slight indentations with a sharp prick punch on all bend lines.*

6. *Remove the weights or vise-clamp wrench and cut out the outline using the proper hand snips.*

7. *Check the pattern before forming to shape.*

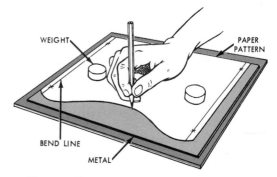

Fig. 7-21. Transferring paper pattern to metal.

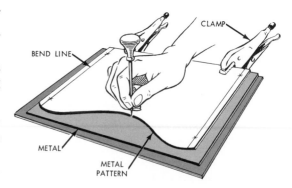

Fig. 7-22. Transferring metal pattern to metal.

Squaring a Piece of Metal

Aim. To develop skill in squaring metal with the squaring shears and to develop an understanding of the operation of the machine.

Specifications. Square the four sides of a piece of metal to any convenient size.

Operations

1. *Place the sheet to be squared between the cutting blades with one side against the right-side gage.*

2. *Extend the edge to be trimmed about 1/4" beyond the lower cutting blade. This distance should never be less than the thickness of the sheet.*

3. *Pull the hold-down handle to clamp the sheet in place.*

4. *Keeping both hands on the metal, step on the foot treadle to cut the piece of metal. Be sure the fingers are free of the cutting blades.*

5. *Release the foot treadle gradually, keeping the foot on the treadle until it is back in place.*

6. *Release the hold-down handle and remove the metal.*

7. *Place the edge that has just been trimmed against the right-side gage, again extending the sheet about 1/4" beyond the lower cutting blade, and repeat the cutting operation.*

8. *Set the front gage to required size.*

9. *Place the squared edges of the metal against the front and right gage.*

10. *Hold the metal in place with*

your hands and repeat the cutting operation.

11. *Reset the gage to the size desired.*

12. *Cut the remaining edge.*

Cutting a Piece of Metal to Size Using the Front Gage

Aim. To develop skill in squaring metal and cutting to any desired length.

Specifications. Cut a piece of metal 4" × 10" with the corners squared.

Operations

1. *Place the sheet to be squared between the cutting blades with one side against the right-side gage.*

2. *Square a corner (two edges) of the piece of metal.*

3. *Set the front gage to 10".*

4. *Place a squared edge against the front gage.*

5. *Clamp metal into place using the hold-down handle.*

6. *Press down on the foot treadle to cut the metal. Keep the foot on the treadle until the treadle is back in place.*

7. *Reset the gage to 4", the desired width, and complete the operation.*

Drawing the Stretchout for a Rectangular Pipe

Aim. To learn how to use the stretchout of a pipe in laying out a pattern on paper.

Specifications. Draw the stretchout for a square pipe 4" × 4" and 6" long.

Operations

1. *Obtain paper and drawing instruments.*

2. *Draw a line equal to the stretchout of the pipe.*

3. *Draw another line parallel to and 6″ away from the first.*
4. *Square up one end and mark off 4″ intervals for the corner lines.*
5. *Turn the drawing in to the instructor for checking.*

Drawing the Stretchout for a Round Pipe

Aim. To practice determining the stretchout for round pipe.

Specifications. Draw the stretchout for a round pipe 6″ long and 4″ in diameter.

Operations

1. *Obtain paper at least 8-1/2″ × 14″ and drawing materials.*
2. *Determine the stretchout by the method as shown in this chapter.*
3. *Draw out the pattern according to this stretchout and length and have it checked by the instructor.*

Cutting Metal with Snips

Aim. To develop skill in cutting metal with snips.

Specifications. Using thin scrap sheet metal, lay out the shapes shown in Figs. 7-23 and 7-24 and then cut them out.

Operations

1. *Using dividers, lay out the circles shown in Fig. 7-23.*
2. *Use the squaring shears to trim the excess metal. Leave about 1/2″ from the line to trim off with snips.*
3. *Use combination blade snips or airplane snips to cut the outside circle.*
4. *Punch a large hole inside the inner circle, or make a slit with a hammer and chisel.*
5. *Using aviation snips, cut out the excess metal from the inside. Stay about 1/2″ away from the line.*

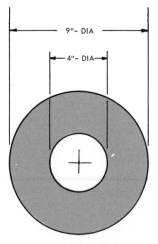

Fig. 7-23. Cutting circular shapes on sheet metal.

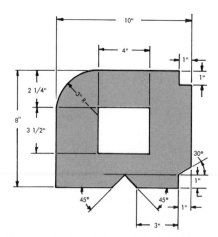

Fig. 7-24. Cutting notched shapes on sheet metal.

6. *Trim off the metal to the inside circle, using airplane snips. Turn the circle in to the instructor.*
7. *Lay out the shape shown in Fig. 7-24.*
8. *Trim off excess with the squaring shears.*
9. *Following the rules for using snips given in this chapter, cut*

the outside shape and the corners of the notches.
10. *Make a hole inside the center square and use airplane snips to trim off excess metal and then trim to the line.*
11. *Turn in the finished piece to the instructor.*

STUDENT QUESTIONS AND ACTIVITIES

1. Describe a master pattern.
2. Name five tools used for cutting metal.
3. What tool scribes metal patterns?
4. What is the difference between a pictorial drawing and a mechanical drawing?
5. What type of shears is used for cutting a pipe into two sections?
6. Explain how to avoid wasting metal when cutting out patterns.
7. With the circumference rule, find the circumference of the following sizes (diameters) of pipe: 3″, 5″, 7½″, 11″.
8. What cutting tool is used to cut an inside circle?
9. Why should a piece of metal be squared before using?
10. Without looking at the list of tools in Chapter 2, see how many you can remember. Explain their uses.
11. Give two ways by which patterns are transferred onto metal.
12. What is the difference between a paper pattern and a template?
13. Name two tools used for cutting circles in metal.
14. What shears are used to cut a metal disk?
15. Describe ten of the principal mechanical parts of the squaring shears.
16. What is meant by a stretchout?

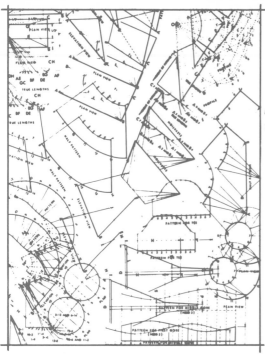

punching, drilling and riveting

When you finish this chapter, you should be able to:
1. Select the best tool or machine to use to form holes in sheet metal.
2. Make a riveted sheet metal seam.
3. Remove rivets without damaging the sheet metal.

Whenever sheet metal is fabricated, holes must often be drilled or punched in it for bolts, rivets, or attachments of some type.

Though not used as often as formerly, the riveted seam is still used in the shop. Its applications are where spot welding is not practical, and the metal is too heavy for seaming. In such cases, rivets are the best means of making the seam.

Making the holes in the proper size and spacing for the riveted seam determines to a large extent the strength and the appearance of the riveted seam.

This chapter will give general rules to follow in hole forming and riveting. However, it is only through practice that you will gain the proficiency needed.

Making Holes

A successful riveting operation depends upon the accuracy and size of the rivet holes and upon the correct size and spacing of the rivets. The holes for the rivets may be punched or drilled, depending upon the thickness of the metal.

Light sheet metal is usually punched, while the heavier metal is drilled. Drilling is more accurate and distorts the metal less.

Size of Holes

The size of the hole depends upon the size of the rivet, which in turn depends upon the thickness of the metal. A good job of riveting is controlled to a great extent by the size of the hole, as shown in Fig. 8-1. If the hole is too large for the rivet, as shown in Fig. 8-1*A*, the head will not be properly formed and will pull out easily. If the hole is smaller than the rivet, the rivet is not inserted entirely through the metal, resulting in insufficient material for forming the head. This is shown in Fig. 8-1*B*. The best hole size is one that will allow the rivet to be inserted easily and quickly and with a sufficient amount of rivet protruding to allow forming a proper head, as shown in Fig. 8-1*C*.

Solid Punch

The solid punch, as shown in Fig. 8-2, is sometimes used to make holes for rivets and for starter holes for sheet metal screws. Although mechanized punches or drills are more commonly used for these purposes, it is occasionally more convenient to use the hand punch. Proper backing is essential when using the solid punch to prevent excessive distortion of the metal around the hole. The materials used for backing are either a lead cake or a block of wood. When using a wood block, always place the metal on the *end grain* of the wood. This way, the wood absorbs most of the pressure, minimizing distortion of the metal.

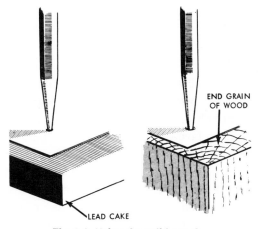

END GRAIN OF WOOD

LEAD CAKE

Fig. 8-2. Using the solid punch.

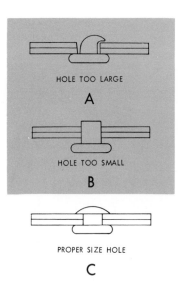

HOLE TOO LARGE

A

HOLE TOO SMALL

B

PROPER SIZE HOLE

C

Fig. 8-1. Correct and incorrect rivet hole sizes.

Turret Punch

Modern sheet metal shops generally have a turret punch such as the one shown in Fig. 8-3. These punches are of different capacities and sizes. The size

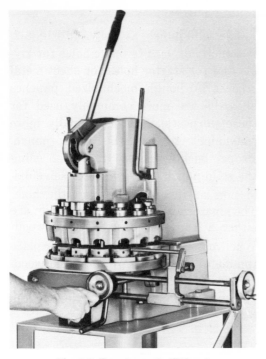

Fig. 8-3. Turret punch. (DiAcro)

punch, the student should check and double check that he has the same size punch and die aligned. If a large punch is aligned with a small die, the result will be either a broken punch or a damaged machine.

Hand Lever Punch

The hand lever punch is used by the sheet metal worker for punching holes in sheet metal and button punching.

In button punching, the die is set so that it makes an indentation in the metal but does not punch completely through, as shown in Fig. 8-4A. Button punching is used in duct and similar work where little strength is required. The ends of the duct are fastened with bolts or rivets and the space in between is button punched, as shown in Fig. 8-4B.

The general operations of all hand lever punches of the type shown in Fig. 8-5 are the same but the methods of changing the punches and dies are dif-

most used is for holes from ⅛" up to 2" in diameter. Small punches are capable of punching ⅛" thick metal (11 gage) and the largest size is capable of punching metal 1/20" thick (18 gage) or lighter. These punches are designed so the upper punch and the lower die are mounted on two revolving tables or turrets. The turrets can be released and turned instantly to allow for immediate setting for the hole desired. They have an advantage over hand lever punches in that they have a deeper reach (generally 18"), and they have an immediate setting. The lever punches require several minutes to change and involve the hazard of misplacing the loose punches and dies. In using a turret

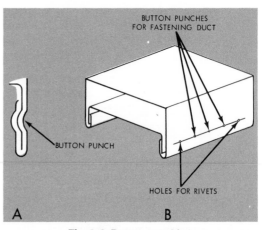

Fig. 8-4. Button punching.

Fig. 8-5. Hand lever punch.

ferent. In general, the punches and dies are changed in the following steps:

1. Remove the die with a screw driver or key provided for the purpose.
2. Open the punch.
3. Remove the threaded collar.
4. Remove punch from collar.
5. Replace the correct size punch in collar.
6. Replace the threaded collar.
7. Return the levers to normal position.
8. Replace the correct size die.
9. Adjust the die with a screw driver until the punch just barely punches a clean hole.

While the gage can be used to punch holes a uniform distance from the edge of the metal, it is better to lay out centers and then punch the holes. The centers are marked with a prick punch. In punching the hole, the centering point of the punch is placed in the prick point on the work. The hole is then completed by pressing down the upper lever.

Drilling Holes

Sheet metal workers sometimes find it necessary to drill holes when working with heavy material. The holes can be drilled by hand or by drill press. When drilling by hand, the electric hand drill is used. Twist drills are used as the cutting tool when drilling holes. The size of the drill is marked on the shank of the drill. The principal parts of a twist drill are *body, shank,* and *point,* as shown in Fig. 8-6. The size may be designated by one of three systems—fraction, number, letter.

Though there are other types of shanks, the most common is the straight shank twist drill. The portable electric hand drill can be obtained with chuck capacities of $\frac{1}{4}''$, $\frac{3}{8}''$, or $\frac{1}{2}''$.

In drilling a hole by hand, make sure that the work is securely clamped. If possible, back up the work with a piece of wood. This will stiffen the sheet metal and will prevent damage to the work, the table, or the drill. Select the proper size drill by checking the size on the shank. Be sure the drill is straight and sharp. Insert the drill in the chuck and rotate the drill to see if it runs true. Enlarge the prick punch in the work by center punching it. Place the point of the drill in the center punch mark and rotate the drill briefly, then check to see that the drill is properly centered in the hole. (If the drill is not properly centered, it may be drawn over with the center punch by making a center punch mark on the side toward which the hole is to be drawn.) Return the drill to the hole and continue drilling until the drill is about to break through the metal. At this point relieve the pressure slightly and continue drilling until the hole is completed. If you do not relieve the pressure just as the drill begins to break through the metal, it will catch on the metal and can pull the drill motor from your hands or break the twist drill.

When using the electric drill press, see Fig. 8-7, remember the following rules:

1. Make sure the holes are properly located and center punched.

2. Check the drill size. If the number is not clear, use a drill gage (device with holes corresponding to drill sizes).

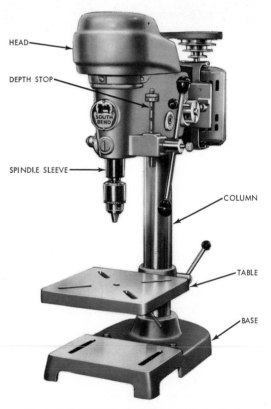

Fig. 8-7. Drill press. (South Bend Lathe Co.)

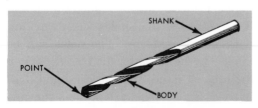

Fig. 8-6. Principle parts of a straight shank drill.

3. Use high speed drills when using a drill with a high speed motor, as such drills are designed for high speeds.

4. Know what type of material is being drilled.

5. Be sure the drill is properly centered in the chuck by turning on the power for an instant.

6. Be sure the work is mounted properly in a holding device such as a vise or C clamp.

7. Adjust the table so that the point of the drill is slightly above the work, using the adjustable stop to secure the proper depth of the hole to be drilled. Be sure the drill does not bore into the table.

8. To reduce friction, use lubricants such as lard, or soluble oil and water for low carbon steels.

9. Check the centering of the drill after the point has just started in the metal; relocate the hole with a center punch if necessary.

10. Feed the drill with a light, even pressure to prevent bending the drill.

11. Remove and return the drill to its proper place when finished.

12. If the drill does not produce a chip, it is dull. Stop immediately and have it sharpened.

13. Never leave the chuck key in the chuck.

Riveting

Riveting may be done by hand or by machine. When the job is performed by hand, as is usually the case in sheet metal work, it is done with a hammer and rivet set.

Types of Rivets

There are many types of rivets used in sheet metal work. The four most common types are the tinners', flathead, roundhead, and countersunk head as shown in Fig. 8-8. Tinners' and flathead rivets are used in most jobs of fabrication. The countersunk head is used when a flush surface is desired, and the roundhead when exceptional strength is required. Setting of these rivets is explained in following pages.

Each rivet consists of a head and a cyclindrical body or shank. These are shown in Fig. 8-9. The end of the rivet which is upset is referred to as the formed or upset head. The length and diameter are measured as shown in Fig. 8-9.

Rivet Sizes

The size of tinners' rivets is determined by the weight of 1,000 rivets. For example 1 lb. rivets weigh 1 lb. per thousand, 2 lb. rivets 2 lb. per thousand.

Flathead rivets vary in diameter

117

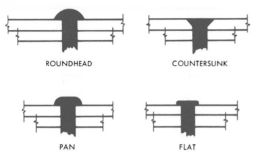

ROUNDHEAD COUNTERSUNK

PAN FLAT

Fig. 8-8. Types of rivets.

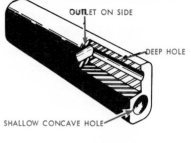

OUTLET ON SIDE

DEEP HOLE

SHALLOW CONCAVE HOLE

Fig. 8-10. Rivet set.

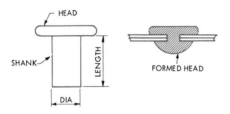

HEAD

SHANK

LENGTH

DIA

FORMED HEAD

Fig. 8-9. Parts of a rivet.

from $\frac{3}{32}''$ to $\frac{7}{16}''$ in $\frac{1}{32}''$ steps. Other rivets vary in diameter from $\frac{3}{8}''$ up to $1''$ in $\frac{1}{16}''$ steps.

Flathead, roundhead, and countersunk rivets may be purchased in various length depending upon the thickness of the sheets being joined.

There are no definite rules to follow in selecting the size of a rivet. In general, the length should be sufficient to protrude through the pieces being joined from one, to one and one-half times the diameter of the rivet. This allows ample material for forming the upset head.

Forming Rivet Heads

The shallow, cup-shaped hole shown by the cross-section view of a rivet set, Fig. 8-10, is used to form the head on the rivet. The deep hole is used to draw the sheets and the rivet together, and also to draw the rivets directly through thin metal without previously punching a hole. The outlet on the side allows the sheet metal slugs to drop out. The rivet set selected should have a hole slightly larger than the diameter of the rivet.

A good job of riveting can be done with not more than six normal blows of the hammer, and after a little practice this number can be cut in half. A skilled mechanic will perform the operation in sequence, as shown in Fig. 8-11, by striking one blow on the rivet set to draw the sheets together around the rivet: one blow to flatten the rivet down and another blow on the rivet set to complete the formed head of the rivet.

Spacing Rivet Holes

Rivet holes should be spaced according to the specifications of the job. *The space from the edge of the metal to the center of the rivet line should be at least twice the diameter of the rivet,* as shown in Fig. 8-12 to prevent the rivets from tearing out. The minimum distance between rivets should be about three times the rivet diameter. The maximum dis-

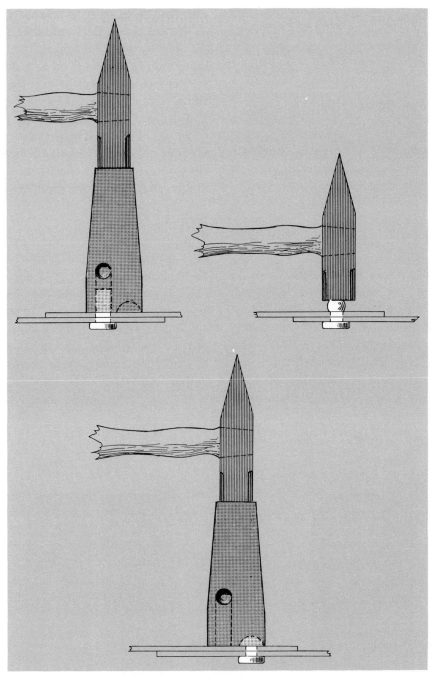

Fig. 8-11. Steps in forming rivet head.

tance between rivets should never be such that the material is allowed to buckle between rivets.

The method of spacing rivet holes for longitudinal seams in pipe is somewhat different from the manner in which the

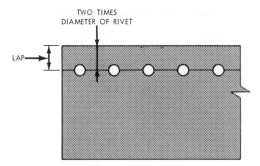

TWO TIMES
DIAMETER OF RIVET

LAP

Fig. 8-12. Lap required for riveting.

rivet holes are spaced for cross seams. See Fig. 8-13.

Although there are various methods of laying out holes for longitudinal seams, the metal strip procedure is generally preferred when the same job is laid out repeatedly. This method consists of using a narrow strip of metal in which the required number of holes have been evenly spaced and prick

punched. The strip is laid on the edge of the metal and the location of the holes marked by prick punching through the strip onto the metal. The only drawback to this method is that as the strip is continually used, the holes become enlarged and accurate marking becomes difficult. Care should be taken to see that the strip is not reversed when switching to the opposite side of the work, since the distances for the end holes are not alike.

Riveting Seams

When making round pipe with a riveted seam, the section of pipe should be formed so that the burred edge of the holes is on the outside of the pipe. After selecting the proper size rivets, rivet set, and hammer, place the job to be riveted on the stake. Insert a rivet in one end of the cylinder, draw the sheets together with the rivet set, remove the rivet set and flatten the rivet just

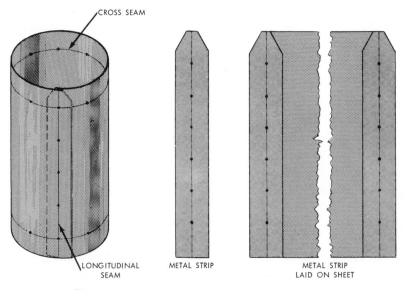

CROSS SEAM

LONGITUDINAL SEAM

METAL STRIP

METAL STRIP LAID ON SHEET

Fig. 8-13. Spacing rivet holes for longitudinal seam.

enough to hold the rivet in place. Repeat the operation on the other end. Then start with the center hole and rivet alternately, right and left, toward the ends of the pipe. It may be that a bulge between the two pieces will develop due to slight misalignment of the holes. If this happens, working from the center out will allow the bulge to be worked to the end of the pipe. The end rivet can still be removed and the bulge eliminated.

Removing Rivets

There are occasions when it is necessary to remove a rivet. One method used for heavy gage material is to place the head of the rivet into a common nut a little larger than the head of the rivet and then punch the stem out through the formed head as shown in Fig. 8-14 and as described by the following steps.

1. Place the rivet on a solid stake with the formed head upward (A).
2. With a riveting hammer, flatten the head as much as possible without distorting metal (B).

3. Center punch the center of the head (C).
4. Place the head of the rivet into a nut a little larger than the head of the rivet. With a solid punch slightly smaller than the size of the rivet shank, punch the shank out of the head (D).

On light gage sheet metal, the most satisfactory method of removing a rivet is by drilling. In this method the following steps are used.

1. Flatten and center punch the exact center of the head.
2. Select a twist drill slightly smaller than the shank of the rivet.
3. Drill into the head of the rivet just up to the surface of the metal.
4. Remove the rivet head with a cold chisel.
5. Remove the sheared rivet with a solid punch and nut as previously described.

Still another method is to cut off the formed head using a sharp cold chisel, the remainder of the rivet being removed with a solid punch. In any method it is important to keep from distorting the metal or elongating the rivet hole.

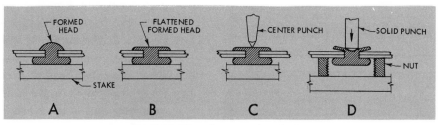

Fig. 8-14. Steps for removing rivets.

Shop Activities

Laying Out the Pattern for a Riveted Seam

Aim.   To learn the method of direct layout on metal.

Operations

1. *Cut two pieces of light scrap metal, 3″ wide, 18″ long, as shown in Fig. 8-15.*
2. *On both sheets, scribe a rivet line parallel to the edge and in from it a distance equal to twice the rivet diameter. (The rivet size will be 1 lb.)*
3. *Mark off the spaces for the end rivets, 1″ from the left end and 2″ from the right end.*
4. *With the steel dividers, space off equal distances between the two end points A and B. (Six rivets are to be used with five 3″ spaces between.)*
5. *Place the piece of metal on a flat wood surface and make the indentation marks using a prick punch and hammer.*

6. *With a lever punch or a turret punch of the proper size, punch holes through the indentation marks.*

Making a Riveted Seam

Aim.   To develop the method of making a riveted seam and skill in the use of the rivet set.

Operations

1. *Place together the two pieces of metal cut for the previous project with the burrs of the holes turned up and the lap on the under side as shown in Fig. 8-16.*
2. *Using 1 lb. rivets, insert the rivet in the end hole; place the deep hole of the rivet set over the rivet, and strike the set a sharp blow with a riveting hammer. Keep the rivet head on a solid foundation.*
3. *Remove the rivet set and strike the rivet one or two blows with the riveting hammer, flattening the rivet sufficiently to make it fit tightly in the hole.*
4. *Place the indentation of the rivet set over the partly flattened rivet, and form the head. If the rivet head has been flattened too much in step 3, the rivet set will touch the sheet metal and leave scars when the rivet head is formed.*
5. *Insert the rivet in the hole at the opposite end and rivet as just described.*

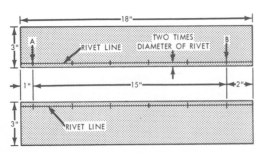

Fig. 8-15. Laying out pattern for riveted seam.

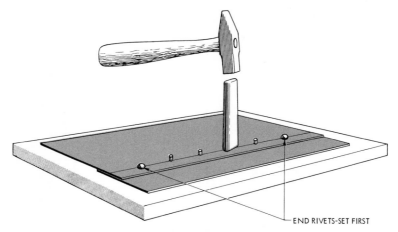

END RIVETS-SET FIRST

Fig. 8-16. Riveting a seam.

6. *Beginning with the nearest center hole, rivet alternately in each direction.*
7. *Turn in the finished seam to the instructor.*

Removing Rivets from a Seam

Aim. To give practice in removing rivets from a seam.

Specifications. Remove three rivets from the riveted seam made in the last project.

Operations

1. *Using a nut and a solid punch as explained in this chapter, remove every other rivet from the riveted seam completed in the previous project.*

STUDENT QUESTIONS AND ACTIVITIES

1. For what is a solid punch used?
2. What is the advantage of a turret punch?
3. What is meant by the term button punching?
4. What is the purpose of the centering point on the end of the hand lever punch?
5. Sketch four types of rivet heads.
6. What is the total weight of 500, four pound rivets?
7. What is the recommended rivet size for seaming 26 gage?
8. What is the purpose of the hole in the side of the rivet set?
9. How is the width of the lap on a riveted seam determined?
10. Why is there an indentation in the rivet set?
11. When making a riveted seam, why is it necessary to rivet the ends first?
12. What is a metal strip used for when making a riveted seam?
13. What is meant by the term featheredging a seam?
14. Give two ways to remove a rivet.

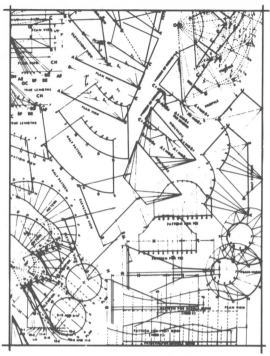

folding edges and making seams

When you complete this chapter, you should be able to:

1. Use the bar folder, making all normal adjustments.
2. Use the bending brake safely, making all the ordinary adjustments for bending sheet metal.
3. Describe by use of sketches how forming molds are used on a bending brake.
4. Name, sketch a sectional view and give the allowances for at least 5 commonly used edges in sheet metal work.
5. By use of sketches, show a sectional view and give the allowances for the following seams:
   - A. Grooved seam
   - B. Standing seam
   - C. Pittsburg lock
   - D. Double seam
   - E. Dovetail seam
6. By use of sketches show how the drive-clip and the S-clip are used to join sections of duct.
7. Sketch a sectional view of a government clip and show how it is used to join sections of duct.

Folding sheet metal to form edges and seams of various kinds is one of the most important operations in sheet metal work. The edges and seams have several purposes. They are used to improve the appearance of finished projects, to strengthen, and to fasten pieces of metal together. The equipment on hand and the amount of strain involved play an important part in selecting the kind of seam used.

Folding Machines

Two types of machines are commonly used in bending or folding metal to form edges or locks for seams: *folders* and *brakes*. The two function differently in that the width of the bend is limited in the folding machine, while in the brake, any width of fold may be made. Each machine will be discussed to acquaint the student with their operations.

Bar Folder

This machine is adapted for bending edges of 22 gage metal or lighter. The bar folder shown in Fig. 9-1 consists of the following parts:

1. *Wing.* The wing forms the edges of the metal over the blade.
2. *Folding Blade.* The folding blade has a sharp beveled edge for forming sharp angles.
3. *Handle.* The handle turns the wing for making bends at various angles.
4. *Setscrews.* One setscrew is located in the shoe at each end of the machine for the purpose of making adjustments for clearance when edging heavy metal or forming double locks.
5. *Gage adjustment screw.* This screw controls the gage for any desired width of edge by setting the dial correctly on the graduated scale.

6. *Graduated scale.* This scale is marked from 3/32″ to 1″ in sixteenth inch divisions.
7. *Locking screw.* This screw is for locking the gage adjustment to keep it from moving.
8. *Wedge adjusting screw.* This screw is located at the rear of the machine and is used for lowering or raising the wing.
9. *Wedge lock nut.* This is used for clamping the wedge adjusting screw firmly in place.
10. *Forty-five-degree stop.* This stop controls the handle making for a 45 degree bend.
11. *Adjustable collar.* This is used for setting for bends at any angle.
12. *Ninety-degree stop.* This stop controls the handle for a 90 degree angle.
13. *Frame.* The frame varies in length from 21″ to 36″ with a 22 gage capacity for mild steel.

Before the student actually begins to operate the bar folder, he should study the various adjustments and operations of the machine. There are six important steps that must be remembered when using the bar folder, namely:

1. *Allowance for the thickness of the metal.*
2. *Sharpness of the folder edge.*
3. *Width of the lock or edge.*

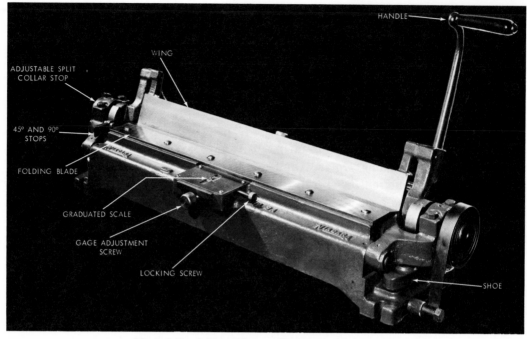

ADJUSTABLE SPLIT
COLLAR STOP

WING

HANDLE

45° AND 90°
STOPS

FOLDING BLADE

GRADUATED SCALE

GAGE ADJUSTMENT
SCREW

LOCKING SCREW

SHOE

Fig. 9-1. Bar folder. (Niagara Machine & Tool Works)

4. *Adjustment for the thickness of metal.*
5. *Angle of the fold.*
6. *Kind of metal.*

Each step should be carefully thought out before forming the edges because after the lock is turned, it is almost impossible to flatten the fold and turn it in the opposite direction without cracking or spoiling the appearance of the metal.

Allowance for Metal Thickness. When making various types of seams from metal of 26 gage or lighter, allowance for the thickness of the metal is not necessary. However, when heavier materials are to be used and accuracy is required, the actual amount of material taken up by the bend or fold must be considered. The amount necessary de-

pends upon the thickness of the metal and the type of the seam or joint. The amount of material to be allowed for the various types of seams will be found under the topic *Seaming* later in this chapter.

Sharpness of Folded Edge. The sharpness of the folded edge is controlled by lowering or raising the wing. The cross-section view of the bar folder illustrated in Fig. 9-2 shows the wing raised for a sharp fold and then lowered for a thick, heavy edge. The wing is regulated simply by turning the wedge adjustment screw to the right for a sharp fold and to the left for a round fold. The wedge lock nut holds the wing in place when it is tightened with a key wrench.

Width of Folded Edge. The illustration in Fig. 9-3 shows the working parts

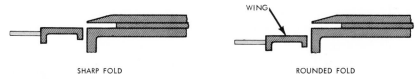

SHARP FOLD   ROUNDED FOLD

Fig. 9-2. Bar folder adjusted for sharp fold and rounded fold.

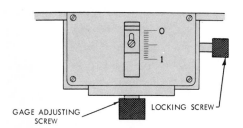

GAGE ADJUSTING SCREW   LOCKING SCREW

Fig. 9-3. Gage for setting width of folded edge.

of the folder that control the width of the folded edge. The gage fingers are regulated by the adjusting screw on the graduated scale found on the front of the machine. The gage adjustment screw moves the fingers forward or backward to the required width of the lock, and the lock screw keeps the gage from creeping. The machine has a range for turning edges up to a width of one inch.

Adjustment for Metal Thickness. The clearance between the jaw and the

folding blade determines the thickness of the metal that is to be bent. The setscrews in the shoes on each end of the folder will raise or lower the jaw for more or less clearance. After making the adjustment, the lock nuts should be fastened to keep the screws from turning.

Operation of the Bar Folder. The procedure for making a single hem is illustrated in Fig. 9-4.

1. Set the gage by means of the gage adjusting screw to the width desired, in this case, 3/8 inch. See Fig. 9-4A.
2. Tighten the lock screw to keep the gage from slipping.
3. Loosen the wedge lock nut in the rear of the machine.
4. Adjust the wedge screw to get the desired fold. For this particular operation, the fold should be sharp. Tighten the wedge lock nut.

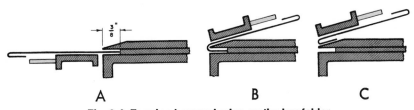

A   B   C

Fig. 9-4. Forming hemmed edge on the bar folder.

5. Set the stop of the adjustable collar to the maximum angle.

6. Adjust the screw in the shoe on each side of the folder for the thickness of the metal. Be sure both sides of the machine are set identically.

7. Insert the metal in place between the blades and the jaw, resting it against the gage fingers located under the blade.

8. With the left hand holding the metal in place, pull the handle forward as far as it will go, making the bend, as shown in Fig. 9-4*B*.

9. Return the handle to its former position and remove the sheet of metal. Do not allow the handle to slam back.

10. Place the sheet of metal back on the beveled part of the blade and as close to the wing as possible in the position shown in Fig. 9-4*C*.

11. Hold the metal with the left hand and pull the operating handle briskly with the right hand, flattening the seam.

Hand Brakes

There are many types of bending brakes used by sheet metal workers. The most widely used machine is the hand brake.

Fig. 9-5 (top views) shows the older style Chicago cornice brake. Fig. 9-5 (bottom) shows a newer model hand brake. There are still many more of the older style brakes in service because brakes are built to give good service for forty to fifty years. For this reason, details are given concerning the older style brake. For the newer style brake, the basic parts are the same and basic operating practices are the same. The only difference is in the way some of the adjustments are made.

Before learning the operation of the hand brake, it is well to make a careful study of the different parts of the brake. The worker should know the name of each part and where it is located. It is always well to keep in mind that skill in the operation of any machine depends on the operator's knowledge of its parts and adjustments.

Parts of the Brake. The three basic parts of the brake are: the bed, top leaf, and bending leaf as shown in Fig. 9-5. In addition the parts indicated by numbers in the *front, rear,* and *right side* views of Fig. 9-5 show the parts necessary for intelligent operation of the brake. These parts are:

1. Clamping handle on each side for holding the sheet in position.
2. Two-position handle on each side, for operating bending leaf.
3. Balance weights, adjustable to make bending operations easier.
4. Upper bending leaf bar, removable when bending small locks.
5. Adjustable stop gage, used to form any desired angle.
6. Clamping link which operates the top shaft.
7. Top shaft.
8. Slot casting for adjusting the bending bar for various gages of metal.
9. Slot-casting pin.

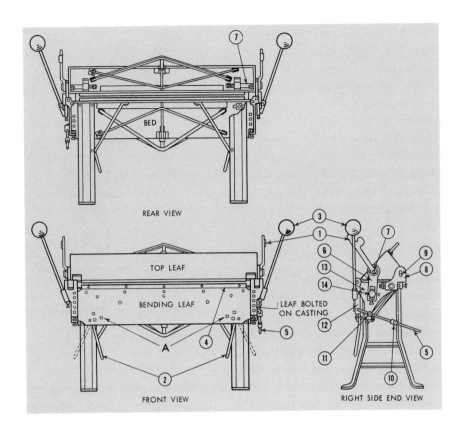

Fig. 9-5. Top: Parts of the bending brake. Bottom: A recent model brake. (Dreis & Krump Mfg. Co.)

10. Adjusting-stop slide on the stop gage for bending locks at various angles.
11. Stop-gage casting.
12. Bending-leaf casting.
13. Bed-end casting.
14. Link-adjusting block.

To regulate the angle of a bend when duplicate work is to be done, the adjusting stop is regulated to allow the bending bar to be raised to the desired angle for making the required number of bends.

Adjustment for Thickness of Metal. The average hand brake in the sheet metal shop has a capacity of 16 gage and can also bend the lightest sheet made. Since 24 and 26 gage are the most common gages in the sheet metal shop, the brake is usually set to work well with these thicknesses. If material much heavier or much lighter than this is to be bent, then the handle tension of the brake must be adjusted for the different thicknesses. A brake set for 26 gage will probably not even clamp down on 16 gage and one set for 16 gage would probably allow 26 gage to slip during the bending operation.

The brake handle is operated on an eccentric. By means of adjusting screws the operating range of this eccentric can be moved up or down for clamping different thicknesses. As a general rule, the handle should be adjusted so that about a ten-pound pull will set it. Fig. 9-6 shows the detail of the handle mechanism as shown by numbers 6 and 14 in Fig. 9-5. In Fig. 9-6, screw A is the set screw that locks the adjustment. To adjust the tension, first loosen this screw. Then turn screw B in to tighten the han-

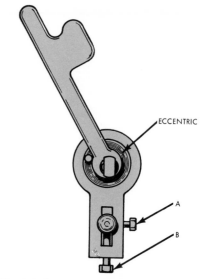

Fig. 9-6. Detail of brake handle adjustment.

dle tension and out to loosen it. By adjusting screw B and testing the handle while a sample of metal is in the brake, the proper tension can be reached. Then tighten screw A to again lock the handle adjustment. The handle adjustment should be made on both ends of the brake. Too much difference in handle adjustment will result in uneven bending by the brake.

In addition to setting the handle tension, it is also very important to adjust the amount of set-back between the top leaf and the bending leaf. Fig. 9-7 shows the importance of this. If there were no allowance for the metal between the top leaf and the bending leaf, then the metal between the top leaf and bending leaf would crack or distort, or parts of the brake would be damaged. The general rule for set-back is to allow 1-1/2 times the thickness of the metal for 22 gage or lighter. For everything thicker than 22

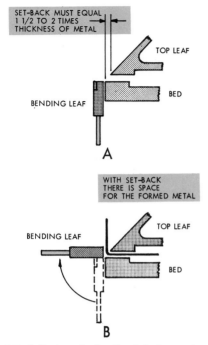

Fig. 9-7. Adjustment of setback between top leaf and bending leaf.

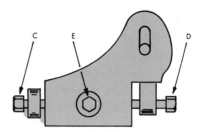

Fig. 9-8. Brake setback adjusting mechanism.

gage, allow 2 times the thickness of the metal. Exceptions for special cases may be made, of course. If for some reason a very sharp corner on the bend is necessary, the set-back could be brought up to the thickness of the metal, but never smaller than this. For very brittle metal which would break when bent, the set-back can be very large to make a radius in the bend. In making a radius bend, a piece of sheet metal is often slipped over the nose of the top leaf to eliminate the sharp edge and further increase the bend radius.

The adjusting mechanism for making the set-back is shown in detail in Fig. 9-8. It is also shown as numbers 8 and 9 in Fig. 9-5. There is a duplicate mecha-nism in the other end of the brake, and both ends must be adjusted exactly the same or the brake will bend the metal more on one end than on the other.

To make the set-back adjustment, first loosen the set screw *E* in Fig. 9-8. Then the two adjusting screws *C* and *D* are moved to obtain the proper set-back screw *C* moves the top leaf back, while screw *D* moves the top leaf forward. When the proper adjustment is made, both adjusting screws and the set screw must be tightened. Otherwise the top leaf will creep when it is clamped on the metal.

Other Adjustments on the Brake. There are other adjustments on the bending brake which are major ones and therefore should only be made by a qualified person.

However, an adjustment the sheet metal worker may be called upon to make is the one shown at Fig. 9-5*A*. This is a bolt and nut through the double wall of the bending leaf. Sometimes, when bending long pieces, the bending leaf will bend to a different angle on the ends than it does in the center. Tightening or loosening these two bolts will equalize the amount bent over the entire length of the brake.

131

Forming Molds. The formers or forming molds shown in Fig. 9-9 are attached to the bending leaf of the brake by friction clamps or dogs. Different types of molds are used when forming curved shapes such as cornices, skylight bars, and many other articles having rounded and reversed bends, as shown in Fig. 9-10.

How to Operate the Bending Brake. Though the cornice brake is generally operated from the right side, it is designed so that it may be operated from either side.

When making a sharp, right angle bend, the clamping bar is opened as shown in Fig. 9-11*A*, by pushing back the clamping handle. The sheet of metal is placed with the prick-punch marks flush with the edge of the top leaf shown at Fig. 9-11*B*. The sheet is held in place with the left hand, and the top leaf is pulled down with the right hand to clamp the sheet to keep it from creeping. The desired bend is made by raising the bending-leaf handle to the proper position, as in Fig. 9-11*C*.

When making narrow or reverse bends of 1/4″ or smaller, the 1/4″ bending leaf is removed, as in Fig. 9-12, which enables the smaller bend to be made. This is done by removing the machine screws. Since removing this bar reduces the bending capacity of the brake, it should be replaced after making narrow bends.

When bending heavy gage metal, a reinforcing bar or angle iron is attached to the bending leaf to give it added support, as shown in Fig. 9-13. The bar is attached to the bending leaf by inserting friction clamps in the holes of the bending leaf.

The method of squeezing a turned edge or closing a seam is shown in Fig. 9-14. The seam is inserted between the

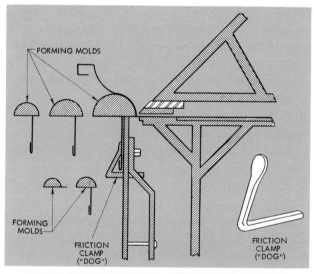

Fig. 9-9. Attaching forming molds to bending leaf bar.

Fig. 9-10. Types of bends made using forming molds.

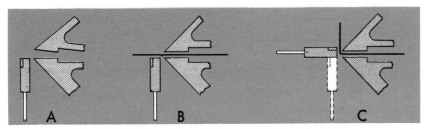

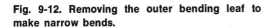

Fig. 9-11. Making a sharp right-angle bend on the brake.

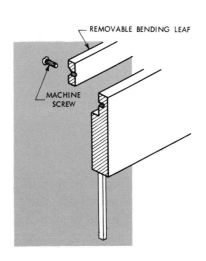

REMOVABLE BENDING LEAF

MACHINE
SCREW

Fig. 9-12. Removing the outer bending leaf to make narrow bends.

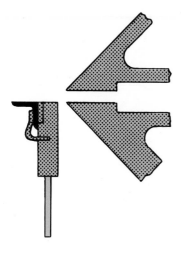

Fig. 9-13. Reinforcing bar or angle attached for forming heavy metal.

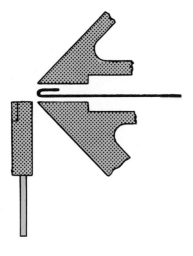

Fig. 9-14. Closing a seam on the brake.

clamping blades and the clamping handle is pulled forward as far as possible, closing the seam.

When forming heavy gage metal, the bending leaf is adjusted for the thickness of the metal by loosening the cap screw and adjusting the setscrews until the bending has the proper amount of clearance.

The method of forming a square duct is shown in Fig. 9-15. Notice that the inside lock is turned before the duct is formed to shape.

This points up the importance of plan-

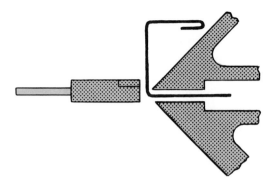

Fig. 9-15. Forming a square duct.

ning the sequence of bends on an object before using the brake. Note that in Fig. 9-15, if the inside lock was not turned first it would be very difficult to bend as the last bend. An aid to making bends is the gap at each end of the brake. This is so that bent edges can swing into this gap and not be distorted when another bend is made. As experience is gained on the brake, it will be easy to plan the sequence of bends. However, the new student should carefully try to visualize the sequence of bends for each object. It will be found that with proper planning, almost every shape can be bent on the brake without distorting the metal.

Care and Safety in Using the Bending Brake. It is important that the sheet metal worker know the safe way of operating the bending brake. Remember that the only correct way of operating a cornice brake is the safe way.

1. Never bend rods or wires in the brake.
2. Pound on metal in the brake with a wooden mallet only.

3. For proper functioning, a brake should be leveled and bolted to the floor. If the top leaf creeps when the handle is clamped down, wedge up one leg on that end until the creeping is eliminated.
4. Oil all moving parts of the brake every three months.
5. Beware of the counterbalance balls and the bending leaf handles when you are near the brake.
6. The capacity of the brake is given on a plate on the end of the brake by a double set of numbers such as 16.8. The first number is the maximum gage of metal that can be bent and the second number is the length of the brake. The capacity is for *mild* or *low carbon* steel, for the length of the brake when the reinforcing bar is in place. Mild steel is both ductile and malleable but has a lower tensile strength and elastic limit than *high carbon* or *hard* steels. Thus, 16-8 means that 16 gage metal 8 feet long can be bent when the reinforcing bar is in place. Without the reinforcing bar, the capacity of the brake is four gages lighter. Metal thicker than the gage capacity given can be bent on the brake so long as it is not for the full length. For example, on a 16-8 brake, 14 gage can be bent for a length of two or three feet, so long as the reinforcing bar is in place. When metal exceeds the thickness of the gage capacity, it depends on judgment and experience of the sheet metal worker as to whether it is beyond capacity.

135

7. When bending heavy metal for seams and similar operations, remember that you can gain considerable mechanical advantage through the leverage principle by clamping down the handle nearest the work first and leaving the handle farthest from the work for last.

8. Do not use pipe extensions on the brake handles to clamp down the work. This will overstrain the machine.

9. The gap in the top leaf of the brake at each end is a considerable aid in forming objects since it allows bent edges to fit in the gap without smashing them down.

Making Edges

Whenever a sheet metal object is made, some type of edge must also be formed. It is seldom that any object is made without some sort of edge to give the product a finished appearance. In addition to providing a finish, an edge eliminates the raw edge of the metal that is likely to cut someone and provides additional strength for the edge. Some edges provide only a small amount of strength, while other edges give maximum rigidity. Figure 9-16 shows some of the sheet metal edges commonly used.

Single Hem

The *single hem* is a folded edge on the metal made in order to increase its strength and to make a smooth finished edge. It is one of the most common of all edges since it is the simplest to form. The hem is folded over in the brake and then inserted in the brake and smashed flat. The allowance for the hem is generally 1/4″. However, on metal heavier than 22 gage, it is common practice to increase the hem to 5/16″ or 3/8″, since the larger edge is easier to bend. A hem is seldom over 1/2″ wide because large hems tend to wrinkle at the edges giving a poor appearance.

Double Hem

The *double hem* is simply a single hem done twice. Again, it is an easy edge to make, but it provides much greater strength than the single hem. The allowance for a double hem is twice the hem size less 1/16″. The inside allowance, shown at *A* in Fig. 9-17 is made to the hem size—generally 5/16″ or 3/8″. The outside allowance, as shown at *B* in Fig. 9-17, is made 1/16″ less than the hem size. This is because the outside line is bent first and it must be short so that it does not cover up the second bend line.

Wired Edges

For a greater amount of strength than that provided by the double hem, the *wired edge* is used. This is done by wrapping the sheet metal around a piece of wire. In manufactured products, wired edges are often formed without

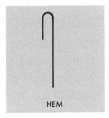

HEM

DOUBLE HEM

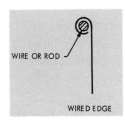

WIRE OR ROD

WIRED EDGE

CAPPED EDGE

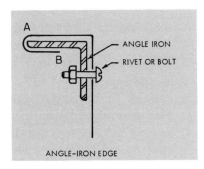

A

B

ANGLE IRON

RIVET OR BOLT

ANGLE-IRON EDGE

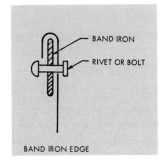

BAND IRON

RIVET OR BOLT

BAND IRON EDGE

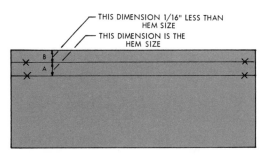

NAILS

WOOD

1/4"

1/2"

A

BLIND EDGE

B

Fig. 9-16. Some commonly used sheet metal edges.

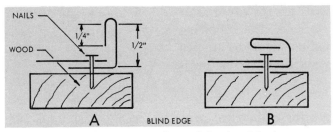

THIS DIMENSION 1/16" LESS THAN HEM SIZE

THIS DIMENSION IS THE HEM SIZE

B

A

Fig. 9-17. Inside and outside allowances for a double hem.

any wire and are simply hollow circles of metal. In the sheet metal shop, however, the wire is always used in the edge. The wired edge is not used as often as it once was because of the time and skill involved in producing it. However, every student who studies the sheet metal trade should know how to make a wired edge.

Allowance for a Wired Edge. The allowance added to the pattern for a wired edge depends upon the diameter of the wire. For 26 gage and lighter, 2-1/2 times the diameter of the wire is added to the pattern. For example, if 1/4″ diameter wire is to be used, allowance for the wired edge would be 1/4″ × 2-1/2, or 5/8″.

For 24 gage metal and heavier, allowances must be made for the thickness of the metal in addition to the diameter of the wire, which varies from 2 to 2-1/2 times the thickness of the metal.

The allowance for a wired edge may also be found by folding a narrow strip of metal around the wire, then straightening it out and measuring it. This gives the exact amount required for the edge.

Preparing a Wired Edge. There are a number of methods by which the edges of sheet metal may be prepared for wiring. The method selected depends largely upon the shape of the article. Cylindrically shaped articles, whenever possible, are wired before they are formed to shape. Tapering articles are wired after they have been formed. The following review of information should be studied carefully before starting wiring projects:

1. Wired edges for cylindrical articles should, whenever possible, be wired while the metal is flat.
2. The cutting pliers or cutting nippers should be used to cut wire.
3. Bolt cutters can be used to cut heavy wire and rod.
4. The bar folding machine should be used whenever possible to form the metal for a wired edge.
5. A bending brake is used to turn the edges of extra long metal.
6. A properly turned edge in the bar folding machine makes it unnecessary to use a mallet to form the metal over the wire.
7. When using the bending brake, it is necessary to use a mallet to form the metal over the wire.

Edges with Steel Angles and Bars

For maximum strength, the bar edge or the angle edge is often used. The bar edge provides as much strength as a wired edge and is easier to form. The angle edge provides more strength than any other edge and is equally easy to form. These two edges are really the same except that they employ different shapes of stock around which the metal wraps. Depending upon the conditions of the job, the bar edge may be most suitable or the angle edge may be best. The amount of metal to allow to wrap around the edges is the thickness of the angle or bar plus 3/8″. Thus, if 1/8″ bar or angle is used, the distance from *A* to *B* in Fig. 9-16 would be 1/8″ + 3/8″ = 1/2″. Generally, 1″ × 1/8″ bar or 1″ × 1/8″ angle is used for the stock. However, any size could be used.

Capped Edges

The capped edge shown in Fig. 9-16 is generally an emergency edge used when the ordinary edge was forgotten or, more often, when a sheet metal object is cut down and a raw edge is exposed that must be covered. The width of the cap is generally about 1/2″ on each side, though it will vary with job conditions. It is simply a strip of metal bent as shown and slipped over the raw edge of the metal. Generally, the cap is held in place by tack soldering, though it is sometimes riveted or bolted.

Blind Edges

The blind edge shown in Fig. 9-16 has many names such as *false edge* and *Dutchman*. It is used to cover nail heads and the raw edges of sheet metal when sheets must be nailed to a wooden surface, such as in covering a door with metal. A formed strip of metal is slipped under the sheet and nails are driven through both pieces of metal, close to the edge as shown in Fig. 9-16A. After the nails are all driven in to secure the sheet, the upright edge is carefully pounded down with a mallet so that the nail heads are covered and the edge of the metal has the appearance of a double hem. See Fig. 9-16B. This same edge can be used in the same way to finish a joint where two sheets of metal must be joined over wood.

Making Seams

In sheet metal construction, there are a variety of methods for joining the edges of sheet metal. These methods, however, may be generally classified as either *mechanical* or *welded*. The choice of the seam is determined primarily by the thickness of the metal, the kind of metal, the cost of fabrication, and the equipment available for making the seam. However, it is obvious that the mechanical seam is used when joining light and medium gage metal and that, when joining heavier metal, a riveted or welded seam is necessary.

In planning the fabrication of sheet metal articles, the worker should be able to visualize the type of seam that is best fitted for the specific job. Fig. 9-18 shows the various types of mechanical seams.

Types of Seams

Grooved Seam. One of the most common types of seams used in joining the edges of light or medium gage sheet metal is called a grooved seam. This seam consists of two folded edges called *locks* as shown in Fig. 9-19A. The two edges are hooked together as in Fig. 9-19B, and locked together at Fig. 9-19C with a grooving tool called a hand groover or with a grooving machine. The width of the lock is shown by W.

When making a grooved seam, it is necessary to make allowance for the amount of material that is to be added for the lock. The amount depends largely upon the width of the lock and the thickness of the metal.

The formula for finding the amount of material for a grooved seam is as follows:

24 gage or lighter $= 3 \times$ width of lock.

22 gage or heavier $= 3 \times$ width of lock plus 5 times the thickness of metal.

Half of the above allowances are to be added to each side of the pattern. Grooved seams are rarely used in metal heavier than 20 gage.

The most accurate method of finding the amount of material for a grooved seam is to take a 1″ strip of metal 6″ long and cut it into two parts at right angles to the length. Turn the required

139

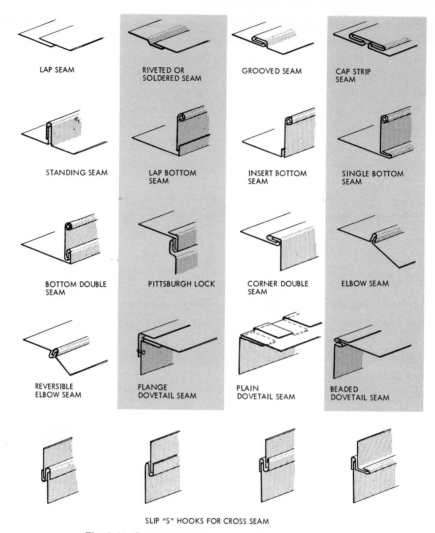

LAP SEAM

RIVETED OR SOLDERED SEAM

GROOVED SEAM

CAP STRIP SEAM

STANDING SEAM

LAP BOTTOM SEAM

INSERT BOTTOM SEAM

SINGLE BOTTOM SEAM

BOTTOM DOUBLE SEAM

PITTSBURGH LOCK

CORNER DOUBLE SEAM

ELBOW SEAM

REVERSIBLE ELBOW SEAM

FLANGE DOVETAIL SEAM

PLAIN DOVETAIL SEAM

BEADED DOVETAIL SEAM

SLIP "S" HOOKS FOR CROSS SEAM

Fig. 9-18. Common seams used in sheet metal work.

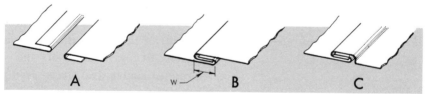

A   W   B   C

Fig. 9-19. Steps in forming a grooved seam.

lock at one end of each piece and groove together. Measure the length of the strip. The difference between this di- mension and the original 6″ length of the strip will be the exact amount which must be added for the seam.

Pittsburgh Seam. This seam is sometimes called a hammer lock or hobo lock. It is used as a longitudinal corner seam for variously shaped pipes such as the duct shown in Fig. 9-20. The seam consists of two parts, the single lock as in Fig. 9-21A, and the pocket lock in Fig. 9-21B. The single lock is placed in the pocket lock, Fig. 9-21C, and the flange is hammered over, Fig. 9-21D.

Fig. 9-20. Ductwork using Pittsburgh seams.

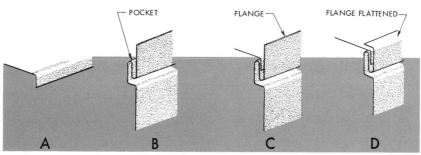

Fig. 9-21. Steps in forming the Pittsburgh seam.

One of the advantages of the Pittsburgh seam is that the single lock can be turned on a curve and the pocket lock can be formed on a flat sheet and then rolled to fit the curve as shown in Fig. 9-22.

The Pittsburgh seam is the most commonly used of any seam in the sheet metal shop. It is so common that special machines called roll-forming machines, such as the one shown in Fig. 9-23 are in every general sheet metal shop. With these machines, the metal is inserted in one end and runs through a series of rolls so that it emerges from the other end with the pocket lock completely formed. In shops where there is no roll-forming machine, the Pittsburgh seam

is formed on the brake. The allowance for the Pittsburgh seam when formed in the brake is 1-1/4″, as shown in Fig. 9-24. Then the Pittsburgh seam is formed as shown in Fig. 9-25.

Step 1—Bend 90° on the 1-1/4″ line.

Step 2—Remove metal and insert 1-1/4″ edge into the brake with the large part of the metal pressed tightly against the leaf of the brake. This makes a second bend 1/2″ from the first.

Step 3—With metal in position of Step 2, bend it as far as the brake will bend.

Step 4—Remove metal and replace in the brake as in position of Step 1. Then bend the 1-1/4″ line which was bent to 90° in Step 1.

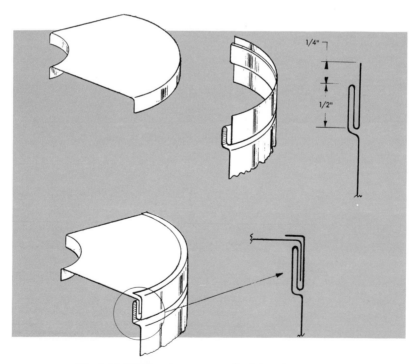

Fig. 9-22. Pittsburgh seams can be formed on curves.

Fig. 9-23. Pittsburgh lock forming machine. (The Lockformer Co.)

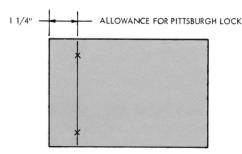

1 1/4" — ALLOWANCE FOR PITTSBURGH LOCK

Fig. 9-24. Allowance for Pittsburgh lock.

Step 5—Metal will be in position shown by dotted line. With wooden mallet, beat metal down to position shown by solid lines in Step 5.

Step 6—Slide metal in brake and flatten with upper leaf.

Step 7—Remove metal and turn it over so edge of upper leaf clamps just back of the point indicated by *A*. This position is determined by holding the point indicated by *B* just past the outside edge of the bending leaf. Since the bending leaf is 1/2″ wide and the distance from *B* to *A* is also 1/2″, this means the metal is in position. After metal is clamped, bend it slightly to approximately a 15° angle as shown by dotted lines. Then pound it down with wooden mallet to position shown by solid lines.

Drive-Clip Seam. This seam is generally used in connection with S clips for connecting cross seams on ducts. However, it is sometimes used for joining other sheet metal objects.

The seam is made by turning edges as shown in Fig. 9-26*A* on the two pieces to be joined. These edges will vary with job conditions, however, the common width is 1/2″. The actual drive clip is formed as shown in Fig. 9-26*B*. Often the clip will have to be driven on with a hammer, which is the reason for its name. Fig. 9-26*C* shows the completed seam.

S Clip Seam. The S clip is an S shaped piece of metal that forms two pocket locks for the joining metal to slip in as shown in Fig. 9-18. As with the drive clip, the most common application of the S clip is in joining sections of duct. However, it is also often used wherever two joining sections of metal need to be held in a flat seam and where there is no need for strength in holding the two pieces together. Often in covering a wall with sheet metal, the S clip is bent on the edge of the sheet and is used as shown in Fig. 9-27.

Fig. 9-28 shows how the S and drive clips are used to join sections of duct.

Slip-Joint Seam. This seam is used

143

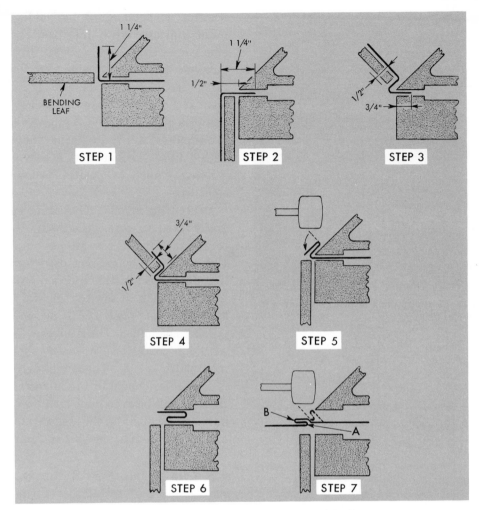

Fig. 9-25. Steps in forming the Pittsburgh lock.

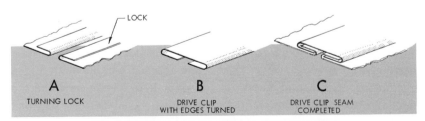

Fig. 9-26. Steps in assembling a drive clip seam.

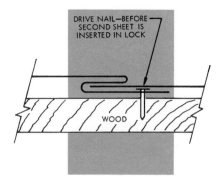

Fig. 9-27. S clips are used to join sheet metal pieces covering a wall.

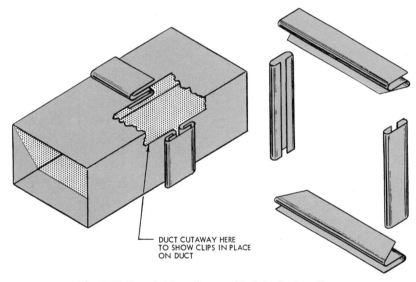

DUCT CUTAWAY HERE
TO SHOW CLIPS IN PLACE
ON DUCT

Fig. 9-28. S and drive clips used to join duct sections.

for a longitudinal corner seam, as shown in Fig. 9-29. It consists of a single lock, as shown at *A* and a double lock, pictured at *B.* The single lock is slipped into the double lock, *C,* completing the assembly of the seam.

When making pipes with a slip-joint seam, as shown in Fig. 9-30*A,* great care should be taken to see that the corners of the metal are squared and the edges are trimmed. Failure to do so will twist the pipe out of shape or cause the edges of the pipe to be uneven as in Fig. 9-30*B.*

Double Seam. There are two types of double seams. One type is used for making irregular fittings such as square elbows, offsets, boxes, etc. The double

145

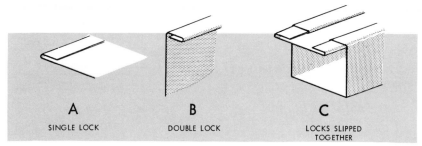

Fig. 9-29. Slip joint seam.

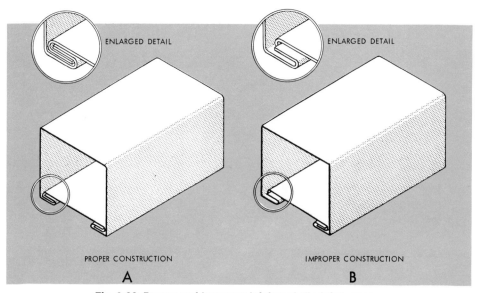

Fig. 9-30. Proper and improper joining of slip joint seams.

seam is made somewhat differently than the slip-joint seam. The single edge is turned at right angles, as shown in Fig. 9-31*A*. The double edge is formed as in Fig. 9-31*B*. It is placed over the single edge as in Fig. 9-31*C*, and is double seamed over a stake, as shown in Fig. 9-31*D*. The completed seam is shown in Fig. 9-31*E*.

Bottom Double Seam. This seam is used to fasten bottoms to cylindrically shaped articles such as pails, tanks, etc. The operations for making this type of seam are as follows: The single edge shown in Fig. 9-32*A* is turned on the body of the cylinder by means of a turning machine. The burr is turned on the bottom, Fig. 9-32*B*, using a burring machine. The bottom is snapped on the body, Fig. 9-32*C*, and is peened down as in Fig. 9-32*D;* the seam is completed by using a mallet as in Fig. 9-32*E*.

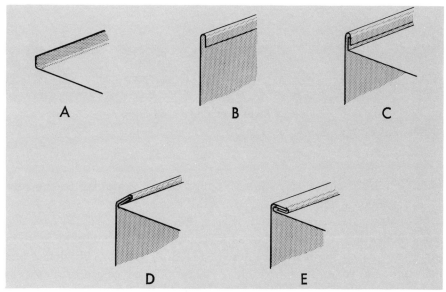

Fig. 9-31. Making a double seam.

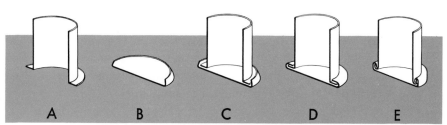

Fig. 9-32. Steps in making a bottom double seam.

Handy Seam. A typical longitudinal seam is shown in Fig. 9-33. Though similar to a grooved seam, it does not require a grooving tool. The seam consists of a double edge turned at right angles, shown in Fig. 9-33*A*, and a single edge, Fig. 9-33*B*. The double edge is placed over the single edge, Fig. 9-33*C*, and is hammered over with a mallet, Fig. 9-33*D*. The handy seam prevents the edges from buckling when two full sheets of metal are being seamed together. It is generally used in large ducts requiring two or more sheets of metal.

Dovetail Seam. This seam is an easy and convenient method of joining collars to flanges. There are three types of dovetails: the plain dovetail, the beaded dovetail, and the flange dovetail. The dovetail seam is principally used on round or elliptical pipe, and seldom on rectangular duct.

Plain Dovetail Seam. This seam is

147

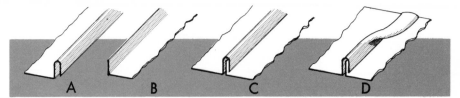

Fig. 9-33. Steps in making a hand seam.

used when joining a collar to a flange without the use of solder, screws, or rivets. It is made by slitting the end of the collar and bending every other tab as shown in Fig. 9-34*A*. The bent tabs act as stops and the remaining straight tabs are bent over the part to be joined, as shown in Fig. 9-34*B*. This seam may be made watertight by soldering around the joint.

Beaded Dovetail Seam. This seam has a bead formed around one end of the cylinder by means of a beading machine. This bead acts as a stop for the flange to rest upon and the tabs are bent over to hold the flange in place. The procedure is similar to the plain dovetail seam.

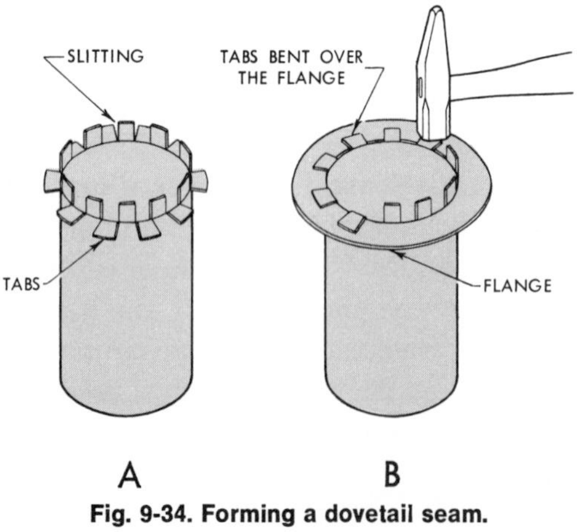

Flange Dovetail Seam. Fig. 9-35 shows the assembly of a flange type dovetail seam for cylindrical pipes. This seam is used where extra strength and neat appearance are important. It is commonly used where pipes intersect with a metal plate such as in furnace flues, ceilings, etc. First, a flange is turned on the *collar* as shown in Fig. 9-35*A*. Next, slits are cut at regular intervals at the end of the *sleeve* and matching rivet holes are drilled in the collar and sleeve as shown in Fig. 9-35*B*. The plate rests on the collar flange and the sleeve is inserted into the collar as shown in Fig. 9-35*C*. The rivet holes are alined and the rivets are installed. Finally, the tabs are hammered over to complete the seam as shown in Fig. 9-35*D*.

Standing Seam. Standing seams on cross seams of large ducts, or any large sheets of metal, eliminate the need for angle steel reinforcement. This lock is easily made and provides greater convenience in fabrication. The seam is shown in the open and closed position in Fig. 9-36.

Another seam used very often for making cross seams for connecting two sections of duct is the *government clip,*

SLITTING   TABS BENT OVER THE FLANGE

TABS   FLANGE

A   B

Fig. 9-34. Forming a dovetail seam.

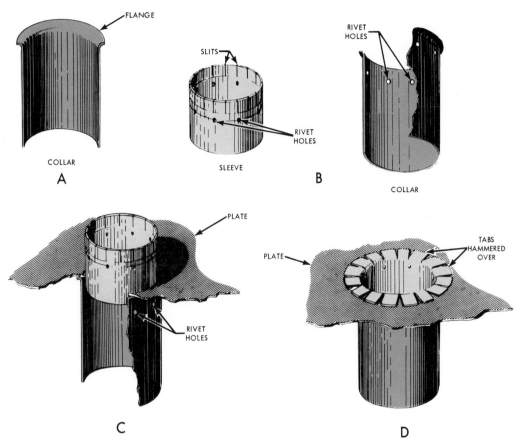

Fig. 9-35. Steps in forming a flange dovetail seam.

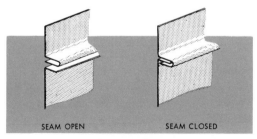

Fig. 9-36. Standing seam.

sometimes called a pocket lock. The government clip is used in the same manner as the S and Drive clips. The difference is that the finished government clip is not flush with the duct but projects out about 1″ as shown in Fig. 9-37, much in the same manner as a standing seam. The government clip is formed as shown in the section view in Fig. 9-37*A*. Figs. 9-37*B* and 9-37*C* show how it is used to join the duct.

Many general sheet metal shops use so many government clips that they have special machines to cut them out. These are called clip punches or clip dies. The metal is cut into 4-1/2″ wide strips and then cut to the proper length

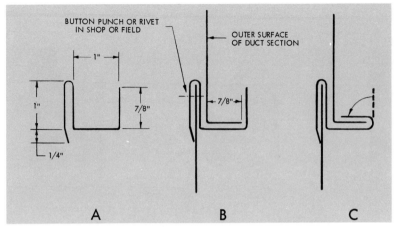

Fig. 9-37. Steps in forming a government clip.

in the clip die. Clip dies are usually foot-operated and are shaped so that one stroke of the die punches the rivet hole and cuts the end of the strip to the proper shape as shown in Fig. 9-38. Then the other end of the clip is turned over and cut in the same manner to give the complete clip blank as shown in Fig. 9-38.

After the clips are cut, they are bent to the proper shape, usually in a small brake set up with special gages for quick bending of clips. When they are formed, the clips are riveted into frames such as the one shown in Fig. 9-39. These frames are then inserted on the end of the duct and punched or riveted securely.

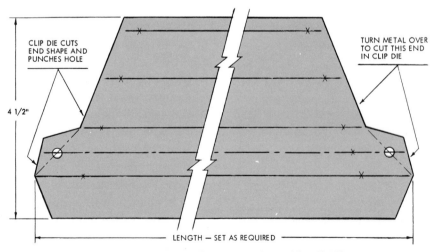

Fig. 9-38. Government clips may be formed by clip dies.

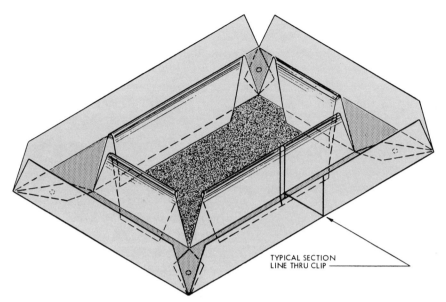

TYPICAL SECTION
LINE THRU CLIP

Fig. 9-39. Assembling and attaching government clips to ductwork.

Shop Projects

Making a Single and Double Hemmed Edge

Aim.   To develop the ability to operate and adjust the bar folder.

Material.   Galvanized steel 3″ × 10″, 26 gage or lighter.

Specifications.   Make a 3/8″ double hem on one side of a strip of metal and a 1/4″ single hem on the other side.

Operations for Single Hem

1. *Cut a strip of metal to the required size.*
2. *Set the gage of the bar folder for a 3/8″ hem, as explained previously. (Before setting the gage, the gage adjustment should be checked by turning the gage adjusting screw until the fingers are flush with the edge of the folding blade. The reading of the gage should then be zero. If it is not, loosen the screw and set the plate.)*
3. *Insert the edge of the metal to be folded between the folding blade and the jaw, as shown in Fig. 9-40A.*
4. *Pull the handle forward as far as possible, as demonstrated by Fig. 9-40B.*
5. *Insert the hem between the folding wing and the blade, with the folded edge facing upward.*

6. *Pull the handle forward as far as possible, completing the single hem, as in Fig. 9-40C.*

7. *Reset the gage for a 1/4" width hem and repeat the operations, completing the single hem.*

Operations for Double Hem

1. *Reset the gage of the bar folder for a 3/8" width edge. (For light metal, both hems may be turned with the same gage setting, it being possible thereby to complete the double-hemmed edge before resetting the gage.)*

2. *Insert the 3/8" hem, with the folded edge upward, between the folding bar and jaw, as shown in Fig. 9-41A.*

3. *Push the handle forward as far as it will go, as pictured in Fig. 9-41B.*

4. *Release the metal by returning the handle to its former position.*

5. *Turn the metal over and insert the double hem between the folding bar and the blade, then push the handle forward as far as possible, Fig. 9-41C, completing the double hem.*

Making a Grooved Seam by Hand

Aim.   To develop the ability to make a grooved seam by hand.

Material.   Two pieces 3" × 12" 28-gage steel.

Specifications.   Make a 1/4" grooved seam by hand, using scrap metal.

Operations

1. *Cut two pieces of metal to the required size.*

2. *Set the gage of the folder for a 1/4" lock.*

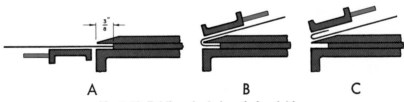

A   B   C

Fig. 9-40. Folding single hem in bar folder.

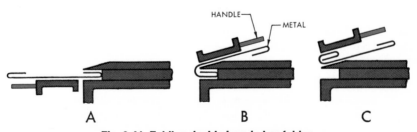

HANDLE — METAL

A   B   C

Fig. 9-41. Folding double hem in bar folder.

3. Turn the lock on each piece of metal as shown in Fig. 9-42A.
4. Hook the two pieces together, Fig. 9-42B.
5. Place the metal to be grooved on a flat stake and flatten the seam slightly with a mallet. Be sure to keep the two pieces tightly hooked.
6. Select the proper size of hand groover, choosing one having a slot about 1/16″ wider than the width of the lock.
7. Place the groover over the seam at one end and strike lightly but firmly with a hammer, making a short groove.
8. Repeat the process and groove the other end.
9. Groove the balance of the seam by moving the groover along the seam, as shown in Fig. 9-42C. Keep the groover moving along the seam. Do not finish the seam in one pass. It will be a neater

job to groove the seam gradually in two or three passes.
10. Flatten the seam with a mallet to make it smooth, completing the grooved seam. The mallet is the only proper tool for this operation. Using a hammer would mar the work.
11. Measure the width of the metal and determine how much metal was used to form the seam.

Making a Pittsburgh Lock

Aim. To develop the understanding and skill necessary to make a Pittsburgh lock.

Material. One piece 28-gage galvanized steel 6″ × 6″, one piece 3″ × 6″.

Specifications. Make a 3/8″ Pittsburgh lock with scrap metal.

Operations

1. Cut out the two pieces of metal to the specified size.

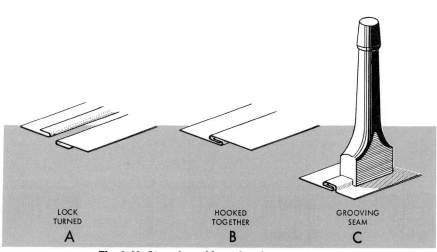

LOCK TURNED
A

HOOKED TOGETHER
B

GROOVING SEAM
C

Fig. 9-42. Steps in making a hand-grooved seam.

2. *Lay out the lines on the two pieces according to the drawing in Fig. 9-43.*

3. *Using the 6" × 6" piece, form the Pittsburgh seam according to the instructions in this chapter.*

4. *Using the 3" × 6" piece, make the single edge to go into the pocket lock.*

5. *Pound over the edge of the seam and turn in to the instructor.*

Making a Duct with a Pittsburgh Seam

Aim. To learn how the Pittsburgh seam is used in making duct work.

Specifications. Make 6" × 4" duct, 12" long, with a Pittsburgh seam on one corner.

Operations

1. *On a piece of 26 gage galvanized steel lay out the pattern shown in Fig. 9-44.*

2. *Form the pocket lock for the Pittsburgh seam.*

3. *Bend the single edge.*

4. *Starting with the side nearest the single edge, bend the corners of the duct.*

5. *Finish the seam and turn in to the instructor.*

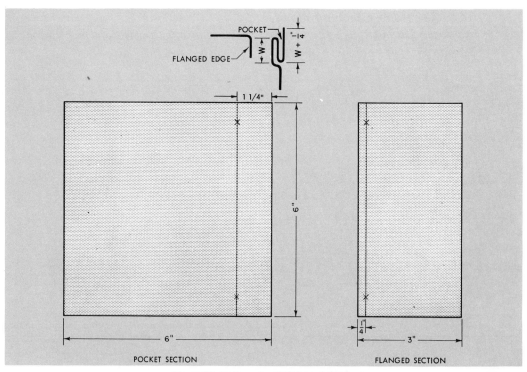

Fig. 9-43. Pattern for Pittsburgh lock.

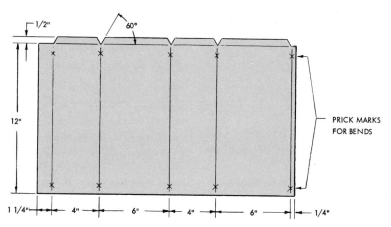

Fig. 9-44. Pattern for duct with Pittsburgh seam.

Making a Duct with a Double Seam Corner

Aim. *To gain practice in using the double seam.*

Specifications. *Make a duct 6″ × 4″ long, with a double seam on one corner.*

Operations

1. *Lay out the pattern for the duct, as shown in Fig. 9-45. Prick* *punch all bend lines. Notice the 1/16″ allowance to prevent binding when the lock is hammered over. The allowance for a double seam is equal to three times the width of the seam, with the measurements distributed as shown.*

2. *Cut out the pattern.*

3. *Bend the 5/16″ edge (right edge in Fig. 9-45) at a right angle, as shown in Fig. 9-46A.*

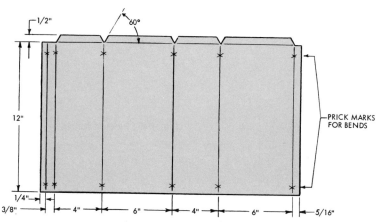

Fig. 9-45. Pattern for duct with double seam corner.

4. *Make the folded lock on the opposite end for the double seam, as shown in Fig. 9-46B.*

5. *Form the remaining bend lines to shape as in Fig. 9-46C.*

6. *Place the duct with the corner to be double seamed on a stake.*

7. *Squeeze the lock together with a pair of tongs.*

8. *Hammer the lock over, using a mallet as in Fig. 9-46D.*

9. *Dress (square up the corner of the seam) with a mallet, not with a hammer. Hold a square head stake on the inside edge of the seam to back it up while dressing the corner.*

Using S and Drive Clips to Join Duct

Aim. To show how to use S and drive clips and to give practice in their use.

Specifications. Make S and drive clips and connect the two ducts as shown in the previous two projects.

Operations

1. *Lay out and cut two pieces of metal as shown in Fig. 9-47 for drive clips. Bend them as described in this chapter.*

2. *Lay out and cut two pieces as shown in Fig. 9-48 for S clips. Bend them as described in this chapter.*

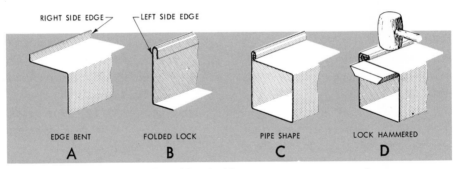

RIGHT SIDE EDGE   LEFT SIDE EDGE

EDGE BENT   FOLDED LOCK   PIPE SHAPE   LOCK HAMMERED

A   B   C   D

Fig. 9-46. Steps in making double seam corner on square pipe.

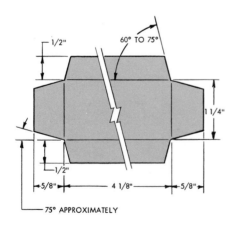

Fig. 9-47. Pattern for drive clip.

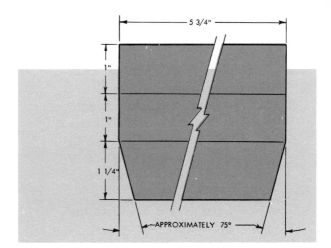

Fig. 9-48. Pattern for S clip.

3. *On the two ducts, use tongs to bend the 1/2″ edge back for taking the drive clip, as described in this chapter. Bend the edges on 4″ sides only. The 6″ sides will remain straight to receive the S clips.*
4. *Slip the S clips on one of the ducts and fit the other duct into them.*
5. *Start the drive clips and tap them on with a hammer.*
6. *Tap the tabs of the drive clips around the corners to finish.*
7. *Turn in to the instructor.*

Setting the Hand Brake

Aim. To give practice in setting the brake for different thicknesses of metal.

Specifications. Set the hand brake for the proper handle tension and set-back for the gage of metal given by the instructor.

Operations

1. *Obtain a sample of metal from the instructor.*

2. *Determine the thickness of the sample to the nearest 1/32″.*
3. *Set back the top leaf of the brake 1-1/2 times the thickness of the metal, according to the instructions in this chapter.*
4. *Set back both ends of the brake equally.*
5. *Put the sample in the brake and set both ends of the brake to the proper handle tension.*
6. *Have the instructor inspect the brake after it is completely set.*

Making a Wired Edge Using the Bar Folder

Aim. To develop the ability to make a wired edge by the use of the bar folding machine, the hand brake, and wiring machine.

Material. Lightweight scrap metal, 1/8″ wire.

Specifications. Make a 1/8″ wired edge on a flat piece of scrap metal.

Operations (using the bar folding machine)

1. Cut a piece of light gage metal to the desired size.
2. Set the gage of the bar folding machine 1-1/2 times the diameter of the wire or 3/16" (1-1/2 plus the wire diameter which is used in the bends equals 2-1/2 times the diameter of the wire, the amount that is added to the pattern).
3. Lower the wing by loosening the wedge lock screw. It should be lowered an amount equal to the diameter of the wire.
4. Tighten the lock nut, insert the edge of the metal, and turn the folded edge, as shown in Fig. 9-49A.
5. Cut the wire to the proper length, using a pair of cutting pliers or cutting nippers.
6. Straighten the wire on a smooth surface, using a mallet.
7. With the wire in the folded edge as in Fig. 9-49B, place the end of the wired edge between the rolls of the wiring machine, as shown in Fig. 9-49C. Note that the edge of the upper roll is set just inside the edge of the metal.

8. Lower the upper roll by turning down the crank screw just enough to start turning the edge.
9. While holding the work in a horizontal position, run the wired edge through the rolls.
10. Tilt the work upward, lower the upper roll, and repeat the operation until the metal is fitted closely around the wire as in Fig. 9-49D, completing the wired edge. It may be necessary to readjust the machine gage to keep the rolls on the edge of the metal.

Making a Wired Edge Using the Hand Brake

Operations

1. Cut a piece of metal to the required size.
2. Measure along the side of the metal 2-1/2 times the diameter of the wire.
3. Place the metal on the hand brake with the bend lines flush with the jaws, then bend the edge at right angles as in Fig. 9-50A.
4. Cut the wire to the proper length, using a pair of cutting pliers.
5. Straighten the wire over a smooth surface, using a mallet.

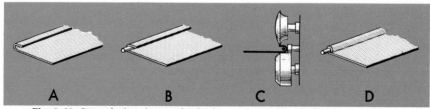

Fig. 9-49. Steps in forming a wired edge on bar folder and rotary machine.

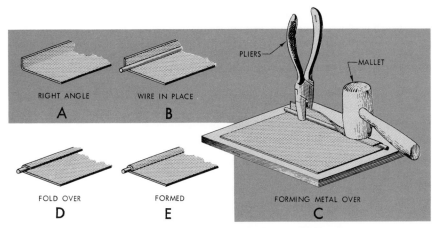

Fig. 9-50. Forming wired edge with the bending brake.

6. *Place the wire in the folded edge. See Fig. 9-50B and hold in place with vise clamp pliers.*

7. *Form the metal over the wire, using a mallet or riveting hammer.*

The steps are shown in Fig. 9-50C and 9-50D.

8. *Complete the wired edge in the wiring machine.*

STUDENT QUESTIONS AND ACTIVITIES

1. What type of seam is used in joining light sheet metal together?

2. Describe the procedure for grooving by hand. Describe the procedure for grooving by machine.

3. What is the formula for finding the proper amount of material for a groove seam regardless of the thickness of the metal?

4. Describe the parts of a Pittsburgh lock. Use sectional drawings if desirable.

5. What types of lock are generally used for assembling cross seams of ducts?

6. Describe the slip joint. Use sectional drawings if desirable.

7. What causes the side of a square or rectangular pipe to twist out of shape?

8. What is the difference between a double-seam joint and a slip joint?

9. Describe the method of making a double seam on the bottom of a cylindrically shaped article. Use sectional drawings if desirable.

10. Why may the handy seam be used to good advantage when joining two or more sheets of metal?

11. Describe two types of dovetail seam.

12. Describe various types of slip S clips.

13. What is the advantage of using the standing seam for large duct pipes?

14. Describe and name the major parts of the hand brake.
15. Where are the clamping handles located on the hand brake?
16. Give the location of the bending leaf handles.
17. Why are the counter-balance weights on the brake adjusted?
18. What is the name of the bar which is removed when bending small locks?
19. Describe the method of adjusting the clamping bar for various thicknesses of metal on the brake.
20. Describe the method of smashing a hemmed edge.
21. Why are bend lines prick punched before forming the object in the brake?
22. When is it necessary to attach a steel reinforcing bar or angle to the bending leaf?
23. Describe the uses of forming molds attached to the brake.
24. Tell how to adjust the brake for handle tension and set-back.

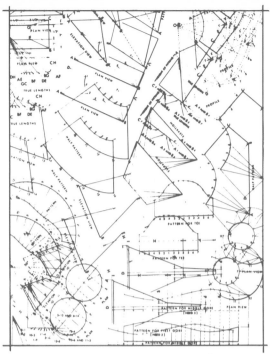

turning, burring and raising

When you finish this chapter, you should be able to:
1. Define or identify:
   - A. Turning machine
   - B. Burring machine
   - C. Combination machine
   - D. Raising
2. Make a turned edge.
3. Make a burred edge.
4. Make a wired edge.
5. Raise a circular piece of metal.

This chapter is concerned with the tools and practices involved in working with circular and cylindrical sheet metal objects. The first part covers the various types and uses of edge forming machines. The second part covers raising circular pieces of metal.

Rotary Machines

The edges for round and cylindrical objects are formed on *rotary machines* such as shown in Fig. 10-1. Rotary machines are available in many sizes and capacities and may be either hand-operated or motor powered. However, the operating principles for all machines are basically the same.

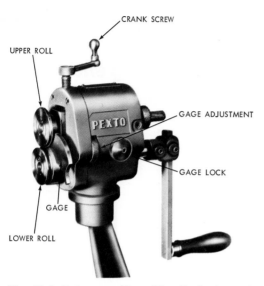

CRANK SCREW

UPPER ROLL

PEXTO

GAGE ADJUSTMENT

GAGE LOCK

GAGE

LOWER ROLL

Fig. 10-1. Rotary machine. (The Peck, Stow, & Wilcox Co.)

Fig. 10-2. Turning rolls. (Niagara Machine & Tool Works)

Turning Machines and Burring Machines

The two types of rotary machines most commonly used for forming edges are the *turning machine* and *burring machine*. Although the operation of the machines and the results are similar, there are some differences between the two. The main difference is in the shape or profile of the *forming rolls* as shown in Figs. 10-2 and 10-3. Note that the edges of the rolls on the turning machine in Fig. 10-2 are rounded, producing a curved bend, or *radius*. The upper roll of the burring machine shown in Fig. 10-3 has a sharp edge which produces an angular bend. Thus, the turning machine is better adapted for bending heavier gage metals in which a sharp, angular bend would cause too much stress at the bend and ultimately weaken the product.

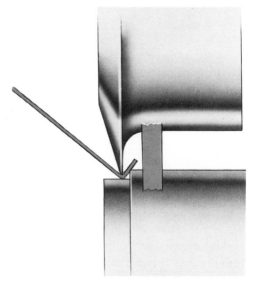

Fig. 10-3. Burring rolls. (Niagara Machine & Tool Works)

162

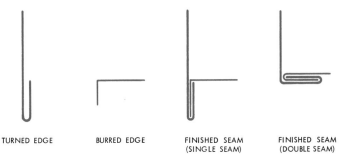

TURNED EDGE   BURRED EDGE   FINISHED SEAM   FINISHED SEAM
(SINGLE SEAM)   (DOUBLE SEAM)

Fig. 10-4. Single and double seaming.

Also, because of the radius bend, the turning machine is commonly used in preparing wired edges. On the other hand, the burring machine is particularly suited for lighter metal fittings which require a narrow, sharply angled edge or flange. Burred edges are usually 1/4″ or less.

An example of the respective uses of the turning and burring machines would be the component parts of a cylindrical object such as a can or bucket. The sides of the object are usually of heavier gage metal than the bottom or ends. Thus, the edges for the sides would be formed by turning and the bottom or end edges would be formed by burring. The parts are usually joined by single or double seaming so, as shown in Fig. 10-4, the use of the two methods of forming are particularly adaptable to this type of fabrication.

Preparing Edges

Preparing a Wired Edge. The turning rolls are used to begin the wired edge as shown in Fig. 10-2. First, the gage is adjusted by turning the knurled knob at the side of the machine as shown in Fig. 10-1. The distance to be taken is 2-1/2 times the diameter of the wire to be used. This distance is measured from the face of the gage to the center of the upper roll as shown in Fig. 10-5. The proper procedure for turning an edge for wiring is as follows:

1. Set the gage to 2-1/2 times the diameter of the wire.
2. Tighten the crank screw just enough to pull the work through the rolls, but not enough to run a groove in the metal.
3. Make one complete revolution of the work.
4. Tilt the work upward, tighten the crank screw enough to keep pulling the work through and make a second pass through the machine.
5. Tilt the work as far as possible, tighten the crank screw, and make the last pass through the rolls, completing the edge for the wire.

Now, the wire is inserted into the prepared edge and the edge is finished on special wiring rolls as shown in Fig. 10-6.

163

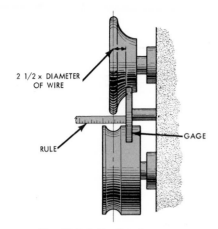

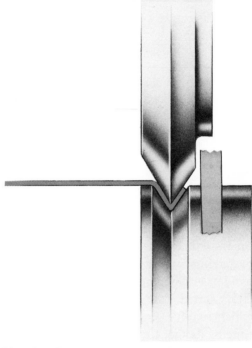

2 1/2 × DIAMETER OF WIRE

RULE

GAGE

Fig. 10-5. Adjusting the gage.

Fig. 10-7. Forming the elbow edge. (Niagara Machine & Tool Works)

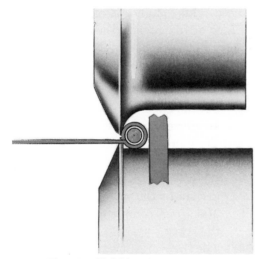

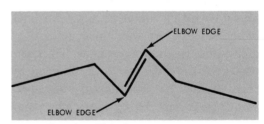

ELBOW EDGE

ELBOW EDGE

Fig. 10-6. Finishing the wired edge.

Fig. 10-8. Finishing the elbow edge.

Preparing an Elbow Edge. Elbow edges are prepared just as turned edges except that special rolls as shown in Fig. 10-7 are often used. The angular rolls allow for the required angle offset of the elbow as shown in Fig. 10-8.

Preparing a Burred Edge. The burring machine is generally used to turn small edges on circular disks for pail covers, bottoms, etc. The operation of the machine, as shown in Fig. 10-9, requires considerable practice to produce neat edges quickly and consistently. It is therefore advisable for the student to cut a number of small disks about 6″ in diameter and practice until he is able to turn a good edge.

If the student will follow the instruc-

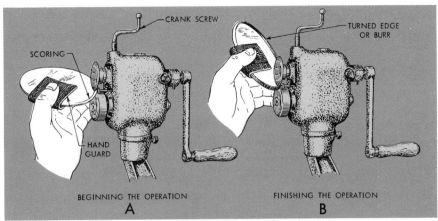

CRANK SCREW

TURNED EDGE
OR BURR

SCORING

HAND
GUARD

BEGINNING THE OPERATION
A

FINISHING THE OPERATION
B

Fig. 10-9. Operating the burring machine.

tions given here, he will produce very good results with practice.

1. Hold the left elbow tightly against the body.
2. Hold the disk tightly between the tip of the thumb and the side of the index finger, as shown in Fig. 10-9*A*.
3. Note the U shaped piece of metal used as a hand guard against cuts.
4. Hold the arm rigid throughout the entire operation.
5. Tighten the crank screw just enough to pull the metal through the rolls. The tightness of the rolls has little effect on the actual bending.
6. Make one revolution, scoring the edge slightly.
7. Without tightening the crank screw, make a number of revolutions, raising the disk slightly after each revolution until the burr is turned to the proper angles as shown in Fig. 10-9*B*. Note

that the actual bending is done by tilting the metal up, and, since the metal is shrinking in this case, the more gradual the bending, the less wrinkles and waves there will be in the edge.

Combination Machines

The combination machine shown in Fig. 10-10 has interchangeable rolls and

Fig. 10-10. Combination machine. (Peck, Stow & Wilcox Co.)

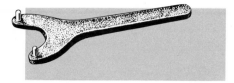

Fig. 10-11. Spanner wrench.

gages for many different types of operations. With this machine, one worker may perform turning, burring, wiring, elbow edging and many other operations simply by changing the rolls on the machine. The rolls are easily changed by placing the prongs of the spanner wrench, Fig. 10-11, in the holes located in the front of the rolls and turning the wrench counterclockwise.

Raising

The term *raising* is applied to the process of raising or bumping flat metal so as to form ornaments for cornice work, curved moldings, sheet metal balls, and covers for various objects. This operation is performed by a raising hammer and a raising block, such as shown in Fig. 10-12.

Raising Hammers

The raising hammers in Fig. 10-12 have various face sizes including 2-1/8″ and 1-3/4″; 2″ and 1-1/2″; 1-5/8″ and 1-3/8″; and 1-3/8″ and 1-1/8″. The selection of the hammer depends largely upon the desired size and depth of the depression to be made in the object.

Raising Block

The raising block is made of various materials which are capable of giving resistance to the blows of the raising hammer. Hardwood or lead cakes having differently sized shallow depressions are well adapted for use in raising operations.

Procedure for Raising

The illustration in Fig. 10-13 shows the cross section view of the raising block and the operations in sequence. To avoid buckling the metal, the following steps should be carefully observed:

1. Begin the raising operation at the outer edge of the disk as shown in Fig. 10-13A.
2. Work inward toward the center, gradually turning the metal as each blow is struck, shown at Fig. 10-13B.
3. Continue working toward the center, gradually raising the disk until the desired depression is completed. This is shown at Fig. 10-13C.
4. Place the inside of the raised disk over the rounded head of the tea-kettle stake. Using a mallet, strike light blows to smooth out all wrinkles.

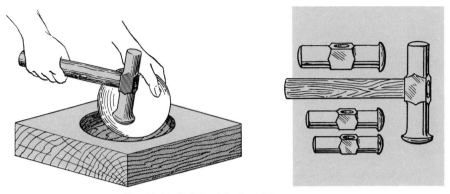

Fig. 10-12. Raising block and hammers.

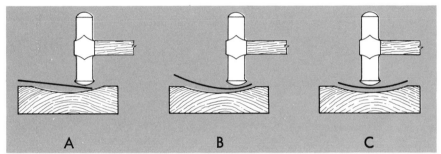

Fig. 10-13. Steps in raising a piece of sheet metal.

Class Activities

1. Be prepared to give the name of the turning machine for any rolls that the instructor shows or draws on the board.

2. Be able to explain to the class why it is said that turning a 90° edge on a circle causes the metal to shrink.

3. If a burring machine were not available, suggest to the class two other

ways in which an edge could be turned on a circular piece of metal. Be able to discuss the disadvantages of these methods as compared to using the burring machine.

4. Be prepared to give to the class at least one example of how raising is used in industry.

STUDENT QUESTIONS AND ACTIVITIES

1. What machine turns burrs on disks?
2. What are the differences between the turning and burring machines?
3. What is meant by the term *raising* metal?
4. Draw the upper and lower turning rolls.
5. Draw the upper and lower burring rolls.
6. Draw the upper and lower elbow edging rolls.
7. Give examples of objects you could make using: (a) turning rolls, (b) burring rolls, and (c) elbow edging rolls.

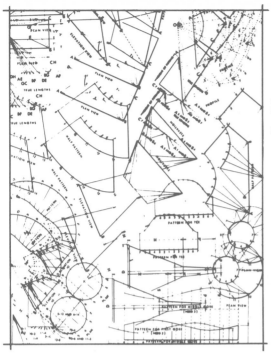

forming, crimping, beading and grooving

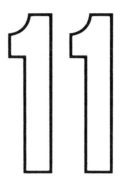

When you finish this chapter, you should be able to:
1. Define the following terms:
   A. Forming
   B. Beading
   C. Crimping
2. Identify and explain the purpose of the:
   A. Forming machine   C. Beading machine
   B. Crimping machine   D. Combination crimping and beading machine
3. Explain the difference between the plain forming machine and the slip-roll forming machine.

In this chapter, you will learn about the four machines most commonly used in fabricating pipes and other cylindrically shaped objects. They are the *plain forming machine, slip-roll forming machine, crimping machine* and *beading machine.*

Forming Machines

The two types of forming machines commonly used in the sheet metal shop are the plain forming machine and the slip-roll forming machine.

Plain Forming Machine. The plain forming machine consists of three rollers through which flat sheets of metal are fed to be formed into cylindrical shapes. The two front rollers are driven either by a hand crank assembly or by an electric motor. Most shops will mainly use the hand powered machine. The rear, or *idler,* roll does the actual forming of the cylinder. It is adjustable to accommodate different thicknesses of metal and the diameter of the piece to be formed.

Slip-Roll Forming Machine. The slip-roll forming machine, Fig. 11-1, operates the same way as the plain forming machine. The difference is that the upper roll on the slip-roll machine can be released and swung away to facilitate removing the formed piece of metal. See Fig. 11-2. On both types of forming machines, the two front rolls act as feeding or gripping rolls while the rear roll gives the proper curvature to the work. The front rolls are adjusted by two screws located at either end of the machine. The rear roll is adjusted by two screws located at the rear of each housing. The grooves in the front and rear rolls are used for forming pieces with wired edges.

Forming Cylinders. The forming process is begun by inserting the work piece between the two front rolls as shown in Fig. 11-3, left. The front rolls are adjusted by turning the knurled adjusting screws on the front of the machine as shown in Fig. 11-1. The front rolls should be adjusted to allow just enough clearance between the rolls to avoid crushing the locks. After the work piece is inserted, it is tilted upward as indicated by the dotted line in Fig. 11-3, left. This begins the curve and allows the work piece to pass between the upper and rear roll. The radius of the curvature is controlled by the position of the rear roll. For a smaller radius, the rear roll is lowered as shown in Fig. 11-3, left. For a larger radius, the roll is raised, as shown in Fig. 11-3, right. The rear roll is adjusted by the two screws located at the rear of the gear housings at either end of the machine.

On the plain forming machine, the work piece can only be removed by passing it all the way through the machine. On the slip-roll machine, the upper roll

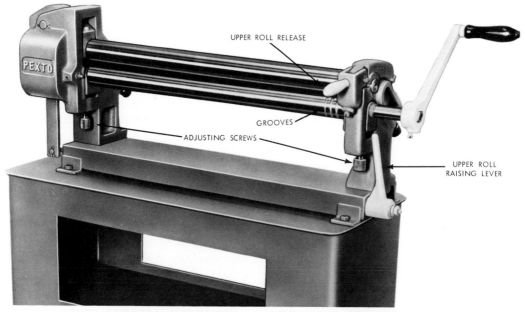

UPPER ROLL RELEASE

GROOVES

ADJUSTING SCREWS

UPPER ROLL RAISING LEVER

PEXTO

Fig. 11-1. Slip-roll former. (The Peck, Stow & Wilcox Co.)

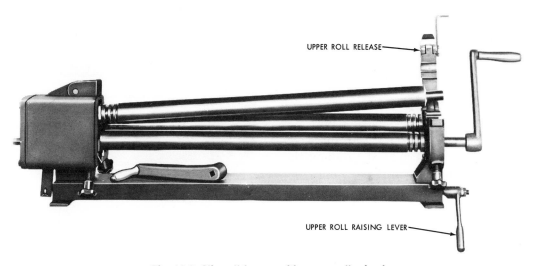

Fig. 11-2. Slip-roll former with upper roll raised.

UPPER ROLL RELEASE

UPPER ROLL RAISING LEVER

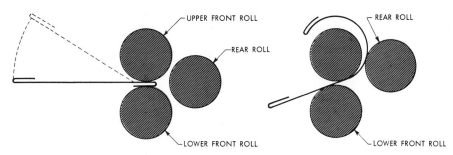

UPPER FRONT ROLL

REAR ROLL

REAR ROLL

LOWER FRONT ROLL

LOWER FRONT ROLL

Fig. 11-3. Starting and forming cylindrical shapes

is released and swung away, allowing the piece to be slipped off the roll.

Forming Cylinders with Wired Edges. When forming pails, cans, and other round articles with wired edges, the wire should extend past the metal slightly at one end. This is the end that should be inserted between the rolls as shown in Fig. 11-4. The wire at the other end should be slightly shorter than the metal to form a pocket to receive the wire from the other end. A short piece

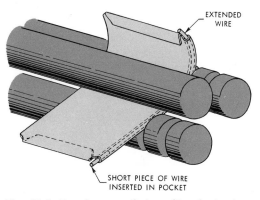

EXTENDED WIRE

SHORT PIECE OF WIRE INSERTED IN POCKET

Fig. 11-4. Forming a cylinder with wired edge.

171

of wire should be inserted to prevent the pocket from being smashed. Continue to form the cylinder to the curvature desired until the ends meet. Insert the end of the wire into the pocket of the wired edge from where the short piece of wire has been removed, and continue until the seam has passed through the rolls. The hand lever is then opened to allow the roll to be raised and the cylinder removed.

Crimping

Crimping is the process used to corrugate one end of a pipe to make it smaller, so it will fit easily into the end of another pipe of the same dimension. This method eliminates the need of making one end of the pattern for the pipe smaller than the other. However, crimping can be used on light gage metal only. Crimping can also be used when turning large flanges on collars since it aids in stretching the metal. A crimped edge is shown in Fig. 11-5.

Fig. 11-6 shows the rolls used for crimping edges.

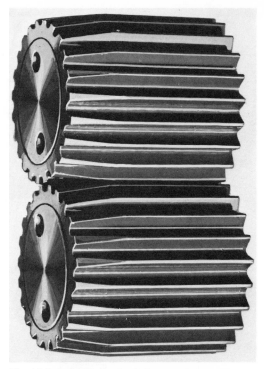

Fig. 11-6. Crimping rolls. (Niagara Machine & Tool Works)

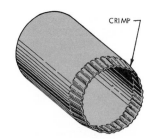

Fig. 11-5. Crimped edge on a pipe.

Beading Machines

Beads are formed on cylindrical objects to serve as stiffeners, reinforcement or ornamentation. The beading machine is a rotary machine equipped with special beading rolls. The standard shapes of beads are the single bead, ogee bead and triple bead as shown in Fig. 11-7.

Fig. 11-8, left, shows the type of hand-operated, bench-mounted beading machine commonly used in the shop. Note the deep throat. This allows for beading several inches from the end of the cylinder. Fig. 11-8, right, shows a power driven beading machine.

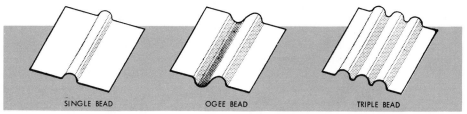

Fig. 11-7. Standard types of beads.

SINGLE BEAD   OGEE BEAD   TRIPLE BEAD

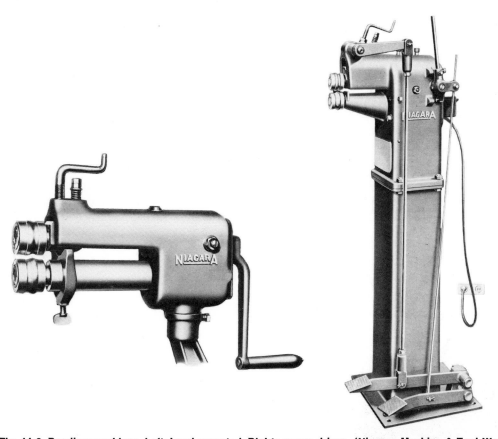

Fig. 11-8. Beading machines. Left: hand operated. Right: power driven. (Niagara Machine & Tool Works)

Fig. 11-9 shows two important steps in setting up and operating the beading machine. First, set the gage as shown in Fig. 11-9, left. The thumb screw on the bottom of the gage should be tightened firmly so that it cannot slip as the bead

173

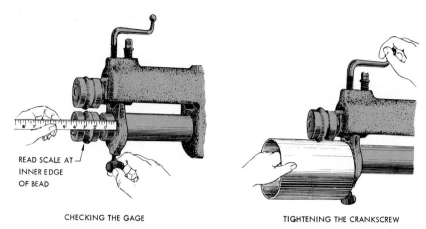

READ SCALE AT
INNER EDGE
OF BEAD

CHECKING THE GAGE

TIGHTENING THE CRANKSCREW

Fig. 11-9. Steps in operating the beading machine.

is being formed. Next, the work piece is inserted between the rolls up against the gage and the crankscrew on top of the machine is tightened. Care should be taken not to set the crankscrew too tight so as to cause the rolls to cut through the bead.

Combination Crimping and Beading Machine

If a work piece is to be both crimped and beaded, this may be accomplished in operation by using the combination machine shown in Fig. 11-10.

Fig. 11-10. Combination crimping and beading machine. (Niagara Machine & Tool Works)

Fig. 11-11. Revolving tool stand. (The Peck, Stow & Wilcox Co.)

Revolving Tool Stand

The revolving tool stand shown in Fig. 11-11 is a great time and space saver in the shop. The top piece holds four machines and may be rotated. Underneath is storage space for more machines. Thus, instead of having to move from machine to machine, a single worker is able to perform up to ten different operations without having to move at all.

Shop Activities

Making a Round Pipe with a Grooved Seam

Aim.   To learn how to make the pattern for a round pipe and to form the groove seam.

Specifications.   Lay out the pattern and make a round pipe 5″ in diameter, 7″ long, with a 1/4″ groove seam.

Operations

1. *Lay out the pattern shown in Fig. 11-12 and cut it out.*
2. *Bend the 1/4" edges for the groove seam on the bar folder.*
3. *Roll up the pipe.*
4. *Finish the groove seam. (See Chapter 9.)*
5. *Turn in the pipe to the instructor for and save for the next project.*

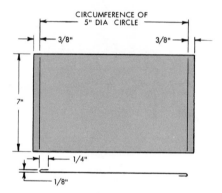

Fig. 11-12. Pattern for round pipe.

CIRCUMFERENCE OF
5" DIA CIRCLE

3/8"   3/8"

7"

1/4"

1/8"

Making a Dovetail Seam

Aim. To learn how to use a dovetail seam to connect a round pipe to a flat plate.

Operations

1. *Use the round pipe made in the preceding project.*
2. *With a pair of dividers, mark a line 3/8" from the end of the pipe, as shown at top left, Fig. 11-13.*
3. *Clip the edge about every 5/8", as shown at top right, Fig. 11-13.*
4. *Bend out every other tab at right angles, beginning with the tab at*

the seam, as at bottom left, Fig. 11-13.

5. *Cut an opening in the flange the size of the collar.*
6. *Place the collar with the notched end in the opening and bend the remaining tabs over the flange, using a hammer, as at bottom right, Fig. 11-13.*

A marking gage (see Fig. 11-14) may also be used to mark off allowances for seams. It is cut out of scrap sheet metal. The notch made is the required width of the allowance to be marked.

Crimping, Beading and Connecting a Round Pipe

Aim. To illustrate how to join round pipe by crimping and beading.

Specifications. Crimp and bead the round pipe from the preceding projects and join it to another round pipe with sheet metal screws.

Operations

1. *Take the pipe and crimp it and beam one end so that it will lap 1-1/2" into another pipe. Read the instructions in this chapter for crimping and beading.*
2. *Make a second pipe according to the layout shown in Fig. 11-12.*
3. *Join the two pipes and secure with three sheet metal screws. Make sure the pipes are straight and the seams are aligned before inserting the screws.*
4. *Turn in to the instructor.*

Making a Round Tank

Aim. To learn how to lay out a round tank with a double seam and to

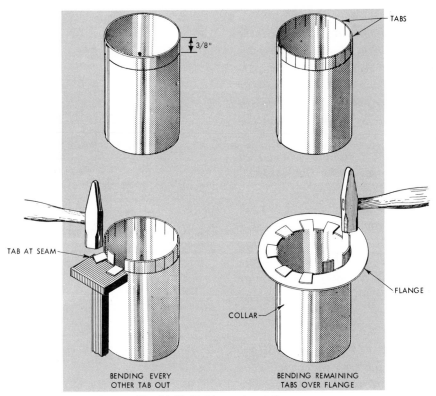

Fig. 11-13. Making a dovetail seam.

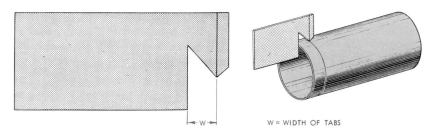

Fig. 11-14. Making a marking gage for seam allowances.

gain skill in making wired edges, double seams and groove seams.

Specifications. Lay out and make a 7" round tank, 4" high with a 1/4" wired edge, a 1/4" groove seam, and 1/4" double seam.

Operations

1. *Lay out the patterns for the tank shown in Fig. 11-15. Extreme accuracy is essential for the patterns on this project. Allow for all seams and edges. Check with the instructor before cutting the patterns.*

2. *Form and complete the wired edge according to the instructions in Chapter 9.*

3. *Bend the edges for the 1/4″ groove seam.*

4. *Roll the tank and the wired edge according to the instructions given in Chapter 11, under Forming Cylinders with Wired Edges.*

5. *Complete the groove seam.*

6. *Turn the edge on the bottom with the burring machine.*

7. *On the bottom piece turn up the outside edge with the burring machine.*

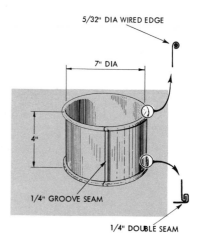

Fig. 11-15. Making a round tank with a wired edge and double seam.

8. *Connect the bottom to the main part.*

9. *Set down the seam and finish it.*

10. *Turn in to the instructor and save the tank for soldering later.*

STUDENT QUESTIONS AND ACTIVITIES

1. What is the difference between a plain former and a slip-roll former?
2. Why is the work inserted between the rolls after they are closed?
3. Describe the method for forming cylinders with wired edges.
4. Give the procedure for forming a length of round pipe.
5. Why is it necessary to crimp one end of a length of pipe?
6. Why is a bead put on the end of a length of pipe?
7. What is meant by a combination crimping and beading machine?

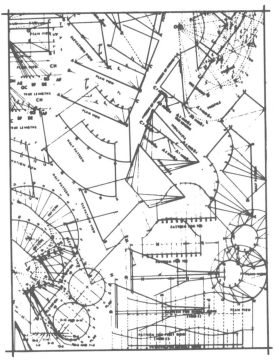

soldering

12

When you finish this chapter, you should be able to:
1. Define the following terms:
   A. Soft Solder
   B. Hard Solder
   C. Flux
   D. 50-50 Solder
   E. Raw Acid
   F. Cut Acid
   G. Tinning
   H. Sweating
   I. Skimming
   J. Tacking
   K. Soldering
2. List at least seven items that will make a poor soldering job.
3. Sweat solder, tack, or skim solder a flat seam of sheet metal.
4. Tin a soldering copper.

Solders applied with a soldering copper are used for fastening many types of sheet metal work and for making seams watertight. To do a good job of soldering, you must know the kind of material being soldered, the kind of solder and flux which are most suitable, and the proper soldering copper for the job.

The material in this chapter is presented so as to give you not only the proper procedures for soldering, but also the reasons for performing each step. For example, students sometimes make the mistake of using too much solder. The result is a job whose appearance and quality is poor.

Solders

The term *soldering* is a broad one but it generally refers to the *joining or uniting of two or more pieces of metal by means of an alloy having a lower melting point than the pieces being joined.* Soldering may be divided into two general classes, *hard soldering* and *soft soldering.* Hard solders are those having a melting point over 750° F and include such processes as silver soldering and brazing. However, it is soft soldering that is generally used by the sheet metal worker and it is this process that we shall be concerned with in this chapter.

Properties of Soft Solder

Soft solder is composed of tin and lead and its melting point depends largely upon the proportions of these two elements. For example, solder composed of half tin and half lead, commonly called *half-and-half,* melts at about 418° F, while solder consisting of 10% tin and 90% lead has a melting point of about 573° F.

Soft solders are classed by the proportion of each element, by weight. Therefore, *50-50* means that the solder consists of 50% tin and 50% lead by weight. It is important to note that the percentage of tin is always given first. Thus, *60-40* contains 60% tin and 40% lead, while *40-60* contains 40% tin and 60% lead. In the sheet metal shop, the preferred solder proportion is 50-50 since this gives a low melting point without using too much expensive tin. Other trades have found that different

proportions of tin to lead are better suited to their particular needs. Generally, increasing the tin content lowers the melting point of the solder. However, this is *only* true up to about 87% tin content. After that point, as the tin content increases the solder's melting point rises.

It is well to remember that the strength or bonding quality of a soldered seam depends on more than the melting point of the solder used. For example, a poorly tinned soldering copper may be over-heated to a temperature of 700° and still not distribute the solder in the seam a satisfactory way.

Bar and Wire Solder

In the sheet metal trade, solder is generally used in bar or wire form. Although solder can be obtained from manufacturers in bars from 1/2 to 1-1/2 pounds, as shown in Fig. 12-1, some sheet metal shops prefer to prepare their own solders by melting the correct proportions of tin and lead into molds that cast their shop name on the bars.

In addition to the bar form, solder is available in triangular or round bars about the size of a lead pencil and about 18″ long. It is also available in 1/8″ or

Fig. 12-1. A typical bar of solder.

1/16″ diameter wire. This can be either solid or hollow wire either with an acid or rosin flux in its center. This is called *acid core* or *rosin core* solder. Manufac-turers of solder will pour the solder in any size or shape that the contractor specifies.

Soldering Fluxes

Flux is required to remove the oxide film that is always present on metal. If no flux were used, this oxide film would make adherence of the solder to the metal difficult if not impossible. Rather than bonding to the metal, the solder would only lie loosely over the oxide film.

There are two general classes of soldering flux: corrosive and non-corrosive. Acids are corrosive and should therefore be washed off immediately after the soldering operation is completed. Rosin is a non-corrosive flux. It may be in the form of a lump, powder, paste, or liquid.

Muriatic Acid

Muriatic acid is the commercial grade of hydrochloric acid used in soldering. It is used for making zinc chloride, for a flux on galvanized steel and for cleaning off dirty parts of the metal before they are soldered. In the sheet metal shop, muriatic acid is usually called *raw acid*.

Though the terms hydrochloric acid and muriatic acid are often used inter-changeably, there is one difference of which the student should be aware. Muriatic acid is the *commercial* term and comes in one strength only—a medium strength acid. Hydrochloric acid is the *chemical* name and can be in any strength from a very dilute to a very concentrated and dangerous acid.

Raw hydrochloric acid is colorless and has a sharp and pungent odor. However, the surest identification of raw acid is to put a small amount on a piece of galvanized metal. If the liquid bubbles and smokes and turns the zinc coating black, it is raw acid.

Zinc Chloride

Zinc chloride is often called cut, cured, or killed acid. It is unequaled as a flux when soldering galvanized metals, zinc, brass, copper, and lead. It is also used for soldering tin which has become tarnished by being exposed to the weather.

Cut acid is colorless and odorless. However, it is as corrosive and danger-ous as raw acid and therefore should be treated with care. One method of distinguishing cut acid from raw acid is by putting a small amount on a piece of galvanized metal. If the reaction discussed previously occurs, the acid is raw. If no reaction occurs, then the liquid is cut acid.

Preparation of Zinc Chloride. Zinc chloride is prepared by pouring muriatic acid into a jar having a large opening at the top. This allows the acid to boil without running over. Place the jar near an open window or out of doors

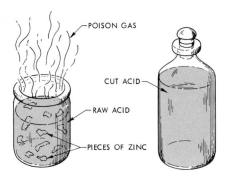

Fig. 12-2. Preparing zinc chloride (cut acid) flux.

where the fumes can escape. Put a small quantity of zinc cut into small pieces into the acid as shown in Fig. 12-2. As the boiling action slows down, continue adding zinc until the acid will no longer boil. The cut acid should be filtered through a very fine copper screen to remove all dirt left by the dissolving of the zinc before putting it in tight glass containers for storage.

Safety. With both raw and cut acid, it is extremely important to remember that these acids are highly dangerous and to be treated with the utmost caution. They will eat holes into clothing and may cause painful skin burns. The greatest danger is that they can cause blindness if allowed to come into contact with the eyes. If this happens, wash the eyes immediately with plenty of cold water. *A doctor should be consulted at once regardless of whether or not there is a burning sensation.* Often the reaction of the acid in the eye is delayed and may not occur for several hours. See Chapter 3 for additional soldering safety precautions.

Rosin

Rosin is the by-product of oil of turpentine and is a common, non-corrosive type of flux for soldering metals such as bright tin plate, terne plate, and copper. Rosin may be applied as a powder melted on the metal with a warm soldering copper, or made into paste by adding enough benzine to make it a semi-solid.

Soldering Coppers

Soldering coppers are made of solid pieces of copper and vary in shape and weight. The body of the soldering copper, called the *head,* is usually octagonal in shape. The pointed end is referred to as the *point* or *tip* and is forged into various shapes for different kinds of work.

Sizes of Soldering Coppers

Soldering coppers are designated by weight *per pair*. For example, a copper marked with a 3 indicates that it and its mate will weigh three pounds. One 3 pound copper will weigh 1-1/2 pounds *without the handle and shank*.

The standard sizes of soldering coppers per pair are 1, 1-1/2, 2, 3, 4, 5, 6, 8, 12, and 16 pounds. The 12 and 16 pound coppers are used for roofing and other heavy soldering operations.

Handles

Soldering copper handles are made of wood or fiber. The cheaper handle is made with small grooves around the ferrule, on which a piece of wire is wound to keep it from splitting. The better grade of handle has a metal ferrule at the end where the rod is inserted. This keeps the handle from burning when the copper is heated. A special handle for heavy coppers has a large flange to keep

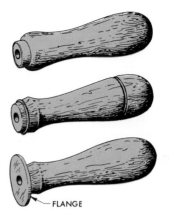

FLANGE

Fig. 12-3. Soldering copper handles.

the heat away from the hand. All three types of handles are shown in Fig. 12-3.

The most common type of handle manufactured cuts a thread on the shank of the soldering copper as it is screwed on. This handle is well protected from burning or charring.

Heating Equipment

Sheet metal workers generally use a bench gas furnace or a butane furnace.

Gas Furnace

The bench type of gas furnace, shown in Fig. 12-4 is especially designed to heat soldering coppers.

The gas furnace is equipped with shutoff valves and a pilot light. The base and the cover of the furnace are lined with asbestos. A steel shelf is located in the rear to protect the tinned points of the copper.

Fig. 12-4. Gas bench furnace. (Johnson Gas Appliance Co.)

For safety, every furnace should be in a well ventilated area. It is preferable that a fume hood and exhaust system be installed over the furnace. When lighting the furnace, observe the following safety precautions:

1. Check the shutoff valve to see that it is closed.
2. Remove any dirt from inside the furnace.
3. Light a small piece of crumpled paper and place it in the mouth of the furnace. At the same time, turn the handle located on the front of the furnace. After the furnace is properly lighted, control the burners by working the valve handle. The small pilot light near each burner will relight the gas when the valve handle is turned to the "on" position. Always stand to one side when lighting the furnace. This will avoid burns in case the fire does flash out when it catches.

When not in use, the furnace burner valve should be turned off, leaving only the pilot light burning. At the close of the day the main line valve and the branch line valve should be turned off.

Fig. 12-5. Butane furnace.

Butane Furnace

The butane furnace, as shown in Fig. 12-5, is often used in the shop. It is portable and simple and safe to operate, providing the manufacturer's instructions and all other shop safety practices are followed.

Soldering

Preparing for Soldering

Forging the Soldering Copper. Sometimes soldering coppers become so misshapen that filing the point will not form it properly. In this case soldering coppers are forged to the desired shape as follows:

1. Heat the copper to a cherry red.

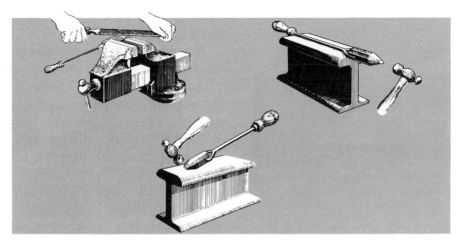

Fig. 12-6. Steps in forging a soldering copper.

2. Place the copper in the vise and file the part to be forged with a coarse file to remove all scales. This is shown in Fig. 12-6, top left.

3. Place the shank end of the copper against the anvil as shown in Fig. 12-6, top right. With a heavy hammer, force the misshapen point back into the body of the copper.

4. Reheat the copper and place it on the anvil, striking solid blows with a heavy hammer, as shown in Fig. 12-6, bottom.

5. Repeat the forging operation when necessary.

Filing and Tinning the Soldering Copper. Tinning a soldering copper means *covering the point with solder.* A well tinned copper is absolutely necessary to a good soldering job. One of the most common mistakes is to try to solder with a poorly tinned copper. *Unless the* *soldering copper is properly tinned, a good soldering job is impossible.*

There are several important reasons for tinning a soldering copper. First, tinning keeps scale and corrosion from forming on the soldering copper point that acts as insulation. This scale and corrosion does not permit the heat to transfer from the copper to the solder. Tinning prevents formation of scale and therefore allows more heat to flow from the copper at the tinned area. If you touch some solder first to the tinned portion of a hot soldering copper and then to the untinned portion, you will note that the solder melts much faster on the tinned portion. This is because the tinning permits proper heat escape from the copper. Second, tinning allows the solder to flow properly from the point to the metal. Also, since tinning keeps the point clean, it keeps dirt and scale out of both the solder and the seam.

The first step in tinning is to heat

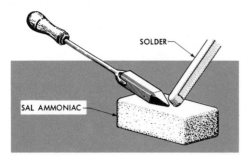

Fig. 12-7. Tinning a soldering copper on a cake of sal ammoniac.

the copper as for forging. The body of the copper is then clamped in a vise and the point is filed, using a coarse file. This removes the pits and old tinning. Then a finer file is used to smooth off the rough edges of the corners of the point.

After the filing operation is completed, reheat the copper enough to melt the solder. When a small portion of solder has been applied, rub the tip lightly back and forth on a block of sal ammoniac, as shown in Fig. 12-7.

If the solder will not adhere to the point, it is because the soldering copper is not hot enough. The point should be hot enough to cause white smoke to rise from the sal ammoniac. *However, care should be taken here because this white smoke is a toxic gas and should not be breathed.* When rubbing the point on the salt ammoniac block, do not wear a hole in the block. Try to rub over the entire surface of the block since using only one spot may cause the block to break before it has received full use.

The soldering copper should be neither overheated nor underheated during the tinning operation. If the copper is too hot, the tin will burn off as fast as it is applied. If it is too cold, the solder will not adhere to the copper.

It is important to keep in mind that the tinned surface will be ruined if the copper is overheated no matter how well it has been tinned. Therefore, when the copper is not in use for a few moments, it should be pulled slightly out of the fire or the flame should be lowered. An indication that the tinning is being burned off the point is a brilliant green flame in the firepot at the tip of the copper. This color is due to chemical reactions as the tinning is oxidized by the flame.

Applying the Soldering Flux. Applying the flux is important. Carelessness in its application has ruined many soldering jobs. Liquid fluxes are applied with a small brush, sometimes called a swab. Care should be exercised to avoid dropping flux anywhere except where the soldering is to be done. Dip the brush in the flux and spread it lightly on the place to be soldered, as shown in Fig. 12-8. Powdered flux, such as rosin may either be sprinkled on the place to be soldered, or it can be melted on the metal with a hot copper.

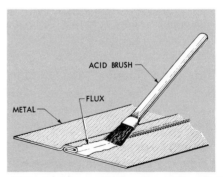

Fig. 12-8. Applying soldering flux with a brush.

Avoid flipping or dropping an acid brush. As noted previously, serious burns and eye injury can be sustained through such carelessness.

Using Dipping Solution. In the process of heating the soldering copper, the tinned part of the point becomes discolored and should be cleaned off before beginning the soldering operation. This is done by plunging the point of the soldering copper into a solution composed of 1/2 ounce of powdered sal ammoniac and one quart of clean water. This is done immediately after removing it from the fire. This operation is shown in Fig. 12-9.

SAL AMMONIAC
SOLUTION

Fig. 12-9. Cleaning tinned soldering copper in sal ammoniac.

Another method, though not as efficient as the dip, is to wipe the copper lightly and quickly with a rag. However, never use woolens since this will spoil the tin coating on the copper.

The dip is also a handy method of determining whether the copper is hot enough to use for soldering. With prac-

tice and observation, the sound of the copper in the dip will tell you whether the temperature is correct. A dull, slow, bubbling sound is characteristic of a cold tin. A sharp, fast, sizzling sound indicates that the copper is hot enough to do a good job.

Tinning for Various Jobs. The number of sides of the tip to be tinned depends on the type and position of the work. For example, when soldering vertical or upright seams, the copper should not be tinned on more than two sides. Most craftsmen prefer only one side, since a soldering copper tinned on all sides will not retain the solder. This is because solder will flow around the tinned sides of the point dropping off at the bottom. If the tip is tinned on only one or two sides, this will not happen.

Position of the Soldering Copper

The position of the soldering copper is important because the copper does two things as it is applied to the parent metal:

1. It heats the metal to the melting point of the solder.
2. It melts the solder and keeps it in a liquid state while soldering.

To do the former, it is important that as much of the point of the copper is resting on the metal as possible to allow maximum heat transfer from the tip to the metal. See Fig. 12-10. It should be remembered that the greater part of the heat is in the body and the base of the point—not in the tip. However, special work sometimes requires soldering with only the tip of the copper.

Since melted solders will flow to the hottest point on the metal, the soldering

Fig. 12-10. Position the copper so that the solder will flow freely.

copper should be held as shown in Fig. 12-10 so that the solder will be pulled into the seam.

Soldering Different Types of Metals

Soldering Galvanized Metal. When soldering galvanized metal, the principal question concerns whether one should use raw acid or zinc chloride as the flux. If the galvanized metal is bright and clear, zinc chloride can be used to make a well-bonded joint. However, if the metal is dull and dirty, raw acid definitely should be used. There are also good commercially marketed fluxes for soldering galvanized metal.

Soldering Tin and Terne Plate. Steel, coated with tin or lead, can be soldered with a variety of fluxes. Whenever possible, rosin should be used because of its non-corrosive action upon metal. If the metal is dull, as would be true of used or old tin plate, zinc chloride can be used satisfactorily. Always wipe or wash the flux from the metal immediately after completing the soldering.

Soldering Copper and Brass. If the surface of the sheet copper or brass is free of oxide, it can be easily soldered by using zinc chloride as the flux. If the copper or brass is dull, it can be cleaned by applying raw acid directly to the metal with an acid brush. The raw acid should be washed off with a damp rag before applying the zinc chloride for soldering. All flux should be washed off of the metal after soldering.

Soldering Stainless Steel. Stainless steels can be soldered easily with prepared soldering fluxes designed especially for that purpose. If these special fluxes are not available, prepare the surface of the metal in the same way as the surface of tarnished copper is prepared. Scratch the surface with sandpaper and, with a small brush, apply raw acid to the parts to be soldered. After the acid has been left on the metal for the required time (which varies with the type of stainless steel and the strength of the acid), it should be wiped clean with a damp rag. The metal is then soldered in the same manner as copper, using regular half-and-half solder with zinc chloride as the flux. The flux should be thoroughly cleaned from the metal surface after soldering.

Soldering Lead. Rosin flux is considered best for soldering lead. However, with lead, the surface must be scraped with a tinner's scraper or a knife immediately after cleaning, since this metal quickly oxidizes. The soldering copper must be well tinned and colder than usual. There should be some solder between the hot copper and the lead at all times to keep the lead from melting.

Soldering Seams

Soldering Flat Seams. The illustrations in Fig. 12-11 show the proper and improper methods of soldering a flat seam. The seam at Fig. 12-11, left, shows how it looks when it is properly "sweated" together with a well-tinned and properly heated soldering copper. The seam at Fig. 12-11, right, shows the same seam when soldered with a copper which is too small, improperly tinned, and not sufficiently heated. Notice the blocked opening at the joint of the seam which does not permit the solder to fuse the seam properly.

The two seams illustrate the difference between *sweating* and *skimming*. Generally, soldered sheet metal seams are sweated. Sweating means holding the soldering copper in the proper manner, at the correct temperature, and in the proper position so that the solder flows completely through the seam. Sometimes joints are pre-tinned and sweated. This means that the pieces of metal are covered with a thin coat of solder before they are joined. Then the joint is sweated in the usual manner. A pre-tinned joint will show little solder on the surface but will have a completely sweated joint.

Skimming, as shown in Fig. 12-11, right, is generally an improper method of soldering. It only skims over the surface of the seam and therefore is weak and likely to leak.

Another term commonly used is *tacking*. This refers to the process of melting small drops of solder at intervals along a seam for the purpose of holding it in place until it is properly soldered.

Soldering Copper Seams. When soldering copper seams, the same condition will be found as is shown in Fig. 12-12, right, if the parts to be soldered are not properly tinned. There is another important fact to be remembered when soldering copper. *Never use raw acid as a flux for soldering copper.*

Soldering Upright Seams. *Pointing up* is the term used to describe soldering vertical seams. This operation is different from flat soldering since a portion of the soldering is done with the tip of the soldering copper. To solder a vertical seam, place a well-heated copper with the tinned side of the point toward the top edge of the seam and keep the handle higher than the tip itself. Begin the

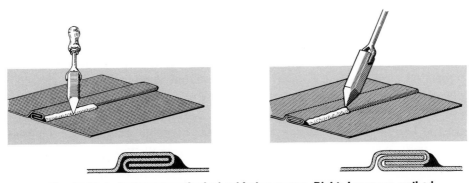

Fig. 12-11. Left: Proper method of soldering seams. Right: Improper method.

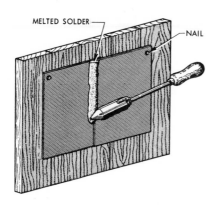

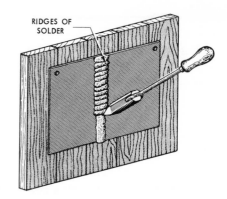

Fig. 12-12. Steps in soldering vertical seams.

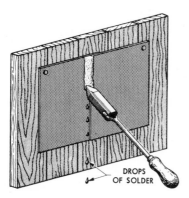

Fig. 12-13. Incorrect position for soldering vertical seams.

sweating and tinning operation by rubbing the soldering copper back and forth across the seam. This is shown in Fig. 12-12. When the tinning operation has been completed, a reheated copper is again placed at the top of the seam with the tip of the copper touching the seam and with the handle elevated above the body of the iron. Apply a small portion of the solder. Move the tip back and forth across the seam, making small

ridges as shown in Fig. 12-13, right. Continue until this seam is completed.

The illustration in Fig. 12-13 shows the soldering copper held in the wrong position. Note that the solder is dropping off the soldering copper. The illustration shows that it is impossible to solder a vertical seam correctly with the soldering iron handle lower than the iron.

Requirements for Successful Soldering

The successful application of soldering depends upon several elements including: properly tinned copper, application and type of flux, properly blended solder, type of soldering tip, correctly heated copper, properly prepared surface, oxidation of metal, the skill of the individual doing the soldering, etc.

When you learn the requirements of successful soldering technique, you have made a good beginning. Thereafter, soldering skill will increase with application and with practice.

The illustrations in Fig. 12-14 demon-

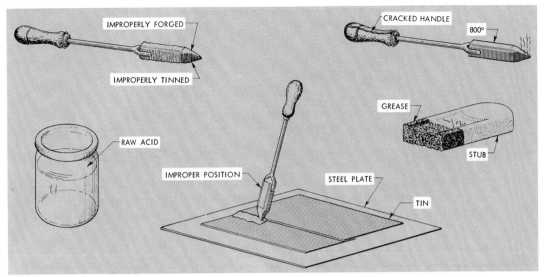

Fig. 12-14. Examples of poor soldering procedures.

strate some things to avoid when soldering. They are presented as an aid to forming proper soldering technique and show such pitfalls to good soldering as:

1. *Poorly forged and tinned copper.* It is impossible to solder with a poorly forged or tinned copper.

2. *Overheated copper.* The temperature of the soldering copper should never be so hot that it will not hold a proper tinned coating.

3. *Broken handle.* Obviously, it is impossible to control the copper effectively when the handle is broken.

4. *Using raw acid as a flux on anything but galvanized metal.* Solder will not correctly adhere to other metals with raw acid as flux.

5. *Dirty solder.* It is impossible to solder with dirty or greasy solder.

6. *Bar too small.* A stub or small piece of solder is too short to hold in the hand.

7. *Soldering with the tip of the copper.* It is impossible to get the proper flow using only the tip of the soldering copper.

8. *Soldering over a piece of steel.* A steel plate under the metal being soldered absorbs heat thus chilling the solder as it is applied. This makes for a poorly soldered joint.

9. *Cold copper.* The soldering copper must be hot enough to make the solder flow smoothly over the metal.

The following review should be studied before proceeding to the projects at the end of this chapter.

1. Solder used in the sheet metal shop is generally a 50-50 composition of lead and tin.

2. Tacking means melting drops of solder along a lap seam to hold it in place.

3. The two general classes of soldering are soft and hard.

4. A soldering copper must be tinned in order to do proper soldering.

5. A sal-ammoniac solution is used to clean tarnished coppers before soldering.

6. Zinc chloride is also known as killed, cut, or cured acid.

7. Zinc chloride is used as a flux for soldering copper.

8. Muriatic acid is a commercial term for medium strength hydrochloric acid.

9. Zinc chloride is made by putting small pieces of zinc into muriatic acid.

10. A coarse file is used to prepare the hot soldering copper point for tinning.

11. A fine file is used to finish the corners of the soldering copper before tinning.

12. When soldering vertical seams, the soldering copper should not be tinned on more than two sides.

13. *Pointing up* is a term used to describe soldering vertical seams.

14. The melting point of soft solder depends upon the proportions of tin and lead in the solder.

15. The term *sweating* means soldering surfaces so as to make the solder to run between the two surfaces, completely filling the joint.

16. Sheet copper should be tinned before soldering it.

17. Gas furnaces should always be turned off when not in use.

18. Red-hot soldering coppers cannot be tinned.

19. Wipe all corrosive fluxes from the metal immediately after the soldering is completed.

20. The brush used to apply acid is called a swab.

21. Soldering copper handles should be kept tight.

22. The heated soldering copper heats the metal surface being soldered as well as the solder itself.

23. Keep soldering flux free of dirt.

24. Always apply a lighted match before turning on the gas furnace.

25. Never stand directly in front of the gas furnace when lighting it.

26. When making zinc chloride, avoid inhaling fumes.

27. Sal ammoniac is used in the soldering dip solution.

28. Short stubs of solder may be attached to a new bar by melting the ends together.

Shop Activities

Forging and Tinning a Soldering Copper

Aim. To teach the proper method of preparing a soldering copper for soldering.

Operation A. Forging the soldering copper.

1. *Select, if possible, a badly worn,*

blunt, soldering copper for practicing purposes.

2. *Heat it almost red in the gas furnace.*
3. *Place the soldering copper in the vise and file it with coarse file until the scales are removed.*
4. *Replace the copper in the furnace and heat to a cherry red.*
5. *With the handle of the soldering copper in the left hand and a heavy hammer in the right hand, place the end of the body of the copper against the anvil. Strike the point or tip of the copper, forcing it back into the body as previously explained in the chapter.*
6. *Reheat the soldering copper and place it on the rail at the required angle and force into shape, turning the copper around as it is being forged.*
7. *Reheat the copper and repeat this operation until the copper is smooth and drawn to the required shape. The soldering copper is now ready for tinning.*

Operation B. Tinning a soldering copper.

1. *Heat the soldering copper body.*
2. *Place the heat of the copper in the vise at a slight angle.*
3. *File the point on the sides to be tinned with a coarse file.*
4. *File the corners and tip smooth with a fine file, removing all burred or rough edges.*
5. *Reheat the copper. Rub the point on a block of sal ammoniac and apply some solder at the same time.*

Soldering a Flat Seam on Various Types of Metals

Aim. To teach the method of flat soldering.

Operation A. Soldering galvanized metal.

1. *Make a groove seam 8" long with two pieces of galvanized metal.*
2. *Place the seam to be soldered in the proper position.*
3. *Apply some raw acid on the seam with a swab.*
4. *Dip the point of the copper in the dipping solution or wipe with a damp cloth. Apply beads of solder to the opening of the seam.*
5. *Hold the soldering copper in the right hand, placing the copper on the metal with the side of the point on the seam.*
6. *Draw the copper along the seam, adding more solder whenever necessary. Always begin at the end of the seam and draw the copper forward.*
7. *Reheat the soldering copper from time to time so the sweating effect will be uniform throughout the seam.*
8. *Wash the acid from the metal.*

Operation B. Soldering sheet copper.

1. *Make an 8" grooved seam with two pieces of copper.*
2. *With an acid brush, apply raw acid to the seam. Let it stand a few minutes and then wipe it off with a clean damp rag.*
3. *Heat and tin the soldering copper.*
4. *Apply the soldering flux, in this case zinc chloride.*
5. *Begin the soldering with a hot*

soldering copper starting at the end and drawing the soldering iron forward.

6. *Reheat the soldering copper often to keep it hot during the entire soldering operation.*

7. *Wash the flux free of the metal. When soldering sheet copper, the parts to be soldered may be tinned before making the groove seam.*

Operation C. Tinning sheet copper for soldering.

1. *Clean the parts to be soldered by applying clean, raw acid.*

2. *Wash off the acid with a slightly damp cloth.*

3. *Melt some solder on the metal with a hot soldering copper, holding the iron on the metal until the solder begins to flow.*

4. *Draw the soldering copper along and at the same time add solder to tin the copper with a thin coating of solder.*

5. *Reheat the soldering copper whenever necessary.*

6. *The used flux should be removed and new flux applied before the soldering is completed.*

Soldering an Upright Seam

Soldering vertical or upright seams requires practice and patience. The student should study the illustrations in Fig. 12-12 of this chapter. Notice that the seam is tinned with the flat side of the pointed soldering copper. At the same time, the solder is sweated into the seam. This is important, since it makes the process of pointing or leading the seam easier to perform and it strengthens the soldered seam.

Aim. To teach the method of soldering a vertical seam, using tin, copper, and galvanized metal. Tools and equipment required include an acid brush, soldering copper, furnace, necessary tools for making a flat seam (grooved, lap, or folded), pieces of scrap metal, 50-50 solder, and fluxes.

Operations

1. *Make the flat seam, using scraps of tin, copper, and galvanized metal. Hammer the seams smooth.*

2. *Nail the metal to the wall or to a vertical board.*

3. *Apply the soldering flux.*

4. *Begin at the top and sweat the seal with a correctly prepared soldering iron, using the flat side of the pointed copper.*

5. *Apply a little flux.*

6. *With the soldering copper reheated, begin at the top and move the tips of the iron back and forth across the seam. Apply a little solder as the soldering copper is moved down the seam.*

7. *Apply the solder as needed.*

8. *Solder the remaining seams.*

STUDENT QUESTIONS AND ACTIVITIES

1. What is meant by the term sweating?
2. What type of flux is used to solder sheet copper?

3. What type of flux is used to solder tin plate?
4. What type of flux is used to solder galvanized metal?
5. What is meant by a dip?
6. What are the two general types of soldering?
7. Describe how a soldering copper is tinned.
8. Describe how a soldering copper is forged.
9. What is the common tin to lead ratio in soft solder used in sheet metal shops?
10. Describe the procedure for making zinc chloride.
11. What is meant by the term tacking?
12. What is the commercial name for hydrochloric acid?
13. What is the difference between hard and soft solder?
14. Why should a soldering copper be filed before forging?
15. Why should corrosive fluxes be washed off of the metal after soldering?
16. Describe the procedure for soldering upright or vertical seams.
17. What are the principal corrosive fluxes?
18. What is the principal non-corrosive flux?
19. When making zinc chloride, why should the jar in which it is being made be placed in ventilation?
20. Name several causes of a poor soldering job.

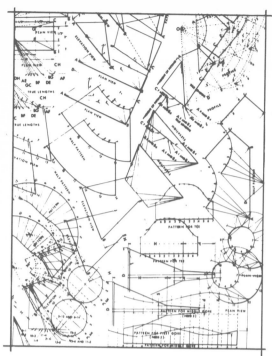

drawing for pattern drafting

13

When you finish this chapter, you should be able to:
1. Identify and use basic drafting equipment, such as:
   A. Scales
   B. Triangles
   C. T squares
   D. Drafting instruments
2. Identify and define the following:
   A. Right angles
   B. Acute angles
   C. Obtuse angles
   D. Rectangles
   E. Triangles
   F. Right triangles
   G. Pentagon
   H. Hexagon
   I. Octagon
   J. The parts of a circle
   K. Ellipse
   L. Cone
   M. Pyramid
3. Divide a line into equal spaces by *stepping off*.
4. Divide a circle into equal parts.
5. Erect a perpendicular to a straight line.
6. Construct any regular polygon.
7. Connect 90° lines to a 90° arc of a given radius.

Pattern drafting plays a vital part in the development of many sheet metal projects. Therefore, this chapter is a general review of the drafting equipment necessary to produce such patterns as well as the geometric constructions which are frequently used in layout work. Much of the pattern layout work done by the sheet metal worker applies the principles of geometric constructions such as found in describing perpendiculars, bisecting angles, and dividing lines into equal parts. It is also important to be familiar with the lines and angles used to produce such constructions since obviously all patterns are composed of such lines and angles.

Professional sheet metal craftsmen must be able to perform mechanical operations both by hand and by machine, and must be able to design and develop their own patterns. The information in this chapter is presented to help the student in subsequent chapters dealing with specific methods of developing patterns.

Methods of Developing Patterns

A *pattern* is a flat outline of the object that is to be made. When this outline is cut and formed into its final shape, it becomes the desired object. When patterns are used repeatedly, they are generally made of metal and are termed *templates* or master patterns.

The commonly used methods by which such patterns are developed for sheet metal objects are: *parallel line development, radial line development,* and *triangulation.* Each of these methods will be discussed in subsequent chapters.

Drafting Equipment

The sheet metal worker and the student should have a complete set of drafting tools. The following tools make up the basic drawing kit for pattern drafting.

Drafting Board

The purpose of the drafting board is to hold the paper in place when a development is being drawn. The sides of the board act as a guide for the T square. Conventional drafting boards are usually 18″ × 24″, but larger boards are available.

T Square

The purpose of the T square is to aid in drawing horizontal lines and to act as a guide for triangles. The T square is shown in Fig. 13-1.

Triangles

Two triangles are necessary—the 45° and the 30°-60°. See Fig. 13-1.

Irregular Curves

Irregular (or French) curves are used to connect points not in a straight line and to draw irregular curves. See Fig. 13-1. However, the student is urged to practice freehand drawing for this purpose since it will be found useful in making larger developments.

45° TRIANGLE   30°–60° TRIANGLE

Fig. 13-1. T square, triangles and French curve.

Fig. 13-2. Set of drafting instruments. (Frederick Post Co.)

Drafting Instruments

Some of the more important of such instruments are shown in Fig. 13-2. A drawing set should include: a large pencil compass for large arcs and circles, a small bow pencil compass for small arcs and circles, large and small dividers for spacing profiles, circles, etc.

Scales

The triangular scale shown in Fig. 13-3 may be used for making measurements. However, a common rule which is graduated in 1/16″, 1/8″, etc., can also be used for this purpose.

Protractors

Protractors, also shown in Fig. 13-3 are used to construct angles.

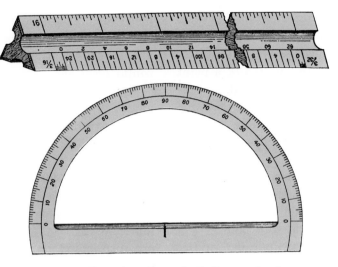

Fig. 13-3. Top: triangular scale. Bottom: protractor.

Lines

A variety of lines are used in the design and development of sheet metal patterns. The more important of such lines are shown in Fig. 13-4.

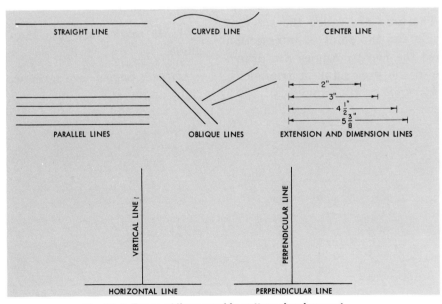

Fig. 13-4. Types of lines used in pattern development.

The following information concerning lines should be studied carefully.

A line is a measurement of length. It is produced by the motion of a point and may be straight or curved.

A straight line is one having the same direction throughout. It is the shortest distance between two points.

A curved line is one whose direction is continually changing.

Parallel lines are lines having the same course which do not meet. They are equally distant at any point.

Horizontal lines are parallel to the horizon.

Vertical lines are at right angles or perpendicular to the horizontal line.

Oblique lines may be drawn at any angle *between* the vertical and horizontal positions.

Perpendicular lines are lines at right angles to a given line.

Center lines are used to show the axes of symmetrical parts, circles, and paths of motion.

Dimension and *extension lines* are used with figures to show the sizes of objects. Dimension lines show the extent and direction of a dimension and are terminated by arrowheads. Extension lines indicate the ends of a dimension.

Angles

An angle is formed by the meeting of two straight lines as shown in Fig. 13-5. The lines are called the *sides* of the angle and the point of intersection is called the *vertex*. Angles are drawn by use of the protractor or triangle.

Right angles are angles of 90°, formed by one straight line perpendicular to another.

Acute angles are less than a right angle.

Obtuse angles are greater than a right angle.

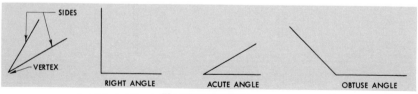

Fig. 13-5. Angles.

Plane Surfaces

Polygons

Plane surfaces have only two dimensions—length and width. A polygon is defined as any figure made up of plane surfaces and having many sides. The illustration in Fig. 13-6 shows only those polygons related to pattern devel-

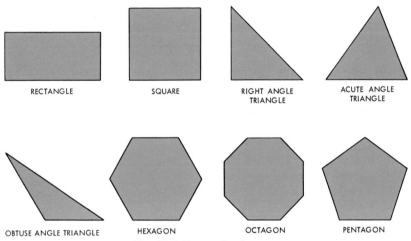

RECTANGLE   SQUARE   RIGHT ANGLE TRIANGLE   ACUTE ANGLE TRIANGLE

OBTUSE ANGLE TRIANGLE   HEXAGON   OCTAGON   PENTAGON

Fig. 13-6. Types of polygons.

opment. In addition, the following definitions of some of the more familiar polygons will be helpful.

A *rectangle* is a four-sided figure whose angles are right angles.

A *triangle* is a figure bounded by three straight lines and having three angles.

A *right-angle triangle* is a triangle with one of its angles a right angle.

An *acute-angle triangle* has all acute angles.

An *obtuse-angle triangle* has one obtuse angle.

A *pentagon* has five equal sides.

A *hexagon* has six equal sides.

An *octagon* has eight equal sides.

Circles

A circle is a plane figure bounded by a curved line called the *circumference*, every part of which is equally distant from the center. The illustration in Fig. 13-7 shows the following parts of a circle.

An *arc* is any part of the circumference of a circle.

A *chord* is a straight line joining the extremities of an arc.

The *diameter* of a circle is a straight

201

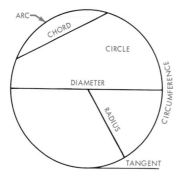

Fig. 13-7. Parts of a circle.

line drawn through its center to opposite points on the circumference.

The *radius* of a circle is a straight line drawn from the center of the circle to any part of the circumference.

A *tangent* is a straight line of unlimited length which touches the cir-

cumference of the circle at only one point.

Ellipse

An ellipse is a plane figure bounded by a curved line described about two points in such a manner that the sum of the distances from every point in the curve to the two fixed points is always the same. The two points are called *foci*, the two lines are the major and minor axes. See Fig. 13-8.

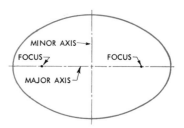

Fig. 13-8. Ellipse.

Solid Geometric Figures

The following solid geometric figures are often found in sheet metal pattern drafting. Solids have three dimensions: length, breadth, and thickness.

A *cone* is a solid having a circular base and a curved surface joining at a point called the *apex,* as shown in Fig. 13-9.

A *right cone* is a cone having the apex centered above the center of the base.

The axis is perpendicular to the base.

The *oblique cone* is a cone having the apex off center to the base.

The *frustum* of a cone is that portion of a cone included between the base and a plane parallel to the base.

A *pyramid* is a figure whose base is a polygon and whose faces are triangles which meet at a point called the *vertex.*

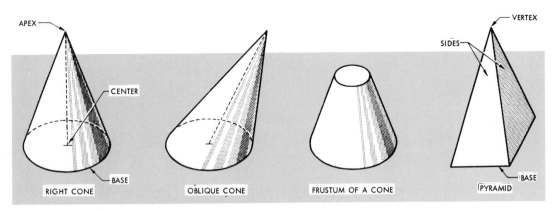

Fig. 13-9. Cones and pyramids.

Geometric Constructions

Many of the situations which arise in pattern drafting layout work can be solved by employing the following geometric constructions.

Bisecting a Straight Line

See *A* of Fig. 13-10. Let *ST* be the line which is to be divided into two equal parts. From the ends of *ST* as centers, with any radius greater than half but less than the length of *ST,* scribe the intersecting arcs *UV* and *WX.* A line drawn through the intersecting points will bisect the line at *Y.*

Dividing a Line Into Equal Parts

See *B* of Fig. 13-10. Let *ST* be the line to be divided. Bisect *ST* at *U.* Bisect lines *SU* and *UT* at *V* and *W.* Continue bisecting until the required number of parts (2, 4, 8, 16, etc.) are found.

A method, shown in *C* of Fig. 13-10, of dividing a line into any number of equal parts is as follows: draw line *ST* to the required length; draw a slant line *SU* to any angle and to a length that can be conveniently divided with a rule into the required number of spaces as shown by the numbers. Connect point *V* (last division) with the end of the line *ST* at *T* to give the line *TV.* Lines drawn parallel to *TV* through the numbered points will give the required number of equal divisions.

Stepping-off Equal Divisions on a Circle

In pattern drafting, one of the more common operations is dividing a circle into equal parts and dividing the stretchout of the circumference of this circle into the same number of parts. The methods discussed above can be used to accomplish this. Most sheet

203

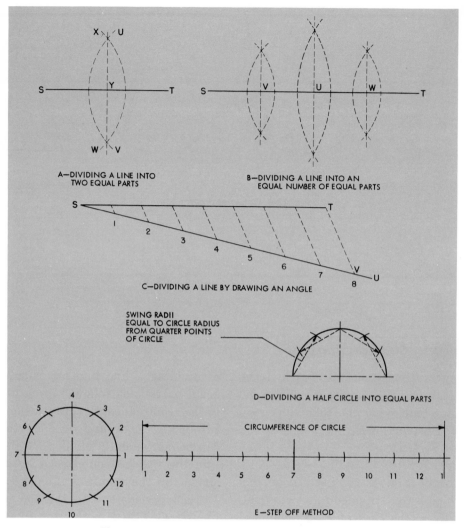

Fig. 13-10. Dividing lines by geometric constructions.

metal men, however, use a system called *stepping-off*.

Whenever a circle must be divided into equal parts, the usual number chosen is six spaces to the half-circle since this is the most convenient. The drawing in *D* of Fig. 13-10 shows how to divide a half-circle into six equal spaces. After the half-circle is drawn, leave the dividers set equal to the radius of the circle. Swing this radius from the quarter points of the circle (*A,B,C*) to divide each quarter-circle into three equal parts.

After the circle is divided into equal parts, as shown in *E* of Fig. 13-10, determine the circumference of the circle from the circumference rule and draw a line equal to this circumference. Next measure the mid-point on the circumference line. This can be done by bisecting the line as shown in the preceding section. By dividing the circumference in half, the first stepping-off can be done on half of the circumference to save time.

To step off the equal spaces, set the dividers to one of the spaces on the circle. This will not be precisely the space for the circumference line since the dividers are measuring across a chord rather than around the arc. Step the distance off on one half of the circumference line. In six steps the dividers will probably be short of the half-way mark on the circumference line. Adjust the dividers to approximately one-sixth of this error and step off again. When the total number of spaces equals the half-way mark exactly, then step off the other half of the circumference to divide the line into the same spacing as the circle. With a little practice, you will be able to set and step off the correct distance in the second or third attempt and you will find that this is the most practical method.

Bisecting Angles

The method of bisecting angles is shown in Fig. 13-11. To bisect a right angle, proceed as follows: draw the right angle *BAC* to any desired size. With *A* as center and any convenient radius, describe the arc *BC*. With *B* and *C* as centers and a radius great enough to intersect, scribe arcs *DE* and *FG*. Draw a straight line from *A* through the intersecting point of arcs *DE* and *FG*. This line will be the bisecting line.

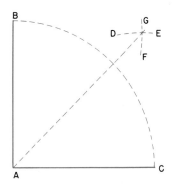

Fig. 13-11. Bisecting an angle by geometric construction.

The same procedure is followed for bisecting other angles.

Erecting a Perpendicular to a Straight Line at a Given Point

See Fig. 13-12. Let *AB* be the line and *C* the given point. With *C* as center and any radius, draw semi-circle *AD*. With *A* and *D* as centers, strike arcs *GH* and *EF*. A line drawn from the point of intersection of the arcs to point *C* will be the perpendicular line.

Constructing Polygons

The construction of regular polygons

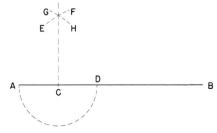

Fig. 13-12. Erecting a perpendicular to a straight line.

is shown in Fig. 13-13. The steps for each figure should be followed carefully since understanding the procedure will help the student in shortening his pattern development work time.

Constructing a Square Within a Circle. See Fig. 13-13. Draw the circle, dividing it into quarters by drawing two diameters at right angles to each other. Connect points *A, B, C,* and *D,* completing the square.

Constructing a Hexagon. A hexa-

gon, as shown in Fig. 13-13, may be constructed as follows: Draw the circle to the required size. Draw two diameters at right angles. With a compass set to equal the radius of the circle and with *A* and *E* as centers, scribe the arcs *CD* and *FG* as shown. Connect points *A, D, G, E, F,* and *C* with straight lines, completing the hexagon as shown.

Constructing an Octagon. Draw the circle in Fig. 13-13 to the required size, dividing it into quarters. Bisect the

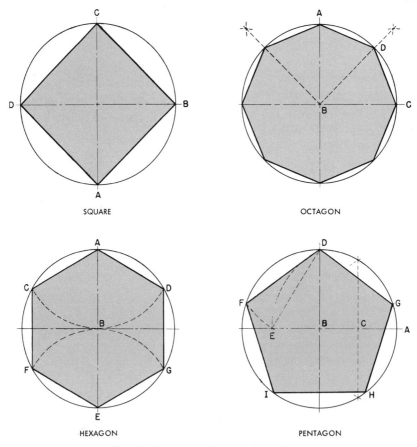

Fig. 13-13. Constructing regular polygons.

angle *ABC* at *D*. Thus, *AD* and *DC* equal two sides of the octagon. Repeat this procedure for the remaining three quarters to complete the construction of the octagon.

Constructing a Pentagon. As in Fig. 13-13, scribe the circle to the desired size, drawing the two diameter lines at right angles. Bisect the radius *AB* at *C*. With *C* as center and radius *CD*, scribe arc *DE*. With *D* as center and radius *DE*, scribe the arc *EF* and point, *G*. With *G* and *F* as centers and the same radius, strike arcs *H* and *I*. Complete the pentagon by drawing the chords, *GD*, *DF*, *FI*, *IH*, and *HG*.

Drawing a Circle through Three Points not in a Straight Line

Let *A*, *B*, and *C* in Fig. 13-14 be the given points. With *B* as center, scribe the arcs *EK* and *DJ*. With *A* and *C* as centers, scribe arcs *IF* and *HG*. Draw

the two perpendicular bisectors until they meet at *O*. This gives the center to complete the circle. This method may be used when finding centers for metal disks, completing circles, etc.

Finding the Opposite Point on the Circumference of a Circle

Let *A* in Fig. 13-15 represent one point on the circumference. With the blade of the steel square on the circumference of the circle at point *A*, and the heel of the square touching the circumference of the circle at any other convenient point, as *D* or *C*, the point where the blade touches the circumference of the circle, *B*, will be a point opposite *A* on the circumference of the circle. This method is used for locating holes for pipe dampers, placing ears on pails, etc. No measurements are necessary in this procedure.

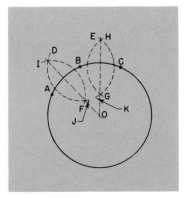

Fig. 13-14. Drawing a circle through three points not in a straight line.

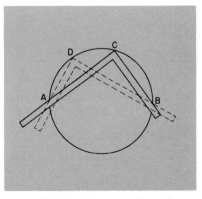

Fig. 13-15. Finding the opposite point on the circumference of a circle.

Class Activities

Drawing a Line Parallel to a Given Line

Aim. To apply the principles of geometric construction to pattern layout work.

Operations

1. *Draw a straight line of any length.*
2. *From points A and B, erect perpendiculars as shown in Fig. 13-16.*
3. *With points A and B as centers and any given radius, strike arcs cutting the perpendiculars as shown.*
4. *Draw a line through the points of intersection of the arcs and the perpendiculars. This line will be parallel to line AB.*

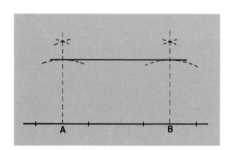

Fig. 13-16. Drawing a line parallel to a given line.

Connecting 90° Lines with a 90° Arc of a Given Radius

Aim. To learn how to make radius corners as required in pattern drafting.

Operations

1. *Draw a right angle of any size, such as ABC in Fig. 13-17.*
2. *Set the compass to the radius required for the 90° arc.*
3. *With B as center, scribe arcs cutting the lines at D and E as shown.*
4. *With points E and D as centers, and with the same radius, scribe intersecting arcs as at F.*
5. *With F as center and the same radius, scribe DE, which is the required 90° arc.*

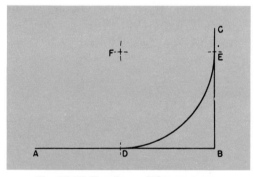

Fig. 13-17. Drawing a 90° corner arc.

Drawing Polygons

Aim. To learn the various shapes of polygons.

Operations. Draw the following to full size: 1. hexagon inscribed in a 3″

diameter circle, 2. *pentagon inscribed within a 3" diameter circle, 3. right angle triangle with 2" sides, and 4. acute triangle of any size.*

Drawing the Parts of a Circle

Aim. To give practice in learning the parts of a circle.

Operations. Draw a circle with the diameter, radius, chord, tangent, and circumference labeled.

Stepping-off Equal Divisions on a Line

Aim. To develop practice in stepping off equal spaces on lines.

Specifications. Draw three lines and step them off into twelve equal spaces.

Operations

1. *Draw a straight line 7" long and step it off into twelve equal spaces according to the instructions in this chapter.*

2. *Repeat this process with a line 9-1/2" long, and with a line 8-1/4" long.*

Dividing a Half-Circle into Six Equal Spaces

Aim. To give practice in dividing a circle into six equal spaces.

Specifications. Draw a half-circle with a 2" radius and step it off into six equal parts.

Operations

1. *Draw a half-circle with a 2" radius.*

2. *Divide the half-circle into quarter-circles.*

3. *Following the directions in this chapter, divide the half-circle into six equal parts.*

4. *Turn in to the instructor for checking.*

STUDENT QUESTIONS AND ACTIVITIES

1. What are the purposes of dimension and extension lines?
2. What is meant by a polygon?
3. Name four kinds of polygons.
4. Name three common geometric angles used in pattern drafting.
5. What are the parts of a circle?
6. What is an ellipse?
7. Describe the frustum of a cone.
8. Describe a right cone.
9. Describe an oblique cone.
10. What are the principle drafting instruments used in pattern drafting?
11. What are three principle methods by which patterns are developed?
12. What are the purposes of the drafting board?
13. Describe a hexagon.
14. Name several objects which are hexagonal in shape.

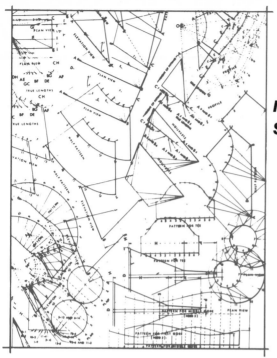

making and notching simple patterns

14

When you finish this chapter, you should be able to:
1. Lay out any *simple* pattern.
2. Notch and clip any *simple* pattern.

In the first 12 chapters, you were primarily concerned with the tools, machines, and materials which are used in the sheet metal trade. Chapter 13 presented you with the instruments and the commonly used geometric constructions which are used to produce sheet metal patterns. However, to usefully apply the information in Chapter 13, it is clearly necessary to be able to actually lay out such patterns on metal. Many of the layouts in sheet metal work are known as *simple patterns*. These patterns are so called because no advanced drafting knowledge is required in order to execute them, but only a basic understanding of how to measure, draw, and apply the principles of straight lines, arcs, circles, and the other geometric constructions.

Laying Out a Simple Pattern Directly on Sheet Metal

Though the patterns the sheet metal worker lays out may vary, the steps by which such patterns are laid out remain the same. By applying the following steps in the process of laying out a pattern, you will avoid both errors and waste.

1. *Check the sheet metal on which your pattern will be made.* Often the bottom of a sheet will have a slight bow in it from the rolling process. Check the bottom edge of the sheet with a straight-edge since any such bowing or warping in the metal will necessarily affect accuracy.

2. *Square up the left-hand edge of the sheet.* The edges of the sheet are seldom perfectly square. Therefore, it is necessary on any layout to square to the left-hand end of the sheet to the bottom edge. The usual method is to use a two-foot or three-foot square and draw a line about 1/4″ from the edge so as to be square with the bottom edge.

3. *Always make your layout in the lower left-hand corner of the sheet.* One of the chief characteristics of the true craftsman in any trade is the ability to do a job with the least amount of waste material. When the pattern is laid out as close to the lower left-hand corner as possible, the metal above and to the right of the pattern will then be usable for other patterns.

4. *Measurements should be from the bottom and left-hand square line.* In Fig. 14-1, the line measurements shown would be taken from left to right, and from the bottom up. Never try to cut your metal exactly to size before making the layout. This increases the chance of error since it is then much more possible to miscalculate the size or get the metal slightly out of alignment. If the sheet is left uncut and measured from left to right and from the bottom up, the entire width and length of the sheet is available on which to work.

5. *Make measurements at both ends of each line and draw a line through the two points.* Ordinarily, only one line at the left-hand end of the sheet is squared. Do not try to square other lines from the edges as would be done in mechanical drafting. In Fig. 14-1, if line *AA′* is to be 1″ from the squared line, the proper method is to measure 1″ at *A* and 1″ at *A′* and then draw a line through these two points. Line *BB′* is 3″ away from *AA′* so 3″ from *A′* and *A* should be marked and a line drawn through these two points.

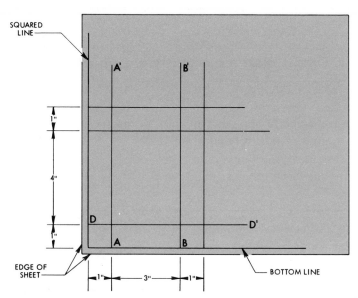

Fig. 14-1. Layout measurements taken from left to right and from the bottom up.

The horizontal lines, such as *DD'* are handled in the same way. One inch from the bottom line is measured at *D* and *D'* and the line is drawn through these two points.

6. *Draw in all the vertical lines and horizontal lines.* Then add lines for miters, notches, seams, edges, and laps. If all vertical and then all horizontal lines are drawn, the basic pattern is generally complete. It is therefore important to be sure that all lines are drawn *before* starting to cut out the pattern.

7. *Prick mark all bend lines.* Before starting to form the pattern, prick mark all bend lines about 1/4″ from the end of the line. In addition to making bends from the unmarked side of the metal, you may want to mark some other

patterns from the first pattern. In that case, prick marks will show the bend lines. Do not depend upon the corners of notches for bend locations.

8. *Study the shape of basic patterns.* Box patterns, for example, may be in a variety of sizes and may use different seams and edges. However, they will always be in the same basic shape. One of the most important considerations in developing a pattern is the ability to visualize the finished job from the flat pattern.

9. *After you have made the layout, check overall dimensions on each side of the pattern.* This is particularly important on patterns drawn with parallel lines. When, as in Fig. 14-1, parallel lines are employed, the width of the pat-

tern at the top and bottom should obviously be the same. If they vary more than 1/16″, this indicates an error in measurement.

Notching and Clipping

Notching and clipping are used to cut away portions of the metal to prevent overlapping and bulging on seams and edges.

Square Notch. The square notch, as illustrated in Fig. 14-2, is used on pans and boxes to enable the corners to fit together. The size of the notch is determined by the bend lines as shown in the illustration.

45° Notch. The 45° notch made in the form of a V is used when double-seaming the ends of projects such as pans, or when making a 90° bend on any job with an inside flange, as illustrated in Fig. 14-3. When the bend of an inside flange meets at an angle other than 90°, the notch must be marked to the necessary angle.

Straight Notch. Fig. 14-4 shows how to make a straight notch or slit edge.

Notches for Wired Edges. In places where wired edges cross seams, the pattern is notched to prevent the material from overlapping. The angle of the notch is usually 30°, and the distance from which the notch is started is 3-1/2 times the diameter of the wire, as is shown in Fig. 14-5.

Clipping. When a single hem meets at right angles, the pattern is clipped at a 45° angle as shown in Fig. 14-6. Angles other than 45° may be used depending upon the shape of the pattern. On some patterns, a combination of these processes may be necessary.

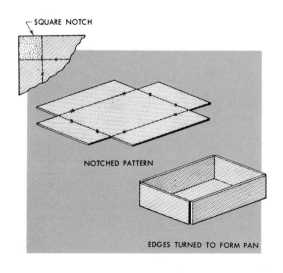

Fig. 14-2. Square notches used on pans and boxes.

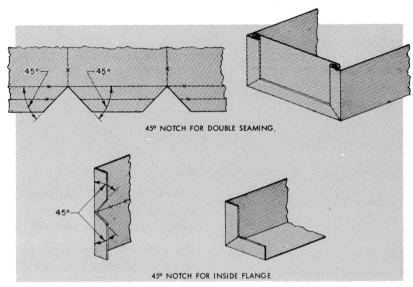

45° NOTCH FOR DOUBLE SEAMING.

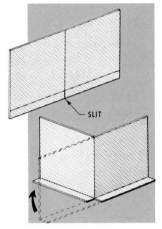

45° NOTCH FOR INSIDE FLANGE

Fig. 14-3. 45° notches used on inside flanges and double seams.

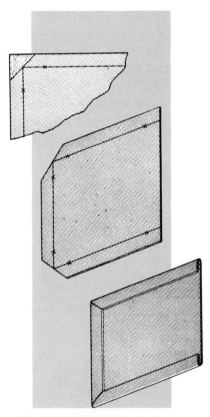

Fig. 14-4. Straight notch.

SLIT

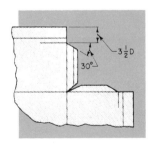

Fig. 14-5. Notches for wired edges.

Fig. 14-6. Clipping for single seam.

Basic Patterns

While many of the patterns used by the sheet metal worker may differ in size or in the various operations used, many patterns follow the same basic forms. The basic pattern forms shown in Figs. 14-7 through 14-14 represent the commonly used patterns and notches. The student should study these patterns for their general shapes as well as for the allowances for seams and edges and for the method of notching.

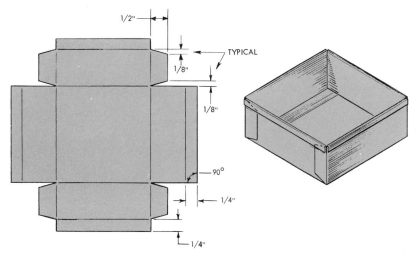

Fig. 14-7. Pattern for one-piece box with 1/2″ lapped corners and 1/4″ single hem.

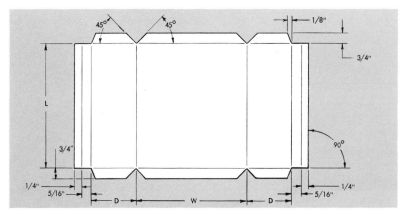

Fig. 14-8. Pattern for three-piece box with 3/4″ laps and 5/16″ double hem. Laps are spot welded, riveted or soldered. (Continued on page 216.)

215

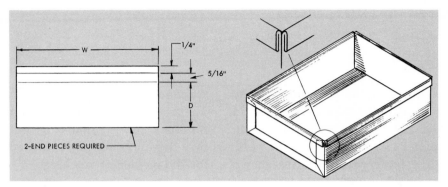

Fig. 14-8. Continued.

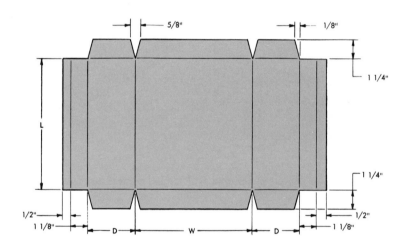

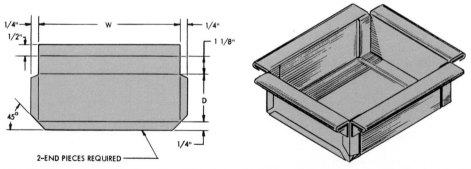

Fig. 14-9. Pattern for box with 1″ x 1″ x 1/8″ angle steel edge. Ends are set in with Pittsburgh seam.

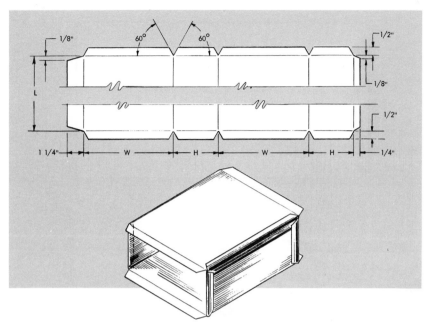

Fig. 14-10. Pattern for one-piece duct with Pittsburgh seams and edges for S and drive clips.

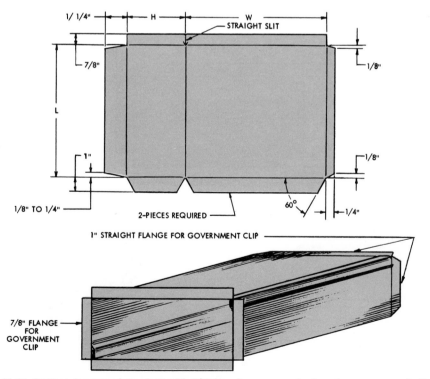

Fig. 14-11. Pattern for two-piece duct with Pittsburgh seams and edges for government clips.

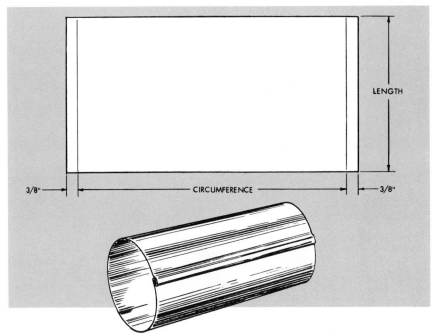

LENGTH

3/8" CIRCUMFERENCE 3/8"

Fig. 14-12. Pattern for round pipe with 1/4" groove seams.

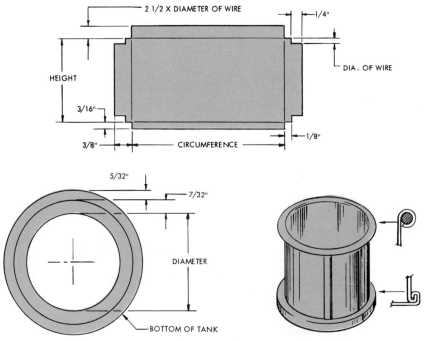

2 1/2 X DIAMETER OF WIRE

1/4"

DIA. OF WIRE

HEIGHT

3/16"

3/8" CIRCUMFERENCE 1/8"

5/32"

7/32"

DIAMETER

BOTTOM OF TANK

Fig. 14-13. Pattern for tank with wired edge.

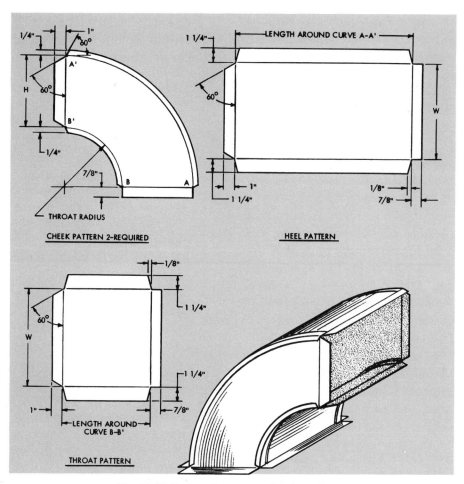

Fig. 14-14. Pattern for rectangular duct elbow.

Shop Activities

Making the Pattern for a One-Piece Box

Aim. To develop skill in laying out patterns for pans and boxes.

Specifications. Lay out and make a one-piece box 6″ × 4″ and 1″ high, with 1/2″ laps and spot welds on the corners and 1/4″ hems around the top.

Operations

1. *Lay out the pattern for the box*

shown in Fig. 14-15. Use 26 gage galvanized metal. Allow for all seams and edges. Check your layout with the instructor before cutting it out.

2. Bend the hems to the outside of the box.

3. If a pan brake is available, bend the opposite sides of the box so that the lap allowances are bent at the same time.

4. Open the ends of the hem so that the laps will tuck under them, and bend the remaining opposite sides on the proper width finger of the pan brake. As the side is bent, guide the laps to the outside of the pan and under the hems.

5. If a pan brake is not available, bend one side of the box and then the adjacent side. Then continue around the box. To make the last bend, one corner of the box will have to be flattened out.

Making a Three-Piece Box with Pittsburgh Seams

Aim. To practice laying out three-piece boxes and to develop skill in using double hems and Pittsburgh seams.

Specifications. Lay out and make an 8″ × 6″ box, 4″ deep with a 5/16″ double hem around the top. Set in the ends with Pittsburgh seams.

Operations

1. Lay out the patterns for the box shown in Fig. 14-16 according to the instructions in this chapter. Allow for all edges and seams. Check with the instructor before cutting out.

2. On the large piece, form the Pittsburgh seam first.

3. Next form the double hems to the outside.

4. Next bend the corners to form the sides.

5. On the end pieces, first form the double hem to the outside. Next bend the single edge for the Pittsburgh seam to the inside.

6. Set the ends into the pocket lock and tap over the seam to finish the box.

7. Turn in to the instructor and then save for soldering practice.

Making a Duct Elbow

Aim. To learn how to lay out and make duct fittings, and to learn how to

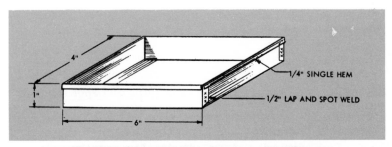

Fig. 14-15. Box with 1/2″ corner lap and 1/4″ hem.

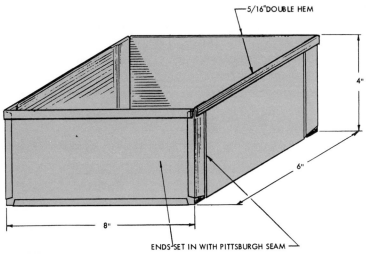

Fig. 14-16. Box with ends set in with Pittsburgh seams.

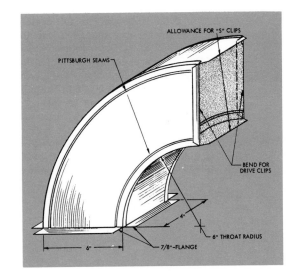

Fig. 14-17. Duct elbow with Pittsburgh seams.

use a Pittsburgh seam on a curved section.

Specifications. Make a 90° duct elbow, 6″ × 4″ with a 6″ throat radius.

Operations

1. Lay out the patterns for the duct elbow shown in Fig. 14-17 according to the instructions given in this chapter. Allow for all seams and edges and have the instructor check the patterns before cutting them.

221

2. *Cut out the cheek patterns and notch them.*
3. *Turn the single edges on the curves with the burring machine.*
4. *On the heel and throat patterns, make the bends for the Pittsburgh seams.*
5. *Roll the heel and throat to fit the curves of the cheek.*
6. *Open up the Pittsburgh seams with a screw driver, if needed, to assemble the elbow.*
7. *Turn in to the instructor.*

STUDENT QUESTIONS AND ACTIVITIES

1. What is meant by notching a pattern?
2. What is meant by clipping a pattern?
3. Why should the bottom of a sheet be checked for straightness?
4. Which end of a sheet should be squared?
5. In what part of a sheet of metal should a pattern be laid out?
6. Why is it poor practice to try to cut a piece of metal exactly to size before the pattern is laid out?
7. Make a drawing to 1/2 scale with all dimensions of a box with 1/2″ laps on the corners and a 5/16″ double hem around the top. Make the box 6″ × 8″ and 3″ deep. Draw in the notches with a colored pencil.
8. Make a pictorial sketch of a box. Make it to any convenient dimensions and any edge other than a double hem. Sketch the patterns for the box roughly to scale making it in three pieces with Pittsburgh seams on corners. Insert all dimensions on the sketch and patterns and indicate the notches with colored pencil.
9. Sketch the pattern for a rectangular duct in two pieces. Make it 10″ × 8″ and 18″ long with corners joined by Pittsburgh seams and allowances for S and drive clips on the ends. Make the pattern to scale, but not necessarily to full scale. Draw in the notches with colored pencil.

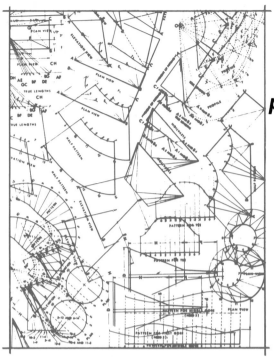

parallel line development

When you complete this chapter, you should be able to develop the pattern for any object that requires the parallel line method to develop the pattern.

All sheet metal patterns are developed by one of three methods—parallel line development, triangulation, or radial line development. In *parallel line developments,* the sides run parallel to one another as in ducts, elbows, and tee joints. In *radial line developments,* all the sides meet at a common center as with cones and pyramids. In sheet metal work, many irregularly formed shapes cannot be developed by either of these two methods. Such shapes are so formed that, although straight lines can be drawn through them, the lines would not run parallel to one another, nor would they all slant at the same angle to meet at a common center. (Examples of such shapes may be found in Fig. 16-1, Chapter 16.) Such surfaces can develop through measurement of the surface, part by part, and adding one part to another until the entire surface is developed. This is the third method of pattern development called *triangulation.*

Developing Patterns for Rectangular Duct

In Chapter 14, you learned how to lay out simple patterns. These were basically parallel line layouts since they involved primarily rectangular shapes with straight sides. Fig. 15-1 shows the patterns for a straight rectangular duct. This is a simple pattern but it involves basic principles which the student should understand. Therefore, the procedure used in constructing this pattern should be studied so that you will understand how they apply to more advanced operations.

Straight Rectangular Duct

In all parallel line developments, the first step is to draw an elevation or side view. After this view is drawn, measuring lines are drawn from it and measured and projected to the pattern. *For plain rectangular duct, the measuring lines on the elevation view are the cor-*

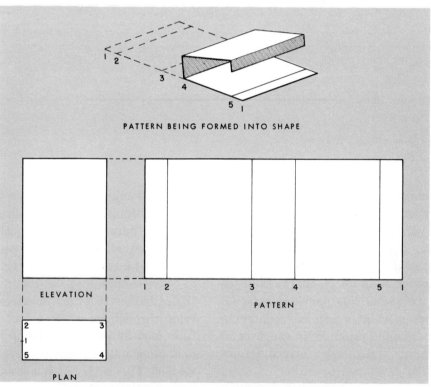

PATTERN BEING FORMED INTO SHAPE

ELEVATION

PATTERN

PLAN

Fig. 15-1. Developing pattern for plain rectangular duct.

ner lines of the duct. After measuring lines are located on the elevation view, then the stretchout of the pattern is drawn and the measuring lines are located on the pattern stretchout in the same relative location as they are on the pattern. In the pattern in Fig. 15-1, measuring lines 2, 3, 4, and 5 are the corner lines, while line 1 is the seam line.

After the measuring lines are located on the pattern stretchout, the lengths of the lines are taken from the elevation or side view and transferred to the same lines on the pattern. In the pattern in Fig. 15-1, all of the lines are the same length and while this step could be eliminated in this particular problem, in subsequent illustrations you will see its importance.

Thus, in laying out this simple duct, you will have used many of the basic principles which parallel line development employs. In developing any pattern by parallel line developments:

1. Draw a side or elevation view of the pattern.

2. Locate the measuring lines on the side view.

3. Draw the stretchout of the pattern. (See Chapter 7 for the definition of *stretchout*.)

4. Locate the measuring lines from the side or elevation view on the pattern stretchout. These lines must be the proper distance apart and in the proper relation to each other as dictated by their location on the side view.

5. Transfer the lengths of the measuring lines from the side or ele-

vation view to the same lines on the pattern.

6. Connect the points located on the measuring lines.

Rectangular Duct Cut at a Miter

Mastering pattern drafting consists of two steps: 1. learning the basic principles, 2. learning to apply these principles to typical problems. The principles explained above and illustrated by Fig. 15-1 apply in the same way to a rectangular duct with an end at an angle. This section will explain how they apply.

Fig. 15-2 shows a rectangular duct with one end cut at an angle. This is a common problem whose solution has many applications.

Step 1 in laying out this pattern by parallel lines is to draw the side (or elevation) view of the duct. This is best done by *first* drawing the plan view and then projecting the lines up to draw the side view, as shown in Fig. 15-2.

Step 2 is to locate the measuring lines on the side view. Since this is a rectangular duct with a plain miter, the corner lines are the only measuring lines needed. Therefore, all of the measuring lines on the side view are already located.

Step 3 is to draw the stretchout of the pattern. Since this is a 2″ × 4″ duct, the total stretchout without seam allowance is 12″.

Step 4 is to locate the measuring lines. Since the corner lines are the measuring lines in this case, the corner lines are drawn on the stretchout at intervals of 4″, 2″, 4″, and 2″.

Step 5 is to transfer the lengths of the measuring lines from the side view to the pattern. The dotted lines in Fig.

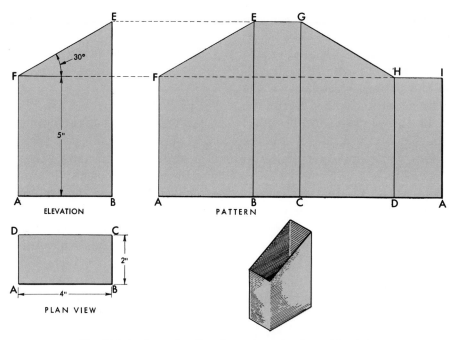

Fig. 15-2. Laying out pattern for rectangular duct with miter.

15-2 show how these points can be projected over to the pattern. Note that line *AF* on the pattern is made to the exact length of *AF* on the side view and line *BE* on the pattern is made the same length as *BE* on the side view. After points, *F*, *E*, *G*, *H*, and *I* are located, lines are drawn to connect them and complete the pattern.

Rectangular Duct with a Double Angle

The previously explained procedures showed how the steps in parallel line layout applied to an actual problem. Here we shall see how the same principles apply to a slightly more complicated operation. Note that the principles used are still exactly the same and only the method of application varies.

Fig. 15-3 shows a rectangular duct with a double angle cut in one end. The steps in laying out this pattern are still the same. First, draw the plan and side views. The measuring lines on the side view are still the corner lines—except that an extra measuring line is added to locate the apex of the angles (point *H* in the side view). This line is shown by line *HE* in the side view.

After the side view and the measuring lines are drawn, the stretchout and the measuring lines on it are drawn. After this, the distances of the measuring lines on the side view are transferred to the pattern and the resulting points are connected by lines to complete the pattern.

Practicing Developing a Pattern for a Duct

To test your understanding of the

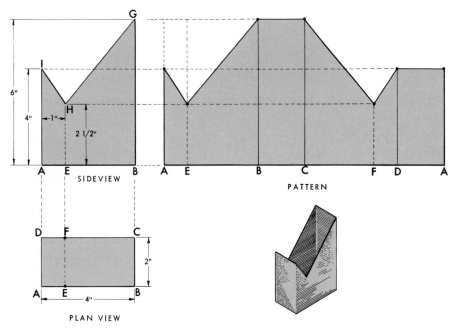

Fig. 15-3. Pattern for rectangular duct with double cut.

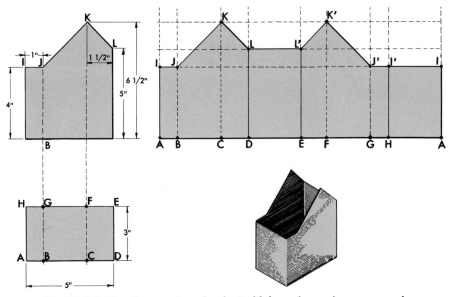

Fig. 15-4. Pattern for a rectangular duct with irregular angles on one end.

principles of parallel line development explained and illustrated thus far, lay out the pattern for the duct shown in Fig. 15-4.

No explanation is given for this layout, but based on information previously presented, the pattern should not prove difficult.

Developing Patterns for Round Pipe

There is another step involved in understanding parallel line layout—the application of parallel lines to round pipe fittings. This is a most common application of parallel line layout since many rectangular ducts can be handled by simple layout methods, but *all* round pipe must be laid out by parallel line development.

Round Pipe with Mitered End

Fig. 15-5 shows a round pipe with one end at a 30° angle. This is a common round pipe layout. All of the principles illustrated in the layout of rectangular duct are used in this layout. In addition, another principle is used to locate the measuring lines on the side view.

Since there are no convenient corners to use as measuring lines, they must be located on the side view in a manner that makes them easy to locate on the pattern. If the plan view is divided into 12 equal spaces on the circumference by the method explained in Chapter 13, then the lines are located in equal spaces on the pattern stretchout. Notice that the lines are projected up from the plan view to locate them on the side view. Though they do not appear to be equally spaced on the side view, they in fact are. The side view is a view of the pipe surface curving away from the view and does not show the distance around the surface in its true length.

This method of dividing the plan view into equal spaces and projecting them up to the side view is a common pro-

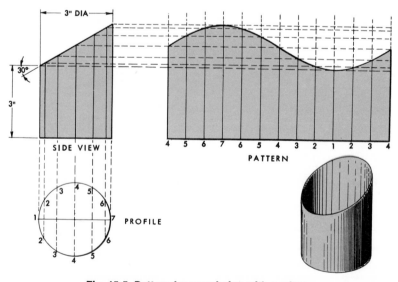

Fig. 15-5. Pattern for round pipe with a miter.

cedure and is used every time a pipe or a curved surface is laid out. When the plan view is used in this manner, it is called a *profile*. A profile is the shape of the fitting at that particular point. The general practice is to draw only half of the plan view when it is used as a profile, since the other half is a duplicate. Fig. 15-5 illustrates this.

After the side view is drawn as in Fig. 15-5, and the measuring lines are located, the stretchout of the pattern is drawn and is divided into the same number of equal spaces as are on the plan view.

Refer to Chapter 13 for methods of dividing a line into equal spaces.

After the side view and the pattern stretchout are marked with the measuring lines, then the next step is to transfer the lengths of the measuring lines to the pattern. This may be done by projecting the lines as shown, or it

may be done by setting dividers to the lengths on the side view and marking this length on the corresponding line on the pattern. After all of the points are located, the curve of the miter is drawn through these points. The curve may be drawn freehand, with a drawing curve, or by bending a flexible rule through these points and marking around the rule with a pencil or scratch awl.

Round Tees

A common group of round pipe fittings laid out by parallel line developments are intersecting pipes, commonly called *tees*. These are laid out as any problem in parallel lines. However, there is one new principle to learn when laying out intersecting pipes. The principle is the development of the intersection line of the two pipes. This line is called the *miter line*.

Fig. 15-6 shows a typical development

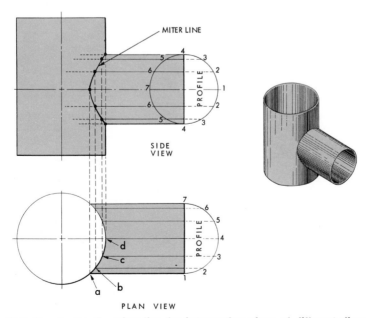

Fig. 15-6. Developing the miter line for intersecting pipes of different diameters.

using a miter line between intersecting pipes. Since this is a common situation, it should be thoroughly understood and studied.

The patterns for this tee cannot be laid out until the miter line is developed. This, therefore, is the first step in laying out such a pattern.

The side view and the plan view are first drawn. Then profiles are drawn for the intersecting pipe on both the side view and the plan view. The profiles are divided into equal spaces—generally six to the half-circle. Lines are then projected from these spaces. On the side view the lines are projected indefinitely for later intersection of lines from the plan view. On the plan view, the lines are projected until they touch the curve of the circle of the main pipe as at

points, *a, b, c,* and *d,* in Fig. 15-6. From these points, lines are projected through the side view to intersect the lines from the side view profile.

Since the profile on the side view and the profile on the plan view locate the same measuring lines, when point *a* on the plan view is projected to intersect line *1* on the side view, this gives the exact spot where line *1* intersects the curve of the main pipe and it therefore is a point on the miter line. When all of the points are found by the intersection of corresponding lines, the miter line is drawn in and then the patterns for both pipes can be laid out by parallel lines. The completed patterns are shown in Fig. 15-7.

There are several short cuts used on the layout in Fig. 15-7. Notice that the

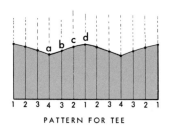

PATTERN FOR TEE

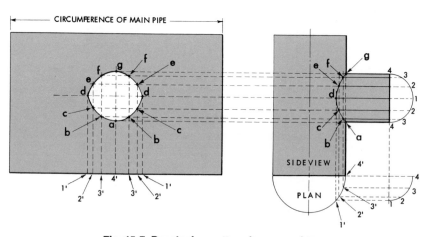

Fig. 15-7. Developing pattern for a round tee.

plan view is attached to the side view and that only half of the plan is drawn. This eliminates many unnecessary lines. Notice also that the pattern for the tee is not developed by projecting the lines from the side view. Instead, the distances on the side view are stepped off by dividers and transferred to the proper lines on the pattern. The distances are taken from line *4-4* to the miter line. For example, for line *2*, the distance on the side view from line *4-4* to point *c* is taken and transferred to line *2* of the pattern to locate point *c*.

The layout of the hole pattern is also done by parallel lines. Notice that the spacing of the vertical measuring lines on the pattern is different. Since the

lines of the stretchout must be the exact duplicate of the lines on the side and plan views, the line spacing is taken from the plan view since this gives the spacing of these lines. In this case, they are not equally spaced, but as long as they are taken in the proper order and the correct spacing, this does not matter.

Tee Intersecting at an Angle

Fig. 15-8 shows the layout for the patterns for a tee intersecting at an angle. This will give you an opportunity to apply the methods of tee layout to a different type of problem. Though the operation appears more difficult than the previous one, the solution is the

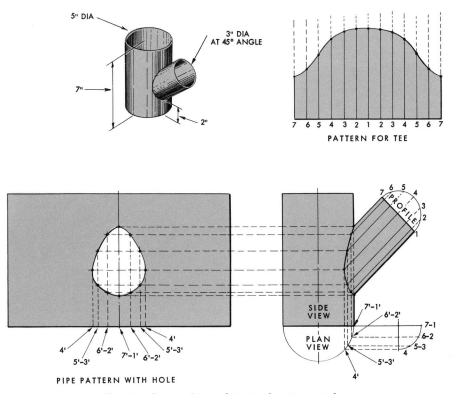

Fig. 15-8. Pattern for tee intersecting at an angle.

same. Thus, you can see how understanding and applying basic principles will help you to handle many varieties of problems. Lay out the patterns for Fig. 15-8 to check your understanding of this phase of parallel line layout.

Round Elbows

Another important application of parallel line layout is laying out the patterns for round elbows. This again is the application of basic principles of layout with one new principle involved. This principle is the location of the miter lines on the elbow.

Before studying the layout of the round elbow, study Fig. 15-9 to learn the parts and nomenclature of the elbow. Just as in tees, *the intersection of two pipes is called a miter*. Note also that the inside radius is called the *throat* and the outside radius is called the *heel*. The throat radius is indicated by r and the heel radius by R. The sections of the elbow are called *gores*.

Just as in any parallel line layout, the first step is to draw the side view and develop the miter lines. For the round elbow, the miter lines are straight lines

with no need for developing. However, the method of spacing these lines is important. The object of the spacing is to make angle a and b in Fig. 15-10 equal so the pattern for the end gore can also serve as the pattern of the middle gore. If these two angles are different, then two different patterns must be laid out. If one space is used for each of the end gores, and two spaces are used for each of the middle gores, then all the angles will be equal. To obtain this spacing, multiply the number of gores in the elbow by two and subtract two from this result. The answer is the number of spaces in which to divide the heel curve of the elbow. After the spaces are stepped off around the curve, then the miter lines are drawn in as shown by the solid lines in Fig. 15-10.

After the miter lines are located, the pattern for the first gore of the elbow is laid out as shown in Fig. 15-11. Other than the special method of obtaining the miter lines, the layout is a typical parallel line development. First draw the profile and space it equally. Project these spaces up into the side view to

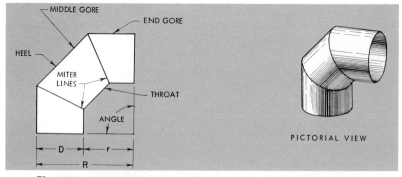

Fig. 15-9. Nomenclature and pictorial view of three-piece elbow.

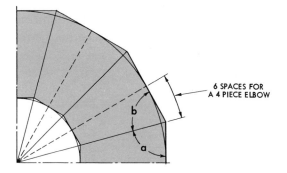

NUMBER OF SPACES = 2 TIMES NUMBER OF PIECES, MINUS 2

$$S = (2 \times N) - 2$$

FOR A 4 PIECE ELBOW:
NUMBER OF SPACES = $(4 \times 2) - 2$
SPACES = 6

Fig. 15-10. How to space miter lines for round elbow.

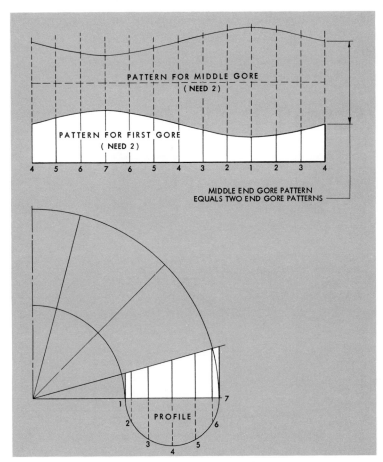

Fig. 15-11. Laying out pattern for first gore.

233

locate the equally spaced measuring lines. Then transfer these lines to the pattern in their proper spacing and length.

The first gore pattern is the only pattern developed. This pattern is cut out of sheet metal and the middle gore patterns are marked from it, since the middle gores are exact duplicates of the end gore except that they are equal to two end gores.

Note that the numbering of the measuring lines of the pattern is arranged so that the seam line of the pattern is on the side of the elbow rather than the heel or throat. It is standard practice to keep the seams on the side and staggered—that is the seams alternate to opposite sides of the elbow at each gore.

The method of numbering and measuring lines need not be the same as shown so long as it is a method which enables you to identify the lines easily.

Practicing Developing a Pattern for a Round Pipe

To test your knowledge of parallel line development as applied to round pipe fittings, lay out the pattern for the fitting shown in Fig. 15-12.

Practicing Developing an Elbow Gore Pattern

Fig. 15-13 gives the layout of a typical elbow pattern. Test your knowledge of parallel line development in this application by laying out the first gore pattern as shown.

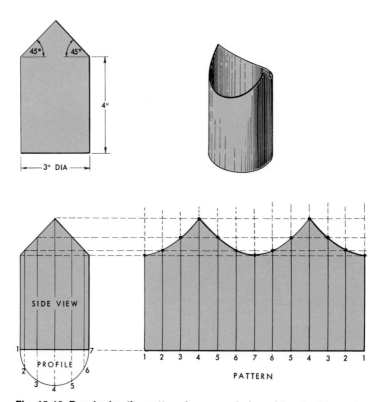

Fig. 15-12. Developing the pattern for a round pipe with a double angle.

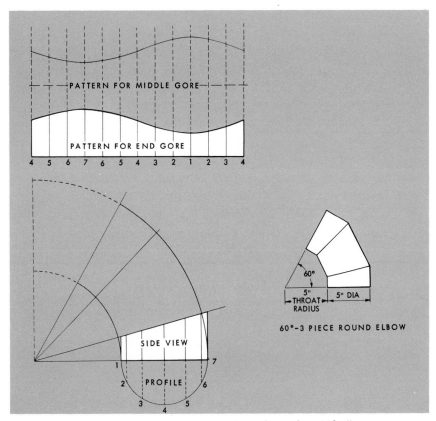

Fig. 15-13. Developing the pattern for a three-piece 60° elbow.

Class Activities

1. *Be prepared to identify which of the sheet metal objects the instructor shows you are ones that can be laid out by parallel line layout.*

2. *Draw a plan and elevation view of an object that can be laid out by parallel lines. Be prepared to demonstrate to the class on the chalkboard how to lay out the pattern for the object.*

3. *Draw a plan and elevation of an object that can be laid out by parallel lines. Exchange your drawing with another student and have the student explain with sketches how to lay out the pattern. Make notes on any procedures you disagree on and discuss them with the instructor.*

STUDENT QUESTIONS AND ACTIVITIES

1. Describe the layouts in which parallel line developments are used.
2. Why is it important to learn basic principles in pattern drafting rather than memorizing steps?
3. List the steps involved in laying out a parallel line development.
4. Explain what a profile is and what its purpose is.
5. Why is the profile divided into equal spaces and projected up to the side view rather than dividing the side view into equal spaces?
6. What is a miter line?
7. Give the number of spaces into which to divide the heel of a round elbow for: (a) four gores, (b) six gores, (c) eight gores.

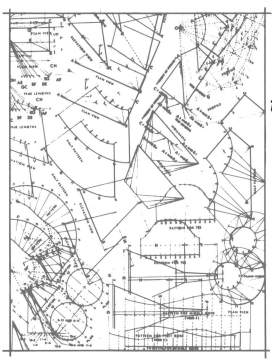

triangulation

When you complete this chapter, you should be able to:
1. Give at least four examples of the type of object for which triangulation is used to develop the pattern.
2. Explain, using sketches, what is meant by true lengths and how they can be identified on a drawing.
3. Given a plan view and the height of a fitting, show by sketches and dimensions how the true lengths of the necessary lines are found.
4. Using triangulation, lay out the patterns for any:

A. Pyramid	D.	Offset fitting
B. Square taper	E.	Square-to-round fitting
C. Round taper	F.	Oval-to-round fitting

Triangulation Method of Layout

Chapter 15 discussed parallel line development. In this chapter, you will learn how to apply triangulation, another of the three basic methods of layout. As stated in Chapter 15, triangulation is the method of developing the surfaces of objects whose sides slant at different angles. Broadly speaking, what triangulation involves is *working from two known points to locate a third point*. Surfaces are measured and laid out one point at a time until the entire pattern

237

is developed. The triangulation method is basically:

1. Dividing the surface into triangles.
2. Finding the true lengths of the sides of the triangles.
3. Drawing the triangles one at a time.

The three main steps involved in the triangulation method are:

1. The construction of the plan and elevation view.
2. The development of the true lengths.
3. The layout of the pattern.

As you did with parallel line develop-

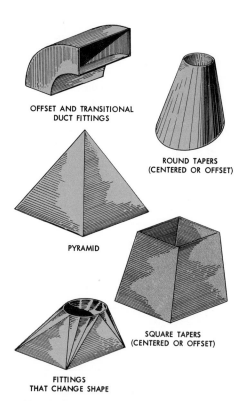

OFFSET AND TRANSITIONAL
DUCT FITTINGS

ROUND TAPERS
(CENTERED OR OFFSET)

PYRAMID

SQUARE TAPERS
(CENTERED OR OFFSET)

FITTINGS
THAT CHANGE SHAPE

Fig. 16-1. Some typical fittings and shapes laid out by triangulation.

ment, concentrate on learning the basic principles of triangulation rather than memorizing of the steps involved in the specific examples presented in this chapter. Mastery of triangulation depends first on understanding these principles and then how to apply them. Do not leave any section of the chapter or any of the practice examples until you thoroughly understand them. An understanding of each section of this chapter depends upon an understanding of the preceding sections.

Fig. 16-1 shows some typical objects which might be laid out by the triangulation method.

Plane Surfaces

To understand triangulation, it is first important that you understand what a plane surface is. Once you understand this, it will be much easier to interpret lines on the elevation and plan views.

A plane surface is a surface having two dimensions—length and width. For example, a desk top is a plane surface as is the surface of a piece of flat sheet metal. Plane surfaces may be at any angle. Thus, a *horizontal plane* has its surface level with the horizon; a *vertical plane* has its surface at right angles or perpendicular to the horizontal plane; a *slanted or oblique plane* has its surface at any angle between the vertical and horizontal planes.

A straight line—by its definition—must lie on a plane surface. Fig. 16-2 shows the three plane surfaces with lines drawn on them to illustrate this. Note that lines may be drawn at any angle on the plane surface. For example, on the horizontal plane in Fig. 16-2, lines *AB* and *CD* are at different angles

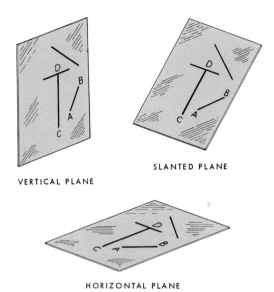

VERTICAL PLANE

SLANTED PLANE

HORIZONTAL PLANE

Fig. 16-2. Plane surfaces may be horizontal, vertical or slanted.

but are on the same plane. This fact will be applied when you work with true lengths.

Identifying True Lengths

On an elevation or plan view, some lines are true lengths, while others are not. Before these true lengths can be found, it is necessary to first be able to distinguish between the lines on the drawing which are true lengths and the lines which are not true lengths. When they are not, the true lengths of the line must be found and it is here that the concepts regarding plane surfaces are necessary.

On any drawing, *lines which are perpendicular to the viewer's line of vision are true lengths.* Lines which are slanted or at an angle to the line of vision are *not* true lengths. This is illustrated by Fig. 16-3. Therefore, on an elevation

view, all lines in a *vertical plane* are true lengths. In the plan view, all lines in a *horizontal plane* are true lengths. *All others are not.*

As an example of this, Fig. 16-4 shows the elevation and plan views of a pyramid with a square base. On the plan view, base lines *AB*, *BD*, *CD*, and *CA* are on a horizontal plane and therefore are true lengths. Lines *EA*, *EB*, *EC*, and *ED* are on slanted plane and are not true lengths.

Likewise, in the elevation view, line *AB* is in a vertical plane perpendicular to the line of vision and is therefore a true length. Here too, lines *EA* and *EB* are on planes slanted to the line of vision and therefore are not true lengths.

To test your ability to identify true lengths, list the true length lines on the plan view of Fig. 16-5. You should have listed lines *AB*, *BC*, *CD*, *DA*, *JE*, *EF*, *FG*, and *GJ*. These are the true length lines on the drawing.

Finding True Lengths

Once you have learned how to identify a true length, you must next be able to find true lengths yourself. There are several methods by which true lengths may be found. However, the method used by sheet metal workers is to draw the line in a true view and then measure it.

One method is illustrated by Fig. 16-6. Here we have a piece of sheet metal cut to a triangle as is shown in the pictorial view. We know that the base of the triangle is 6″ and the height is 8″. What we wish to know is the length of the hypotenuse *AB* (the side of a right-angled triangle that is opposite the right angle). A top view shows only the 6″ base and a front view shows only the 8″

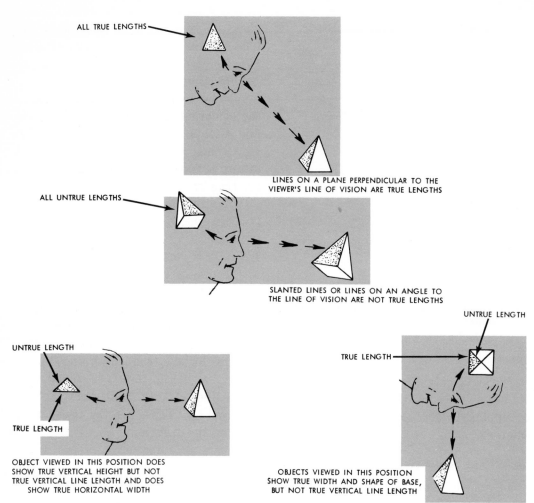

ALL TRUE LENGTHS

LINES ON A PLANE PERPENDICULAR TO THE
VIEWER'S LINE OF VISION ARE TRUE LENGTHS

ALL UNTRUE LENGTHS

SLANTED LINES OR LINES ON AN ANGLE TO
THE LINE OF VISION ARE NOT TRUE LENGTHS

UNTRUE LENGTH

TRUE LENGTH

UNTRUE LENGTH

TRUE LENGTH

OBJECT VIEWED IN THIS POSITION DOES
SHOW TRUE VERTICAL HEIGHT BUT NOT
TRUE VERTICAL LINE LENGTH AND DOES
SHOW TRUE HORIZONTAL WIDTH

OBJECTS VIEWED IN THIS POSITION
SHOW TRUE WIDTH AND SHAPE OF BASE,
BUT NOT TRUE VERTICAL LINE LENGTH

Fig. 16-3. True lengths and untrue lengths.

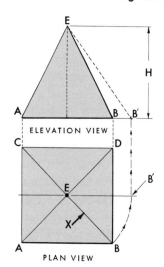

Fig. 16-4. Pyramid with a square base. Lines AB, BC, CD, and DA in the plan view and line AB in the elevation view are true lengths.

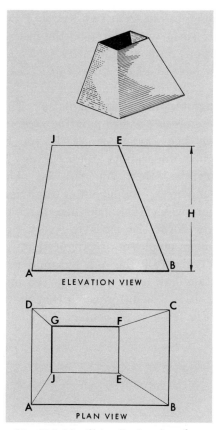

Fig. 16-5. Identifying the true lengths.

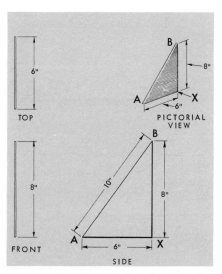

Fig. 16-6. Finding the true length of the hypotenuse of a sheet metal triangle.

height. In both of these views, side *AB* is slanted to the line of vision and therefore not shown in its true length. However, if a side view is drawn, line *AB* is on a perpendicular plane to the line of vision and is shown in its true length which is 10″.

Now let's apply this procedure to the pyramid shown in Fig. 16-4. As stated previously, we know that line *EB* is not shown in its true length in the plan view. To find the true length of *EB* you must change your point of vision to point *X* which is perpendicular to the plane of *EB*. If an elevation view from this point of vision is then drawn, the true length of line *EB* is shown. Fig. 16-7 shows this view. Notice that the triangle in Fig. 16-7 is similar to the sheet metal triangle in Fig. 16-6. If you think of line

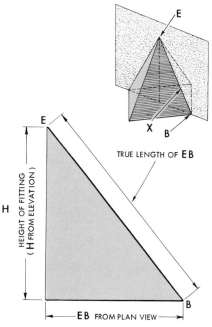

Fig. 16-7. To find the true length of a line, change your point of vision to a point on the line which is perpendicular to your point of vision.

EB in the plan view of Fig. 16-4 as the plan view of a sheet metal triangle, then you can see that *EB* must be the horizontal distance the line travels. Thus, *EB* is the base of the triangle shown in Fig. 16-7. Since the line *BE* runs from the bottom to the top of the pyramid, line *BE* must rise a vertical distance equal to the height of the pyramid. Thus, distance *H* in the elevation view shows the height of the triangle. The hypotenuse of the triangle *EB* is the true length of line *EB*.

From the plan view of Fig. 16-5, draw true length triangles for all lines that are not shown in their true length in the plan view. After you have drawn these triangles, check them against Fig. 16-8.

Triangulating from Two Known Points

If you have understood the preceding sections on how to identify *true lengths* and *how to find a true length,* there is one other basic principle needed for an understanding of triangulation. This is *how to locate a new point by measuring from two known points.* If you thoroughly understand these three basic principles, then you will be able to quickly grasp the layout of any triangulation problem because these three principles form the basis of every layout problem employing triangulation.

Figure 16-9 shows a pyramid with a rectangular base similar to the one in Fig. 16-4. The difference is that the apex in Fig. 16-9 is off-center. We shall lay

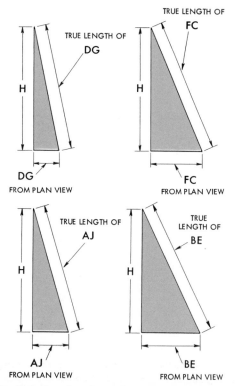

Fig. 16-8. True lengths of lines shown in Fig. 16-5.

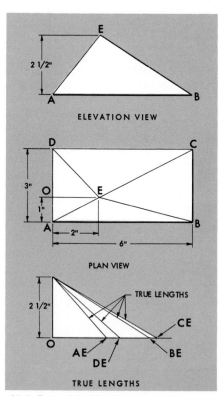

Fig. 16-9. Pyramid with off-center vertex and rectangular base.

out the pattern for Fig. 16-9 to illustrate the principle of locating a new point by measuring from two known points.

The first process in laying out this pattern is to find the true lengths for the lines that are not true lengths on the drawing. This is shown in Fig. 16-9 also. Notice that in finding the true lengths, separate triangles were not drawn for each line. Since each triangle has the same vertical height, time can be saved by drawing all the lines on one triangle as shown. Each of the lines is taken from the plan view and measured out from point O on the true length triangles. This is the way true lengths are commonly found in sheet metal shop layout.

After the true lengths are found, then the pattern can be laid out as shown in Fig. 16-10. *It is suggested here that you follow the steps in Fig. 16-10 with your drawing instruments in order to clearly understand them.* The first step is to draw one of the lines shown as a true length on the plan view. In Step 1 line AB is drawn. Since we know how long this line must be, this locates two points A and B from which we can base our measurements. From the true length triangle, the true length of AE gives the distance that point E is away from point A. Set the dividers to the true length of AE, and using A as a center describe an arc as shown in Step 2. To be the proper distance from A, point E must be on this

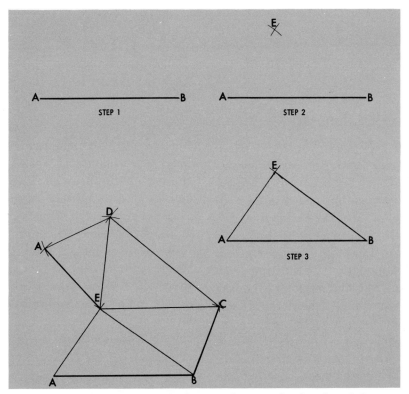

Fig. 16-10. Locating a new point from two known points by triangulation.

arc. However, there is only one place on the arc where E will also be the proper distance from B. To locate the proper distance from B, set the dividers to the true length of BE and swing it from B as shown in Step 2. This intersection of these two arcs gives the location of point E at the correct distance away from points A and B. Connect the points as shown in Step 3 and the first side of the pyramid will be formed. Note that it forms a triangle. Breaking down the surface of an object into triangles and forming these individual triangles on the pattern is the basis of development of the process called triangulation.

After the first side is formed, the same process of measuring from two known points is repeated to form the second side. In this case, point C on the pattern must next be located. This is done by measuring from points B and E. The distance from B to C is a true length on the plan view. Therefore the distance BC can be taken directly from the plan view and swung from point B on the pattern. The true length from E to C is taken from the true length triangle and swung from E. The intersection of these two arcs gives point C and the second side can be drawn in.

The other sides of the pyramid are found in the same manner. After point C is located, then point D is found by measuring from E and C. After D is found, then A is located by measuring from E and D.

Layouts Using Triangulation

Laying Out a Rectangular Transition

To test your knowledge of triangulation methods, lay out the pattern for the rectangular transition shown in Fig. 16-11. In the plan view, the dotted lines are measuring lines drawn on the surface of the fitting to form the triangles necessary for triangulation. This fitting actually amounts to a duplication of the layout of the pyramid except that eight triangles are formed on the pattern instead of four.

The pattern is started by first finding all the true lengths necessary for the lines on the plan view. After all the true lengths are found *and labeled*, then start the pattern by drawing line AB which can be taken directly from the plan. Next swing the true length of AF from A and swing the true length of BF from B to locate point F. After F is found, locate point E next by locating the distance FE from F (this is a true length on the plan) and by locating the true length of AE from A. This completes the first side of the pattern.

The next point to locate is G. This is done by measuring from points F and

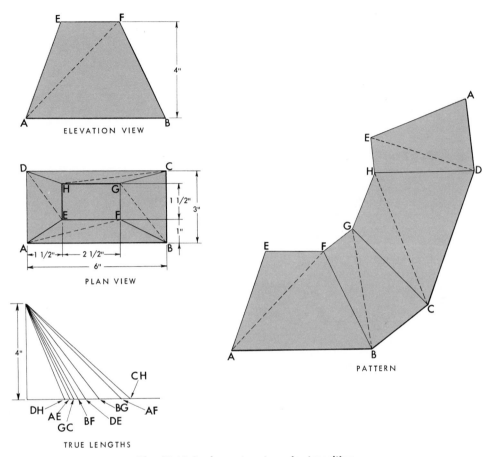

Fig. 16-11. Laying out rectangular transition.

B. Line *FG* can be taken directly from the plan view, while line *BG* must be taken from the true length triangle.

After point *G* is located, then point *C* is found by measuring in the same manner as before from points *G* and *B*. The rest of the layout is repetition, finding points *H, D, E,* and *A* in that order.

Laying Out a Round Taper

You should now have an understanding of the basic principles of triangulation. To fully master this method of layout you should now learn how to apply it

to various typical operations. One very common situation is triangulating a round taper. Though this problem illustrates a round taper, the same methods would apply if the taper were elliptical or any other circular shape.

Fig. 16-12 shows the plan and elevation of a round taper that is offset. The first step in the layout of this problem is to establish the measuring lines on the plan view. This is done by dividing both circles into 12 equal parts. Notice that this is quite similar to one of the procedures in parallel lines. After the cir-

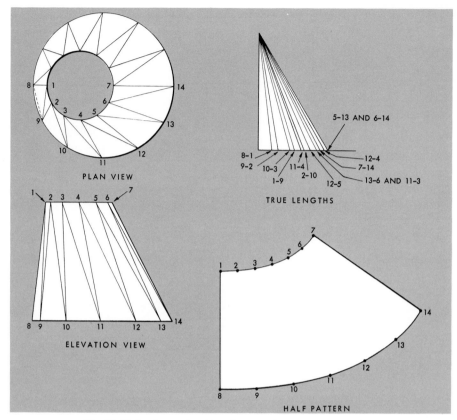

PLAN VIEW

TRUE LENGTHS

5-13 AND 6-14

8-1
9-2   10-3   11-4   2-10   12-4
1-9   12-5   7-14
13-6 AND 11-3

ELEVATION VIEW

HALF PATTERN

Fig. 16-12. Laying out pattern for round taper that is offset.

cles are divided into equal parts then the measuring lines are drawn in as shown. This layout is again the same as the pyramid and the rectangular transition in that triangles are formed on the plan view and on the pattern. For example, the first triangle is formed by *8-9-1*. The dotted line shown in the plan view from *8* to *9* is only to illustrate the triangles formed and are never on the plan view.

After the plan view is drawn, the measuring lines located and the true lengths found, the pattern can be started. This is done by drawing a line and marking the true length of line *8-1* on it. This gives two known points from which to

measure. Next locate point *9* by taking the distance *8-9* from the plan view and swinging it from point *8*. Next take the true length of line *1-9* from the true length triangle. Then swing it from *1*. The intersection of these two arcs gives point *9*.

Point *2* is located next by measuring from points *1* and *9*. After *2* is found then *10* is next located by measuring from *2* and *9*. After *10* is found, then *3* is next located by measuring from points *2* and *10*. Points *11, 4, 12, 5, 13, 6, 14,* and *7* are found in the same manner and in the order given. If you will think of the plan view as a road map and follow the measuring lines, you will have little trouble in finishing the pattern.

Note that only one-half of the pattern is developed. This is because the fitting is symmetrical or "centered" and the other half of the fitting is exactly the same. Therefore it saves time to work on only half of the plan. This is general shop practice in any case when objects are symmetrical.

Laying Out an Oval-to-Round Fitting

Fig. 16-13 shows an oval-to-round fitting. Test your knowledge of triangulation by laying out the pattern. This is an illustration of how the basic principles of triangulation apply to many different shapes.

On this pattern the measuring lines are drawn on only half the plan, since the other half is symmetrical. Actually the measuring lines need only be drawn on one-fourth of the plan since the second quarter is exactly the same as the first quarter, the true length lines will also be exactly the same and there is no need to find them again.

This problem is almost a repetition of the round taper. The only difference is that a straight section is added into the bottom circle to make it an oval. The triangle formed by *11-11'-4* is a flat surface while the rest of the fitting is curved.

This fitting could be started just as with the round taper. However, it is more convenient to start with line *11-11'* and from these two points locate point *4*. Then, since the quarter patterns are duplicates, work from the center toward both ends at the same time. In other words, when the arc for *11-3* is swung,

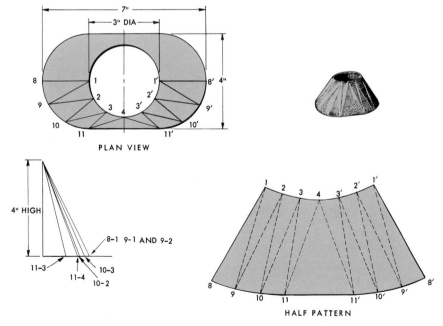

Fig. 16-13. Laying out pattern for oval-to-round fitting.

Sheet Metal Shop Practice

at the same time swing *11'-3'* since this is the same length. This cuts down time involved in setting the dividers by half.

Laying Out a Square-to-Round Fitting

Fig. 16-14 illustrates the triangulation of another common type of fitting. These are commonly called *square-to-rounds* even though the shape may be rectangular-to-round, or even triangular-to-round.

As in previous problems, the method of layout is still that of forming triangles on the plan view and then forming the same triangles on the pattern in their true length.

Since this is a symmetrical fitting, only one-fourth of the plan view is necessary. However, one-half is marked with measuring lines to make the layout clearer. The true lengths of the measuring lines are found in the usual way, as shown.

Again, the method of starting the pattern of the square to round is from the center out. To start the pattern, draw true length line *AB*, which can be taken from the plan view. Next locate point *4* by swinging the true length of *A4* from *A*, and by swinging the true length of

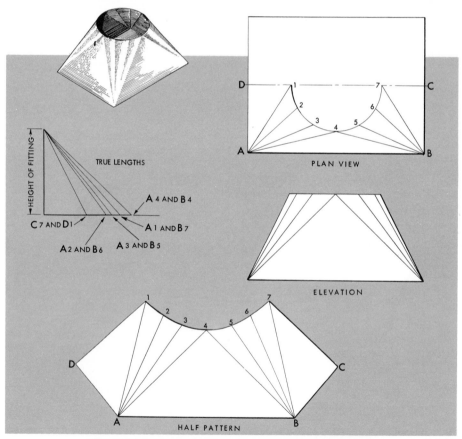

Fig. 16-14. Laying out pattern for square-to-round fitting.

B4 from *B*. After *4* is located, next find point *3*. This is done by swinging the true length of *A3* from *A* and by swinging the distance *4-3* from *4* (*4-3* can be taken directly from the plan view).

Point *2* is found next and then point *1*. After this, the other side of the pattern curve is laid out by locating points *5*, *6*, and *7* in that order. The curve of the pattern is either drawn through these points free-hand or by use of a flexible rule.

After the curve points from *1* to *7* are located, then points *C* and *D* must be found to complete the half-pattern. To find *C* take the distance *BC* from the plan view and swing it from *B* on the pattern. Then take the true length of *C-7*

and swing it from *7*. The intersection of these two arcs gives point *C* and the lines *7C* and *BC* can be drawn in. Point *D* is located in the same way. Take *AD* from the plan view and swing it from point *A*. Then take the true length of *D-1* and swing it from *1*. This locates *D* and the lines can be drawn in.

Laying Out an Offset Square-to-Round Fitting

Fig. 16-15 shows a slightly different square-to-round. This fitting is rectangular on one end and the circle is off center from the rectangle. This, however, makes no difference in the layout of the problem except that the true lengths will all be different rather than

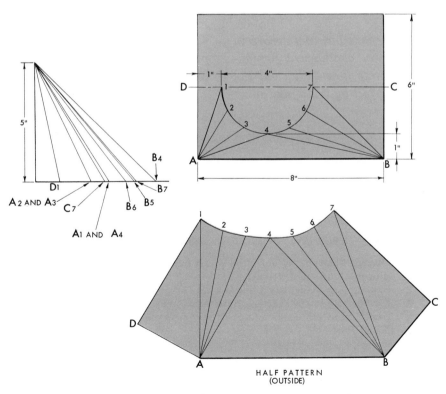

Fig. 16-15. Laying out pattern for offset square-to-round fitting.

being duplicates of corresponding lines. Notice also that no elevation view is drawn of this fitting. In actual shop practice the elevation is seldom drawn unless it is needed to find some of the true length lines. In most cases the only use for the elevation view is to show the height of the fitting, and this can be done by a note on the plan view as shown.

Lay out the pattern for this fitting to check your understanding of triangulation.

Class Activities

1. Draw a plan and elevation view for an object of any of the types listed in item 4 of this chapter and be prepared to demonstrate on the chalkboard how to lay it out.

2. Be able to point out any errors in procedure for any chalkboard demonstrations explaining how to lay out the pattern for an object by triangulation.

3. Be able to identify the true length lines on any plan and elevation drawn on the chalkboard. Also be able to show how to find the true lengths of any lines that are not true lengths.

4. In class, list as many objects as possible that are laid out by triangulation.

STUDENT QUESTIONS AND ACTIVITIES

1. Describe the types of object on which triangulation is used.
2. How is a true length found?
3. Explain how to identify a line is a true length on the plan view.
4. List the basic steps in triangulation that are used in every problem.
5. Under what circumstances is it only necessary to draw half a plan view of a fitting?

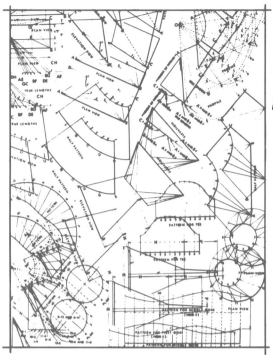

radial line development

17

When you complete this chapter, you should be able to develop the pattern for any centered, round, or square taper, using the radial line method.

Radial line layout is the third method by which the sheet metal worker develops patterns. This method is discussed last for two reasons. First, radial line developments use many of the procedures of parallel line development *and* triangulation which you have already learned in the preceding two chapters. Second, radial line developments are used least of the three methods.

For the radial line method to be used, all lines must radiate from a common center. In addition, the amount of slant of those lines must be relatively large since most radial line developments begin by drawing the side view and then extending the side lines until they meet.

Arcs are then projected from this point. If the side taper is so slight that the point is several feet from the fitting, the radius needed to swing the arc is long and consequently difficult to use. Because of these limiting circumstances then, the conditions under which radial line developments may be effectively employed are necessarily limited.

Fig. 17-1 shows some typical objects which could be laid out using radial line development. Remember, however, that such objects *must* be centered—that is, equally tapered on all sides. Although these objects could also be laid out by the triangulation method described in the preceding chapter, in these particu-

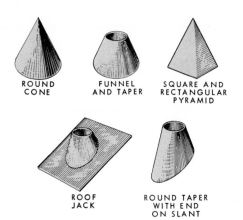

ROUND CONE   FUNNEL AND TAPER   SQUARE AND RECTANGULAR PYRAMID

ROOF JACK   ROUND TAPER WITH END ON SLANT

Fig. 17-1. Typical fittings and shapes laid out by radial line development.

lar cases, radial lines provide a quicker method.

Cones

Fig. 17-2 shows the layout of a pattern for a cone. This is a typical operation and serves to illustrate some of the basic principles of radial line development.

You will notice that radial line developments have several similarities to the pattern layout methods presented in the preceding two chapters. As with many

of the examples presented in those chapters, it is necessary here to have the essential views and to determine true lengths of various elements in the pattern being constructed.

The pattern for the cone in Fig. 17-2 is developed in the following manner.

1. The elevation view, showing the true height of the apex, and the plan view, from which the length of the stretchout is determined, are drawn first.
2. The stretchout arc is drawn with a radius equal to the true length of the side or edge of the object (*AB*).
3. The stretchout arc is swung an indefinite length. Then the circumference of the bottom of the cone is calculated mathematically or from a circumference rule. This would be the circumference of diameter *CB*. This circumference is measured with a flexible rule around the stretchout arc at points *D* and *E* marked as ends of the circumference. Then lines *AD* and *AE* are drawn from the ra-

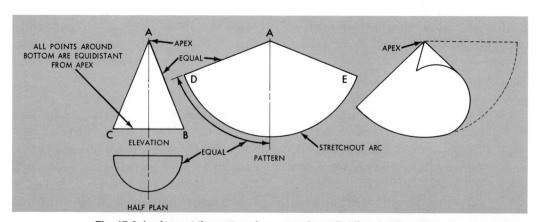

Fig. 17-2. Laying out the pattern for a cone by radial line development.

dius point of the arc. This completes the pattern.

Round Tapers

Any round taper, *provided that it is equally tapered on all sides,* can be laid out by radial line development. The round taper shown in Fig. 17-3 is essentially the same as the cone in Fig. 17-2 except that the top is cut off. In laying out the centered round taper in Fig. 17-3, follow these steps:

1. Draw the side view of the taper.
2. Extend the side lines until they meet. This forms the apex.
3. Use the apex as the center and swing arcs from the top and bottom corners of the taper.
4. The stretchout arc is measured.

In this case, the stretchout is the circumference of a circle whose diameter is the bottom of the taper.

5. Draw lines from the apex to the ends of the stretchout arc.

Pyramid with a Square Base

Pyramids with a square or rectangular base may also be laid out by radial line development, *provided that the sides are equally tapered.* Fig. 17-4 shows a typical example of such a pyramid. This example employs the principles in determining true lengths which were discussed in Chapter 16 and utilizes the steps in the preceding two examples. Here, however, the chords (the line drawn across the curve) are measured

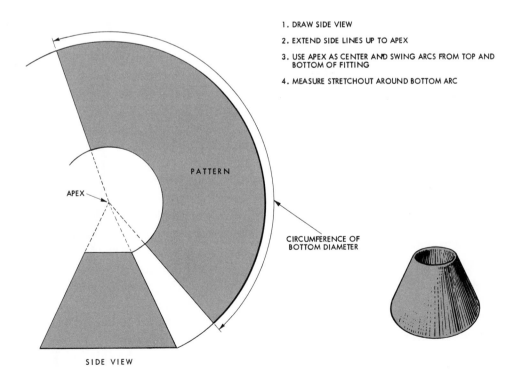

1. DRAW SIDE VIEW

2. EXTEND SIDE LINES UP TO APEX

3. USE APEX AS CENTER AND SWING ARCS FROM TOP AND BOTTOM OF FITTING

4. MEASURE STRETCHOUT AROUND BOTTOM ARC

PATTERN

APEX

CIRCUMFERENCE OF BOTTOM DIAMETER

SIDE VIEW

Fig. 17-3. Centered round tapers may be laid out with radial lines.

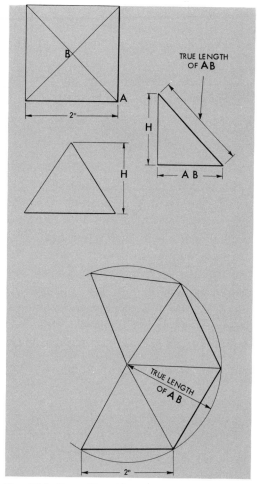

Fig. 17-4. Pyramids with rectangular bases may be laid out by radial line developments when the sides are equally tapered.

both ends of the object are slanted rather than in a plane square to the center line. For objects of this kind, the same basic steps previously outlined are followed. However, new applications of them are made.

Fig. 17-5 shows a round taper with the bottom pitched up at a 30° angle. The first step is to draw the side view shown by *1-A-B-7'*. Then extend the side line *B-7'* down to point *7* to make the complete cone described by *1-A-B-7*. Remember that one of the prime requisites of a radial line development is that all sides *must* be equally tapered. Therefore, *A-1* and *B-7* must have the same slant.

The profile is drawn next. If you will review Chapters 15 and 16, *Parallel Line Development* and *Triangulation,* you will note that this operation is the same here as in those methods. After the profile is drawn and equal spaces are stepped off, project the spaces to line *1-7* and from these points draw lines up to the apex *O* to form equally spaced, tapering lines around the surface of the cone.

You will note that this operation is similar to that you used in parallel line developments. In parallel lines, the profile is drawn to obtain equally spaced *parallel measuring lines* on the surface. In this example of radial lines, the profile is drawn to obtain equally spaced *tapering lines* on the surface.

Since the measuring lines are tapering lines, they are obviously *not* true lengths on the side view. True lengths for them could be found by the method described in Chapter 16, *Triangulation.*

However, since the sides of the fitting all slant the same amount, all the lines

around the arc equal to the length of the bottom side of the pyramid.

Tapers on a Pitch

Though radial line developments are used for the simple tapered objects shown in the preceding examples in this chapter, their greatest use is in laying out more complex fittings. The sheet metal worker often speaks of objects being "on a pitch." He means that one or

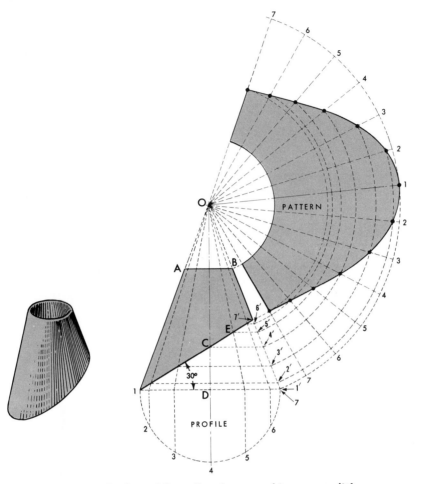

Fig. 17-5. Laying out the pattern for a round taper on a pitch.

on the sides must slant the same amount. This means that the lengths of all the lines can be projected over to the side line to obtain their true length. This is because the side lines are on a plane perpendicular to the line of vision (see Fig. 16-2, Chapter 16) and are therefore true lengths on the drawing.

As an example, in Fig. 17-5 follow point 4 on the profile through the operation. Point 4 is projected up to line *1-7* to locate point *D*. A measuring line is drawn from *D* to *O*. Line *DO* crosses the

bottom of the fitting at point *C*. From *C*, project a line at right angles to the center line over to the side line *B7*. This gives you point *4'*. The distance *O-4'* is the true length of *OC*. Note that all of the points on the side view are projected at right angles to the center line, that is, parallel to line *1-7*. All of the points are projected in this manner. Distance *O-5'*, for example, is the true length of line *OE*.

When all of the true lengths are located along the side line *B-7*, arcs are

255

swung from each of these points with apex *O* as the center. The stretchout of the profile is then measured around the bottom arc (points 7 to 7). Spaces are then stepped off for the measuring lines in duplication of the spaces around the profile. When these spaces are located, lines are drawn from them up to apex *O*.

After the radial lines from the stretchout and the arcs from the true lengths are drawn, then the intersection of the corresponding lines gives the points on the pattern. For example, the point where the arc whose radius is *O-7'* crosses radial line *O-7* is a point on the pattern. The arc whose radius is *O-6'* and radial line *O-6* gives us another point. After all of the points are drawn in, the bottom curve is drawn through these points to form that portion of the pattern. The upper curve of the pattern is an arc swung from point *B*.

Truncated Right Cone
Cut at an Angle

Another round taper with the slant at the top is shown in Fig. 17-6. Check your understanding of radial line develop-

ment by laying out the pattern for this fitting.

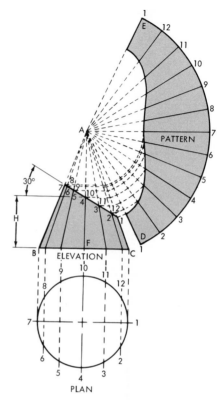

Fig. 17-6. Developing the pattern for a truncated right cone cut at an angle. Base diameter is 6″ and height from base to apex is 8″.

Class Activities

1. *Be prepared to identify which of the sheet metal objects the instructor shows you that can be laid out by radial line development.*

2. *Select one of the objects from item 1. Take its dimensions and from them,* demonstrate to the class on the chalkboard how to lay out the pattern for the object.

3. *Take a plan and elevation view of an unknown object. From it, develop a layout and determine what the object is.*

STUDENT QUESTIONS AND ACTIVITIES

1. On which kinds of objects may radial line development be most effectively applied on patterns?

2. From a review of Chapter 15, how is radial line development similar to parallel line development?

3. From a review of Chapter 16, how is radial line development similar to triangulation?

4. What one characteristic must any object have in order for it to be laid out by radial line development?

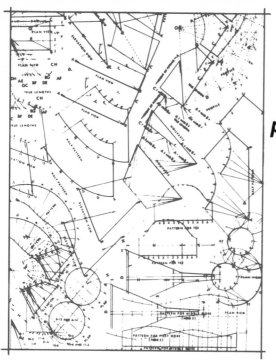

plastics

18

When you complete this chapter, you should be able to:
1. Define "thermosetting" and "thermoforming" plastics.
2. List at least four advantages of plastic over sheet metal.
3. List at least two disadvantages.
4. Describe how PVC plastic is fabricated.
5. Describe how PVC plastic is welded.
6. List at least three different plastics that are used in place of sheet metal for duct, pipe, or fume hoods.

In the sheet metal industry there has been a rapid growth in the use of plastics. First, plastics may outperform the material they replace; second, they may cost less than other materials; and third, they lend themselves to the production of new products previously unavailable. Common uses of plastic materials include exhaust systems conveying highly corrosive fumes from manufacturing processes, and hoods in laboratories that use chemicals in research projects. In addition to these special ex-

haust duct systems, plastics are used in place of metals in a variety of other products which are used or produced by the sheet metal mechanic. Some of these products are fans, fume scrubbers, hoods, tanks, countertops, liners, sinks, laboratory benches, louvers, and many other duct system accessories.

Because plastics have become widely accepted in the sheet metal industry, it is essential that the sheet metal mechanic be well acquainted with the technique of working with plastics as well as the properties of the materials themselves. Since most plastics come to the sheet metal shop in forms familiar to the trade, they are easily adapted to the customary shop practices. Most of the tools and equipment used to work sheet metal can also be used to lay out, cut and assemble plastics. Some special equipment is required to heat, form and weld plastics, and many shops have acquired this equipment in order to serve their customers.

Types of Plastics

The term *plastics* generally refers to any of several man-made (synthetic) materials which are chemically produced and can be molded, cast, extruded, drawn or laminated into many types of objects. Plastics used in the sheet metal industry fall into two main categories: *thermoforming* (thermoplastic) and *thermosetting*. The remainder of this chapter will be concerned with the characteristics and methods of fabrication of these two types of plastics.

Thermoplastic Materials

Because thermoplastics can be heated and formed into various shapes, they are often called thermoforming plastics. All thermoforming plastics can be heated and formed any number of times without losing any of their original mechanical or chemical resistant properties. It is this reversible property of thermoplastic materials that makes them so adaptable to the fabrication of ductwork and fittings. This characteristic is unique in that it allows the continuing use or re-use of material beyond the initial application. For example, a sheet of PVC can be cut, formed and welded into a joint of 18 inch diameter duct. That same section of duct could later be cut along the welded seam, heated and flattened back into a sheet and then re-used to fabricate a fitting or another size duct section. For this reason, the sheet metal mechanic can use thermoplastics in much the same way as a sheet of galvanized iron or hot rolled steel.

Some thermoplastic materials commonly used in ductwork are polyethylene (PE), polypropylene (PP), and, the most widely used thermoplastic in the sheet metal industry, polyvinyl chloride (PVC).

Thermosetting Materials

Thermosetting plastics become permanently rigid when heated or cured. This property of thermosetting materials makes it possible to produce ductwork much the same as concrete, tile and ceramics. However, once these materials are cast or set into an initial shape or form, they cannot be changed or reverted to their original form. A joint of 18 inch diameter duct, for example, could be formed and set using a thermosetting material. However, after the material has set or cured, it cannot be reworked to its original form or any other size duct section.

Production of Plastics

Organic synthetic or processed materials called polymers are very expensive derivatives of petroleum refining. By a highly complicated chemical reaction, polymers are formed to produce a basic plastic material called a *resin*. Resins are further processed by combining them with other chemical substances to attain certain desired physical and chemical characteristics. Some of the important additives are:

Plasticizers—Plasticizers soften the plastic and make it flexible.

Stabilizers—Stabilizers prevent the breakdown of the plastic when it is exposed to heat or light.

Fillers—Fillers add bulk and reduce overall costs.

Colors—Dyes and pigments are added to achieve the desired color in the plastic.

Fibers—Fibers are reinforcing elements which add strength to the plastic.

Solvents—Solvents are added to increase the liquidity and adaptability to processes such as molding, extruding, dipping, brushing, and spraying.

Catalysts—Catalysts are used to start a chemical reaction and speed up the setting or hardening process of plastics.

Basic resins and additives are furnished to the manufacturer of standard products in one of three forms: liquid, granular, or powder.

Liquid plastics may be cast into sheets, used in applications such as spray-on and brush-on coatings or added to paints and adhesives. The base from which plastic foam is made is a liquid plastic. Other products made from liquid plastics include insulation, cushions, styrofoam balls, and sheets used for decorative purposes.

Granular and powdered type plastics are softened by the application of heat and are generally formed by molding, casting or extrusion. Some of these types can also be used to roll sheets or thin films of plastic.

Fabricating Thermoplastics

There are several family groups of plastics that are thermoforming; however, the only materials that are practical for use in duct systems now are polyethylene, polypropylene, and polyvinyl chloride. About 90% of all duct systems made from thermoforming materials utilize one of these three materials. PVC is by far the most widely used because the combination of cost, physical properties, and chemical properties make it the most practical. Consequently, most manuals and handbooks dealing with the fabrication of thermoforming plastics confine their instruction to PVC. Once a mechanic has mastered the techniques of fabricating PVC, he can adapt to other thermoplastics with a little additional knowledge about the particular material.

Polyvinyl Chloride

It is important to know something about the history of a new material as well as its advantages and limitations in order to understand where the material can be used and where it should not be used.

History. PVC was first developed in Germany during the 1930's when military needs consumed most of Germany's steel supply. The shortage of steel coupled with an advanced petro-chemical industry caused Germany to use PVC in place of steel in several places. In the mechanical industry, for example, sheet material was used to fabricate ductwork, and tubular extruded forms were used for ductwork, water piping, and plumbing. It was not until after the war that PVC was used in the United States. Acceptance of the new material was very slow. The engineers and contractors watched the performance of the early systems before specifying the material themselves. By the mid-1950's PVC had passed the test of time and was being installed in many systems requiring resistance to corrosive attack.

Types and Forms of PVC. PVC is produced in two types. *Type I* is an unplasticized sheet that has high chemical resistant properties, but it is quite brittle and is subject to breakage from sharp impact. *Type II* PVC has plasticizer added in the manufacturing stages to soften the sheet and make it less brittle and more resistant to breakage from impact. However, the addition of plasticizer reduces the chemical resistance of PVC. Therefore, when PVC is being considered for a particular system, both the concentration of corrosive agents to be handled and the potential abuse the system may receive must be examined in order to select the correct type.

PVC sheets are produced in both types and are available in thicknesses from $\frac{1}{16}$ inch to 1 inch. These sheets are usually 48 inches wide by 96 inches long. Most duct systems utilize $\frac{1}{8}$, $\frac{3}{16}$, or $\frac{1}{4}$ inch thick material, depending upon the size of the ducts.

Besides sheets, PVC is also manufactured for the sheet metal industry in tubular form. PVC is extruded into round duct usually 20 feet long with a wall $\frac{3}{16}$ inch thick. The diameters available on the market now include 6 through 12 inch (in one inch increments) and 14 and 16 inch diameters as well. Extruded PVC duct is produced only as Type I.

Limitations and Advantages. As in its early applications, PVC is still not a replacement for sheet metal. It is very expensive compared to metal, about four to five times as expensive. In addition, the amount of labor required to work the material into duct and fittings increases the cost of the finished system. For these reasons PVC is used only for those systems requiring superior corrosion resistance and/or light weight.

Compared to steel, PVC is not a strong material. The tensile strength of steel is around 80,000 pounds per square inch, while PVC at room temperature is about 8,000 pounds per square inch, about one-tenth the strength of steel. As the temperature increases, PVC becomes weaker. Manufacturers specify that it should not be used where temperatures exceed 180° F. At this temperature PVC starts to soften and will sag. As a practical matter, PVC is usually not used in areas where the temperature reaches 150° F. Steel does not even begin to weaken until approximately 800° F, and serious weakening does not occur until considerably higher temperatures are reached.

Despite strength and temperature limitations, PVC is outstanding in corrosion resistance. Under very corrosive conditions, where even stainless steel has deteriorated in a short time, PVC has lasted indefinitely. PVC has been

TABLE 18-1

Comparison Chart on Chemical Resistance of Sheet Materials

This chart is based upon the results of laboratory tests on pure chemicals. On-the-job conditions will vary considerably, so that no application involving chemicals should be based entirely upon any chart but should also be based upon tests on the job. The ratings are necessarily only approximate and varying rates of resistance can be expected.

Code: R - - - - resistant
       PR - - - partially resistant
       A - - - - attacked
       N - - - No data available

Figures given are for 68° F

Consult manufacturers' charts for more detailed information

Substance	Stainless Steel Type 316	PVC Type 1	Aluminum	Copper
Acetic acid 80%	R	R	R	R
Aluminum hydroxide	R	R	R	A
Ammonium chloride	R	R	A	R
Antimony trichloride	R	R	N	N
Boric acid	R	R	R	R
Calcium Carbonate	PR	R	N	N
Chlorobenzine	R	A	N	N
Citric Acid	R	R	R	R
Gasoline	R	R	R	R
Hydrochloric acid	A	R	A	A
Hydrofluoric acid	A	R	A	A
Iodine	A	A	N	N
Methyl alcohol	R	R	R	R
Milk	R	R	R	R
Photographic solutions Regular	R	R	N	
Sea water	R	R	R	R
Stannic chloride	A	R	N	N
Sulfuric acide up to 96% solution	A	R	A	R
Zinc Chloride	R	R	R	R

used successfully in high concentrations of fumes from hydrochloric acid, sulphuric acid, nitric acid, calcium carbonate and other highly corrosive chemicals where sheet metals would corrode in a very short period of time. Table 18-1 shows a comparison of corrosion resistance between Type I PVC and the basic sheet metals.

In addition to its high corrosion resistance, PVC has other advantages over metal. First, it is a low conductor of heat. Because of this, extra insulation to prevent heat loss is not necessary and condensation of vapors is less severe than in other systems.

Second, PVC is affected very little by the elements. It is completely unaffected by rain or snow. Sunlight tends to bleach the color of PVC, but it does not impair physical or chemical resistance.

Finally, PVC will not support combustion. While it can be ignited and will burn, it will stop almost immediately when the source of ignition or flame is removed or extinguished. Table 18-2 summarizes the important features of PVC.

Working PVC in the Sheet Metal Shop

Layout and Cutting. Fabricating PVC ductwork and fittings from sheet material requires the same basic procedure as sheet metal. The stretchout of duct sections and sections and patterns of fittings must be laid out on sheets. In layout, the main factor to be taken into consideration is shrinkage. This is a unique characteristic of PVC. Most materials expand when heated; PVC, however, shrinks. The adjustment can be learned very quickly because the amount of shrinkage is uniform and will not vary appreciably from one manufacturer to another.

After the layout is completed, the pieces must be cut to size. If only straight cuts are required, a heavy gage capacity squaring shear can be used to cut sheets up to $\frac{1}{4}$ inch thick. For thicknesses greater than $\frac{1}{4}$ inch, a table saw, hand power saw, band saw, or heavy

TABLE 18-2

POLYVINYL CHLORIDE PROPERTIES

Type I	Type II 25% plasticized	Type II 50% plasticized
1. Most rigid	1. Not as rigid as Type I	1. Pliable as rubber
2. Highest corrosion resistance	2. Slightly less corrosion resistance than Type I	2. Used for gaskets only
3. Impact strength equal to cast iron	3. Higher impact strength than Type I	
4. Grey in color	4. Grey in color but different shade from Type I	
5. 160° F highest safe temperature	5. 120° highest safe temperature	
6. Easily formed and fabricated	6. Easier to form and fabricate than Type I	

duty saber saw can be used to make the cuts. For cutting the various shapes for fittings, a small saber saw is generally used. A band saw may be used if the radius cuts are not sharp.

Layout and cutting of tubular forms is confined to producing elbows and bevels by miter cutting duct sections and welding the resulting joints. The technique of producing these fittings can be accomplished by building a pattern of sheet metal for each desired gore of a round fitting. This pattern can then be clamped to the duct so that it can be scribed. Then the scribe mark can be cut with a hand saber saw.

Forming. The tempering oven is an important piece of equipment in the fabricating shop. It is usually large enough so that an entire sheet 48 by 96 inches can be heated on a shelf. Most ovens have at least two shelves, usually constructed of heavy gage expanded metal. The metal allows the plastic sheet to be laid flat and heated uniformly on both sides. These ovens can be fired by gas, oil, or electric heaters and are usually held at a temperature of 200° F to 220° F.

The procedure for fabricating round duct is to heat the entire piece to be formed in the tempering oven. Tem-

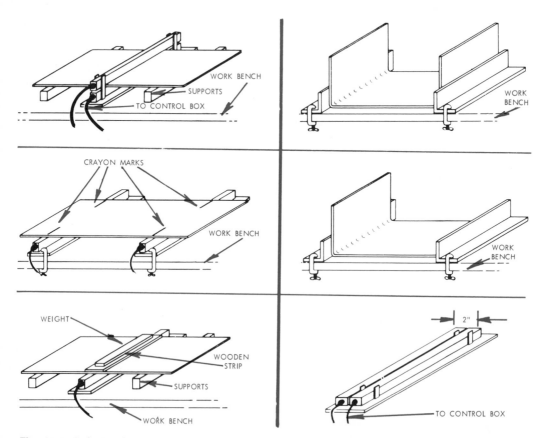

Fig. 18-1. Strip heating device consisting of two electrical heating elements enclosed in aluminum heating bars. Shows heating and clamping for one and two bends. (Kamweld Products Co., Inc.)

pering time for a piece of PVC will vary depending upon the thickness and size. A piece ⅛ inch thick and cut 56½ inches by 48 inches to form a four foot section of 18 inch diameter duct will take five to seven minutes to temper. When the tempered piece is removed from the oven, it is placed around a mandrel of the desired diameter. After the material cools, it is set in the proper shape and will stay that way. To complete the duct section, a longitudinal weld must be made.

To produce fittings such as reducers, elbows, bevels, tees and others requiring tempering, the same procedure is followed. The cut piece is tempered or softened in the oven, then formed on a mandrel of the proper diameter. After the formed piece cools to the set shape, the longitudinal seam must be welded to finish the fitting.

Another special piece of forming equipment is the strip heater used to produce a rectangular duct as shown in Fig. 18-1. Strip heaters are electric heating elements that soften the plastic along the length of a bend or break. After the material is tempered, the bend is made easily and held at the desired

angle until it cools enough to hold its set. After this forming is finished, the longitudinal seams are welded to complete the fabrication.

Welding. Following layout, cutting and forming, the ducts and fittings must be welded. Welding of PVC is the most important single step to be mastered by the sheet metal mechanic. The quality of the duct section or fitting depends on the quality of the weld.

As mentioned earlier, a thermoplastic is capable of being remelted and fused. This property enables the mechanic to weld PVC. Thermosetting plastics cannot be welded. In welding, two edges of PVC are fused together with a filler rod or welding rod also fused into the joint. Besides round rods, triangular rods or flat strips may also be used. Figure 18-2 shows various types of welds using round and triangular welding rods. Fig. 18-3 shows a high-speed welding tool applying a plastic strip to join two sheets of plastic.

Plastic welding guns are light with air-cooled handles. Since plastic welders create no sparks, masks or helmets are not required. However, plastics should

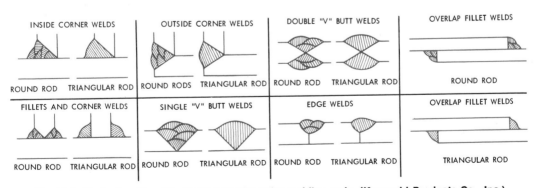

Fig. 18-2. Typical welds with round and triangular welding rods. (Kamweld Products Co., Inc.)

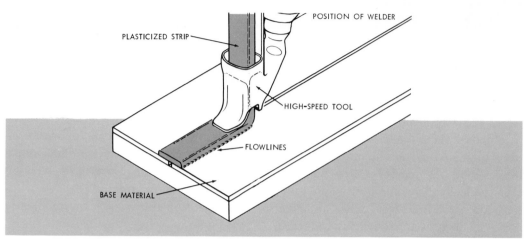

POSITION OF WELDER

PLASTICIZED STRIP

HIGH-SPEED TOOL

FLOWLINES

BASE MATERIAL

Fig. 18-3. High-speed welding gun using flat plasticized strip. (Kamweld Products Co., Inc.)

be welded only in well-ventilated areas. Within the gun, compressed air or inert gas passes over an electrical heating element and is directed through the nozzle and out the welding tip or tool. Fig. 18-4 shows the operation of a welding gun. The temperature of the gas leaving the gun can vary from 400° F to 900° F depending on the wattage of the heating element. When welding PVC, a 350 or 450 watt element is used, and the welding temperature is about 500° F. Regulating the pressure of the gas entering the gun controls the flow through the gun, and thus the welding temperature of the air or gas can be controlled.

PVC base and rod are heated simultaneously and fused. The heated air stream must be carefully controlled to allow just enough heat penetration to melt the pieces without burning them and at the same time assure enough heat penetration so that proper fusion does occur. This delicate balance is attained by a combination of precision welding torch and tips and the positioning of the gun by the sheet metal mechanic.

Preparing the Joint. As a preparatory step to welding, the joint must be shaped by beveling the edges to be joined. This joint design combined with a good weld makes the strongest and best appearing joint. The edges of the base material should be beveled so that when they are butted together they form a maximum angle of 60 degrees. Fig. 18-5 shows the correct angle. A larger angle will require too many passes of welding rod to fill the gap and increase the possibility of a faulty pass and, consequently, a poor joint.

Tack Welding. After the joint has been beveled to approximately 60 degrees, it is ready for the tack weld. Tack welding in PVC serves the same purpose as in metal welding, that is, it holds the materials together during assembly until the permanent weld may be made. After tack welding, the finish weld is applied to the joint.

Tack welding is accomplished by using a special tip on the welding gun. The tacking tip is designed to apply a stream of hot gas at very close range

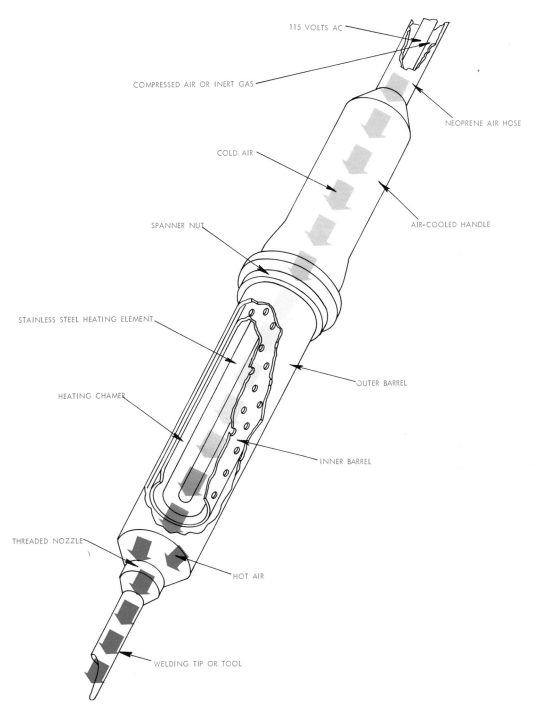

115 VOLTS AC

COMPRESSED AIR OR INERT GAS

NEOPRENE AIR HOSE

COLD AIR

AIR-COOLED HANDLE

SPANNER NUT

STAINLESS STEEL HEATING ELEMENT

OUTER BARREL

HEATING CHAMER

INNER BARREL

THREADED NOZZLE

HOT AIR

WELDING TIP OR TOOL

Fig. 18-4. Plastics welding gun. Compressed air or inert gas is forced through the gun and over a heating element. The hot air leaves the nozzle at the lower end of the barrel and passes through the tip or tool to heat the base plastic and welding rod or strip simultaneously. (Kamweld Products Co., Inc.)

267

Fig. 18-5. The edges of the sheets are beveled at 30°. When they are butted together, they form a maximum angle of 60°.

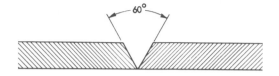

Fig. 18-6. Combination welding and tacking tip eliminates the need for changing tips. (Laramy Products Co., Inc.)

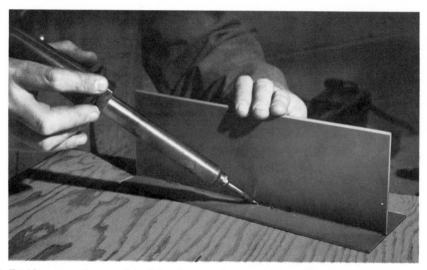

Fig. 18-7. Tacking operation used to join pieces prior to actual welding. (Laramy Products Co., Inc.)

onto the two pieces to be joined. The end of the tip on the top side has an extended tail. This extension is used to press the softened materials together, thereby assisting the fusion process. Figure 18-6 shows a tack welding tip and Fig. 18-7 shows the tack welding step.

The tack weld is very weak and can be split or broken easily. Because it is weak, pieces that are tacked together awaiting finished welds must be handled carefully. On the other hand, if a mistake is discovered in assembly, the tack weld can be quickly broken without destroying the materials. The tack weld is often made the entire length of the seam or joint. This practice, however, is not always necessary, since tack welding

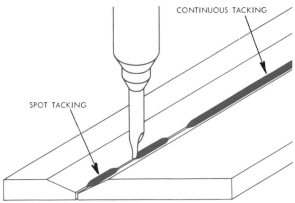

CONTINUOUS TACKING

SPOT TACKING

Fig. 18-8. At times continuous tacking is necessary. Often spot tacking will suffice. No welding rod is used for tacking, only a special tip. (Kamweld Products Co., Inc.)

Fig. 18-9. Round hand welding tip. (Kamweld Products Co., Inc.)

is for assembly and alignment only and not for strength. Fig. 18-8 shows a sample of continuous welding and spot welding.

Hand Welding. After tack welding, the joint is ready for either of two types of finish weld. The hand weld is slow to apply, but it usually results in a nearly perfect weld. The average welding speed for this type of welding is 6 to 8 inches per minute. Hand welding requires a great deal of concentration by the mechanic as he is applying the rod to the joint. To make this weld skillfully, practice and patience are needed in acquiring

the proper touch. The hand weld is accomplished by using a dual purpose tacking and welding tip or a round tip on the welding gun. Fig. 18-6 shows a dual purpose tip; Fig. 18-9 shows a round tip used for hand welding. The round tip is very similar to a tacking tip except it does not have the tail of the tacking tip. It is designed also to direct a stream of hot gas onto a closely confined area.

In hand welding, the mechanic must manipulate the gun in such a manner as to soften both pieces of material plus the welding rod just enough to fuse the ma-

269

Fig. 18-10. Using a combination welding and tacking tip to hand weld a joint. (Laramy Products Co., Inc.)

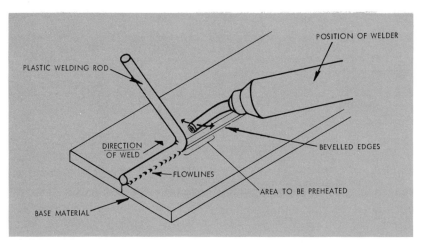

Fig. 18-11. Diagram showing the hand welding operation using a round tip. (Kamweld Products Co., Inc.)

terials. Too little heat will result in a cold weld which is not properly fused. Too much heat will cause burning. In either case the result is a weak, improper weld.

To hand weld, direct the gun into the joint, while holding the welding rod 90° to the materials being joined as shown in Figs. 18-10 and 18-11. Move the gun in a careful fanning motion that keeps both pieces and the welding rod heated to the softened or fusing state. At the same time apply a small amount of downward pressure to the welding rod. This pressure aids the fusing of the rod into the two pieces being welded and moves the whole welding procedure down the length of the joint.

It is important to keep continuous pressure on the rod during the entire weld. If the hand holding the rod must be changed as the rod is fed down, place the third and fourth fingers of the changing hand on the finished weld just behind the point at which the rod curves into the joint. Apply pressure here while grasping the rod with thumb and forefinger. It is possible to touch the rod at the weld due to the low conductivity of PVC and because the rod is heated only on the underside.

In joining one rod to another on a long weld, stop before the rod is too short to hold. At a 60° angle cut off the rod with a sharp knife or snips where the rod contacts the sheet. Cut the new rod at 60° so that it will match the first rod and maintain the round rod configuration. Join the two rods with hot air.

To complete the weld, quickly heat the area of contact between the rod and the sheet. Remove the heat while maintaining a downward pressure on the rod until the weld cools. Then either twist the rod until it breaks or cut the rod with wire snips.

On a good PVC weld there should be no evidence of brown coloration or wrinkles, which indicate overheating. The lines of contact with the sheet on either side of the rod should show a closed, smooth blend of plastic. The rod should not be drawn thinner or compressed much wider than its original form. If the length of the rod has varied more than 10% of its original length, the weld will be weak. The weld bead should appear flattened slightly by comparison with the original round shape of the rod; if the rod appears to be lying on the sheet without any fusion and in its exact round form, insufficient heat is indicated, and the rod may be pulled up with little effort. A good weld will show small flow lines or ripples on either side of the weld where the pressure and heat have caused the PVC rod and base material to soften and fuse.

Speed Welding. Because labor costs for hand welding joints in a duct system were greatly increasing total costs for the fabrication of PVC, an improved method was essential. Speed welding was made possible by the development of the speed welding tip.

Speed welding produces a sound weld about six times faster than a hand weld when applied by a competent mechanic. An average welding rate with the speed tip is about three feet per minute. Speed welding requires less concentration by the welder and, therefore, is not as tiring. In addition it does not require one hand to hold the rod while the weld is being applied. Like the other tips, the speed tip is made so that a stream of hot gas is applied to the materials being welded. The added feature is the tube along the top edge of the tip that holds a length of welding rod. See Fig. 18-12.

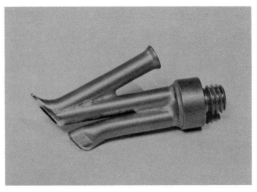

Fig. 18-12. Speed welding tip. (Laramy Products Co., Inc.)

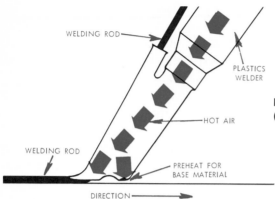

WELDING ROD

PLASTICS WELDER

HOT AIR

WELDING ROD

PREHEAT FOR BASE MATERIAL

DIRECTION

Fig. 18-13. Operation of high-speed welding tool. (Kamweld Products Co., Inc.)

A small orifice in the hot gas tube directs a small stream of hot gas against the bottom of the welding rod just before the rod comes in contact with the softened materials being welded. See Fig. 18-13. The weight of the gun and the welder's hand create all the pressure needed to properly fuse the rod and the two pieces together.

This method of welding is well suited to long, straight seams, curved seams on large diameter ducts, or any seam where the piece being welded can be rolled or turned to keep the seam in a comfortable position for the welder. The tip does not lend itself to tight quarters such as the bottom inside corner of a tank or square back elbow.

To start a weld with the speed tip, hold the gun at 90° to the surface of the sheet. Then insert the rod in the tip until it contacts the materials being welded, as in Fig. 18-14, left. The gun is then repositioned so that the tip is in the

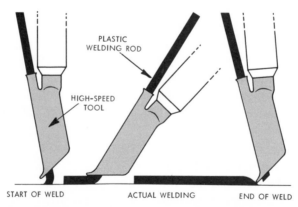

PLASTIC WELDING ROD

HIGH-SPEED TOOL

START OF WELD   ACTUAL WELDING   END OF WELD

Fig. 18-14. Positioning the high-speed welding gun for starting, welding, and ending the weld. (Kamweld Products Co., Inc.)

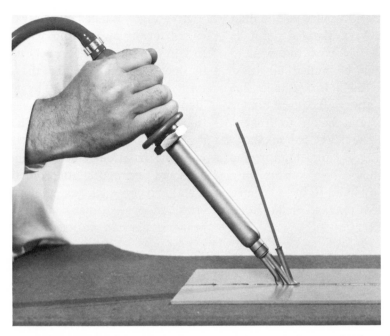

Fig. 18-15. A speed-welding tip used to make a production weld. (Laramy Products Co., Inc.)

weld position on the joint. See Fig. 18-14, center. The rod is fed through the tip for the first inch or two of the weld to be sure it is started properly. After the weld is properly started, the rod will feed automatically as the gun is moved along the joint. See Fig. 18-15. The rod must not be restricted so that it cannot slip through the tube easily as the weld proceeds down the joint.

To finish off a weld, use the tail at the end of the speed tip to pinch off the rod where it is soft and fused into the welded materials, Fig. 18-14, right. A wire snips may also be used to cut the welding rod at the desired location.

Installation Connections

In addition to welding as just discussed, there are several other methods of joining PVC duct sections.

Cementing. Cementing is the application of a solvent cement to the surfaces of the materials to be joined. Solvent cementing cannot be used to join butted pieces as on a longitudinal duct seam. It can only be used where there will be considerable surface to surface contact with a good tight fit. The solvents in the cement produce a surface reaction that dissolves the PVC. The surfaces are placed in contact with each other, solvents evaporate, the reaction stops and the PVC hardens to its original state. Particular care must be exercized that the solvent does not set up in any area prior to mating of the parts.

Bolting. PVC duct sections and fittings can be fitted with flanges so that bolted joints result. The flanges can be flat stock welded at 90° to the duct material, or they can be fabricated from

PVC angle stock and welded to the duct or fitting. Usually, a flanged joint is gasketed with flexible PVC material so that the bolts can be pulled up tight enough to seal the joint. Large flat washers should always be used under both the bolt head and the nut to prevent undue stress on the PVC flange material. When making a flanged joint, the bolts and nuts should be taken up only a little tighter than hand tight to be sure that the PVC is not cracked or damaged by excessive tightening.

Riveting. When PVC first came into use, a means of riveting was employed to join materials. It is rarely used today in duct systems because the resulting joint is not very tight. The method is identical to riveting sheet metal, except that PVC rivets are used. The type of rivet is a self-expanding type that can be installed from one side of a sheet using a special pneumatic gun. Sometimes soft metal rivets such as aluminum pop rivets, copper tinner's rivets, or split brass rivets can be used to join PVC.

Fabricating Thermosets

In the sheet metal shop, the fabrication or manufacturing of ductwork and fittings from thermosetting plastics is more difficult than thermoplastics. As outlined earlier, the basic forms of thermoplastics—sheets, angles, tubes, pipe, etc.—are common in sheet metal and are familiar to the mechanic. These forms and shapes can be worked with some sheet metal equipment and machinery such as a squaring shear, hand brake, saber saw, band saw and layout bench. In contrast, none of the techniques, tools or equipment used in sheet metal fabrication can be used to produce ductwork and fittings from thermosets.

Because the plastic resins used in thermosetting material are expensive, filler materials are used to build up the wall thickness of ductwork. The most common filler is fiberglas cloth or mat. Sometimes asbestos or synthetic fibers are used for the same purpose. In addi-

tion to functioning as a filler, fiberglas adds considerable strength to the product. This type of ductwork is referred to as fiberglas reinforced plastic or FRP.

The fabricating process involves three steps. First, the inside layer of plastic material about $\frac{1}{32}$ inch thick is applied to the mandrel or other form. It contains a very high percent (about 90) of resin to withstand the corrosive attack of the fumes to be conveyed in the duct system. Second, a layer of fiberglas mat or cloth saturated with resin is applied over the first layer. It contains about 75% resin to maintain high corrosion resistance. Additional layers may be added as required to build up the wall to the specified thickness. Finally, a reinforcing layer of woven glass cloth and 60% resin is applied.

The manufacturing methods are complicated and often require special and expensive equipment. As a result, most sheet metal shops purchase duct and fittings prefabricated from companies that specialize in manufacturing FRP products. In the form of prefabricated duct components, FRP is easy to assemble and install. Certain fittings such as tees, bevels, offsets, and elbows can be field fabricated from duct sections by cutting the duct to the proper gores required and assembled with a field "weld" kit. Figure 18-16 shows the six steps required to fabricate a 90° elbow from a section of straight, round duct.

The process of making a joint (Steps 4 to 6 in Fig. 18-16) is also used to make a field connection when installing FRP duct work. Sometimes duct sections and fittings are manufactured with flanges so that field installation can be accomplished with bolted, gasketed joints. Flanges are usually very expensive in FRP material and therefore not used extensively.

Compared to thermoplastics, FRP has three characteristics that make it better suited to corrosive exhaust systems. First, it has higher temperature ranges, and resistance to a wide variety of chemicals, including solvents. Second, it has high impact resistance and mechanical strength. Third, it is rigid and lightweight, requiring less support and hangers than other plastic materials.

However, FRP has two disadvantages inherent in thermosetting materials. First, the material cannot be welded. It can be cemented with special cements or joined by the method outlined in Fig. 18-16. However, both methods require a lengthy set period for the joint to harden and gain sufficient strength for further handling. Second, the material cannot be reworked. If a mistake is made fabricating a fitting or ordering a duct size or setting a bevel, the labor and material are lost.

Conclusion

As stated in the beginning of this chapter, plastics are used in many areas of our lives today. With each passing year more applications for plastics are discovered, better methods of working the materials are found, and improved materials are developed. Nowhere is this more evident than in the sheet metal industry where all components in an entire air handling system are now produced from plastics.

These components include round and rectangular ductwork, an infinite variety of hoods, centrifugal and in-line exhaust fans, fume scrubbers, tanks, stacks and all accessories that make up an exhaust system. A number of industries that use or produce corrosive chemicals in their own manufacturing process use such systems. Examples of some of these industries include aerospace, chemical, steel mills, metal treating and finishing, paper mills, fertilizer, plastics, pharmaceutical, paints, and oil refining, to name a few. In addition, research and development firms, hospitals, medical laboratories, and educational institutions are using plastics to control corrosion in laboratory fume hood exhaust systems.

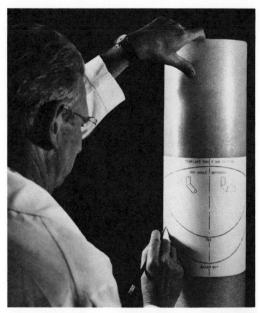

Step 1. Trace ready-to-use template supplied by manufacturer, or make paper template for fast pattern layout.

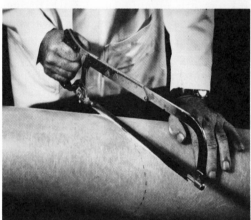

Step 2. Use a hacksaw to start the cut.

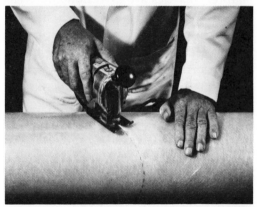

Step 3. Complete the cut with a saber saw.

Fig. 18-16. Working with thermoset tubing. (Apex Fibre-Glass Products Div. of White Consolidated Industries, Inc.)

Step 4. Rough the surface area about 1" in width around the cut with coarse sandpaper and clean it with lacquer thinner or naphtha.

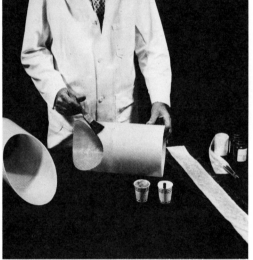

Step 5. Mix resin and a hardener together with a smooth, fold-over action to avoid trapping air bubbles.

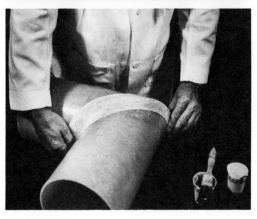

Step 6. Cut a strip of fiberglas cloth large enough to completely cover the joint. Apply the hardening mixture to the tape, wrap it around the joint, and press it with a wood spatula to insure proper resin impregnation. You can achieve more smoothness and even impregnation if you place a strip of cellophane or polyethylene film over the tape before you press it with a spatula. The resin will cure in a few hours at room temperature. The curing process can be speeded up to 15 minutes by the use of an infrared heat lamp placed no closer than 18" to the joint. After curing, the joint may be sanded, feather edged, primed and painted. It is worked as though it were wood or metal.

Fig. 18-16. (Continued)

In all of these applications the sheet metal mechanic will be involved with the fabrication and/or the installation of the system. In order to do his job properly, he must know the material, its advantages and limitations, so that the material is not misapplied or carelessly handled. He must also have a sound understanding of how the materials are worked, to assure a quality system at the lowest possible cost.

Shop Activities

Practicing Stringer Welds on PVC Sheet

1. *Cut a piece of ⅛″ PVC plastic sheet about 12″ × 12″.*
2. *Obtain a piece of ⅛″ diameter PVC plastic welding rod of the same material composition as sheet to be welded.*
3. *Cut the tip of the welding rod at a 60° angle.*
4. *Run a bead with the welding rod the length of the sheet, as described in this chapter. At the end of the weld, leave about 1″ of welding rod sticking up in a vertical position.*

5. *After the weld has thoroughly cooled, try to pull the welding rod away from the sheet with a pair of pliers. If the rod separates from the sheet, it indicates an improper bond. Compare your bead with the cross sections in Fig. 18-17 to determine the reason for failure.*
6. *Continue running stringer beads until they show the proper fusion between rod and sheet. With proper fusion, the rod will break at the end of the weld, not pull away from the sheet.*

	CONDITIONS ROD	SHEET	APPEARANCE	RESULTS
A	COLD	COLD		NO BOND
B	HOT	COLD		POOR BOND ON SHEET
C	COLD	HOT		POOR BOND ON ROD
D	HOT	HOT		ROD AND SHEET OVERHEATED—DECOMPOSED
E	OK	OK		GOOD WELD

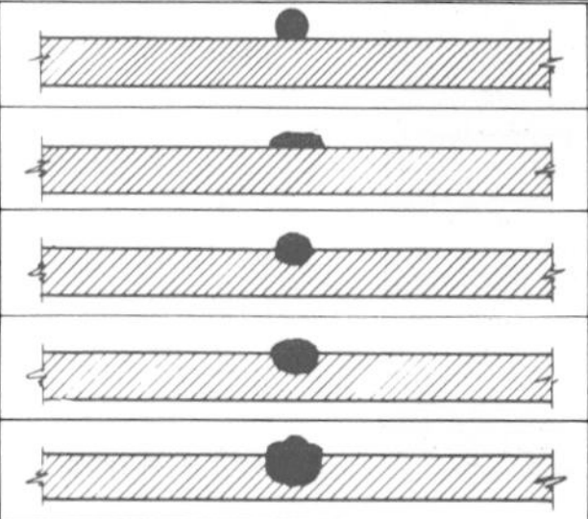

Fig. 18-17. Analysis of "stringer" bead trial welds.

Checking Elongation of the Welding Rod when Welding Plastic Sheet

1. *Measure exactly 5″ from one end of the welding rod and make a small scratch at this point.*
2. *Run a stringer bead on a sheet of plastic using only the marked 5″ of the rod.*
3. *Measure the distance of the stringer bead on the sheet.*
4. *If the stringer bead is longer than 5″, the rod has elongated during the welding.*
5. *Continue practicing in this manner until the length of the finished stringer bead measures the same as the marked rod before welding. A 10% difference in the two is the maximum allowable. In 5″, 10% would be ½″.*

Practicing Manipulation of the Welding Rod and Hot Air Torch

1. *Cut a sheet of ⅛″ PVC plastic approximately 12″ × 12″.*
2. *With a pair of dividers, draw a circle approximately 7″ in diameter on the sheet.*
3. *Run a stringer bead with ⅛″ welding rod around this circle and continue the bead in a spiral inside the circle by joining new rod. Do not move the sheet. The purpose of this circular welding is to have you practice manipulating the torch and the rod in any manner required of you in order to weld a variety of components.*

Running Straight Welds

1. *Cut four pieces of 3/16″ plastic sheet 4″ wide and 6″ long.*
2. *Bevel the 6″ edges of each piece*

to 30°. This means that when the beveled edges of both sheets are butted together the total included angle will be 60° maximum.

3. *Clamp the two sheets together so that the beveled edges form a butt joint with a gap of approximately 1/64″.*
4. *Set and adjust a hot air welding torch so that the temperature ¼″ from the nozzle is 550°.*
5. *Tack weld the seam. Next, run one bead in the bottom of the 60° groove using a ⅛″ diameter rod.*
6. *Using a 5/32″ diameter rod, run two welds side by side over the first weld. No gap or groove should be visible where the welding rod fuses with the sheets.*
7. *Compare your weld with the cross sections in Fig. 18-18.*
8. *When the weld cools, carefully try to break it with your hands. If the weld does not break, it is a solid weld. If the weld breaks, examine the break for indications of the reasons for a poor bond. Normally, the reason for breaking, is a poor bond between the sheet and the rod.*

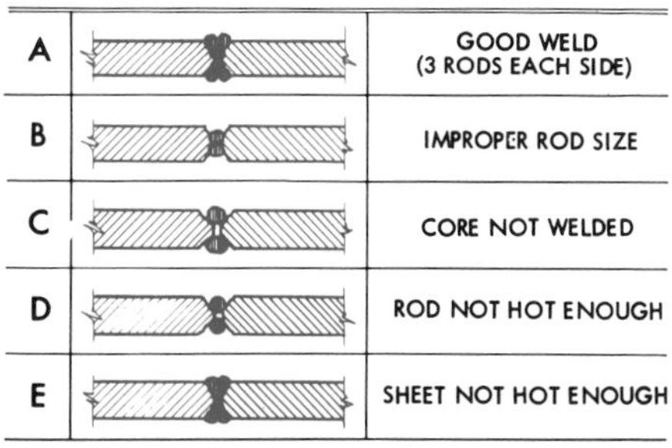

A		GOOD WELD (3 RODS EACH SIDE)
B		IMPROPER ROD SIZE
C		CORE NOT WELDED
D		ROD NOT HOT ENOUGH
E		SHEET NOT HOT ENOUGH

Fig. 18-18. Cross-sections of PVC welds.

9. *If the weld does not break, cut the sheet into two pieces using a band-saw. Make the cut at right angles to the weld. File the cut surface* smooth at the weld and examine it for traces of poor bonding.
10. *Repeat welding and testing with the other test pieces.*

STUDENT QUESTIONS AND ACTIVITIES

1. Explain the difference between thermosetting and thermoforming plastics.
2. Define the following terms:
   a. Plasticizers
   b. Solvents
   c. Catalysts
3. What do the letters PVC signify?
4. List some of the limitations of PVC.
5. List some of the advantages of PVC.
6. What is the difference between Type I and Type II PVC?
7. In outline form, list the steps required to make a round pipe from PVC plastic.
8. How are PVC joints prepared for welding?
9. What is tack welding?
10. What are the characteristics of a good PVC weld?
11. What is the "speed tip" used in plastic welding?

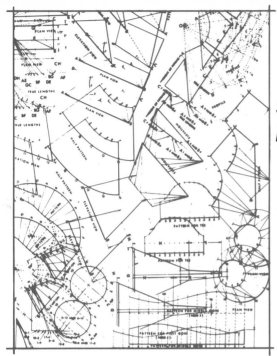

short method of pattern development

When you complete this chapter, you should be able to develop a pattern for any cone, square taper, square to round, or round pipe fitting using the *rollation* method of layout.

In sheet metal work, as in most trades, there are short cuts used in the shop to save time. The short method of pattern development, often called the *rollation* method, is one of these. No extensive knowledge of geometry, drafting, or mathematics is involved in rollation, so it may be employed by apprentices and craftsmen alike. However, it must be considered as a supplement to regular drafting procedures rather than as a substitute for them. Through experience, the sheet metal worker learns the layout approach which is best suited to a particular problem and uses that method for the job.

Rollation is most valuable on jobs where a high degree of accuracy is *not* required and where speed is.

Fundamentals of Short Method Pattern Development

Most sheet metal patterns employ such geometric forms as squares, rectangles, cylinders, and funnels. Therefore, let us examine the short method by applying it to one such form, a simple funnel of the type shown in Fig. 19-1. Viewing the funnel, it is obvious that a pattern for half of the funnel will be the same as other half in reverse.

The short method consists of making a template as shown in Fig. 19-1. The template consists of the side view of the fitting and the top and bottom profiles. The curved edges of the profiles describe the outside edges of the top and bottom of the funnel. Therefore, if this template is rolled on a piece of paper, the shape

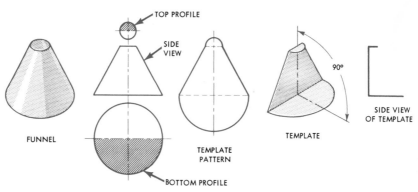

Fig. 19-1. Steps in making a template for a simple funnel pattern.

that these curved edges describe is half of the pattern, as shown in Fig. 19-2. *It should be noted that the absence of symmetry in the object to be made is not a limiting factor in using the short method.* A template may be designed from an off-center pattern, a number of templates may be used, or the template pattern may be used for only one-half of the whole layout and another template used for the other half. However, rollation is generally used on symmetrical objects, since off-center patterns can usually be developed as fast by other methods.

The essence of the short method, therefore, is the design of the half-pattern template. Once ability to visualize the finished product and express it in these terms has been developed, even the most complex job can be laid out quickly and accurately.

Once this template is completed, the edges are chalked and the template is rolled over a sheet of soft black building paper, leaving a clear white outline. An alternate method by which a clear pattern may be obtained is to dip the edge of the template in oil and roll it over the paper.

Another common method is to roll the template slowly over the paper marking the contact points of both profiles with the paper with pencil as it is rolled. This

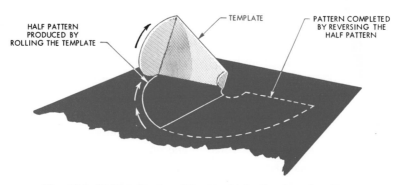

Fig. 19-2. Rolling the template to obtain the funnel pattern.

produces a series of pencil marks that then can be drawn into a smooth curve with a flexible rule.

Important Points to Remember When Using the Short Method

1. *Patterns developed by the short method do not include allowance for seams or for soldering.* Be sure to take this into account and make the necessary additions before cutting the metal.

2. *In order to produce an accurate pattern, the ends of the template must be bent accurately.* Templates for larger patterns should be made of heavier gage metal and reinforced with metal braces or blocks of wood. This is also true for lighter or smaller templates that will be used often.

3. *Remember that the template produces only one-half of the pattern for the final product.* If a full pattern is desired, the template must be reversed and matched before using for the pattern.

4. *Some more complex patterns do not have clearly indicated lines at the points where bends are to be made.* Be sure that these lines are clearly marked on the final pattern during the process of rolling the template.

A Brief Review of the Short Method Process

The finished sheet metal object is visualized by the worker in terms of its geometric construction. The basic geometric form is graphically shown in halves and these halves are combined to make the template. This is shown in Fig. 19-1. The template is then chalked or oiled on its edges and rolled over a piece of paper, as shown in Fig. 19-2. Finally, the half-pattern which results from these operations is reversed and matched, producing the whole pattern.

Representative Applications of the Short Method

At the outset, it is strongly recommended that you try to develop some of the patterns from beginning to end while studying those illustrated in Figs. 19-3, 19-4, 19-5, and 19-6. This is the best means by which to determine those

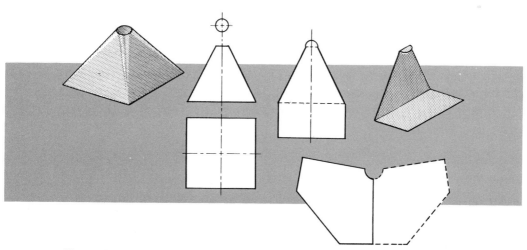

Fig. 19-3. Short method of pattern development for a square-to-round fitting.

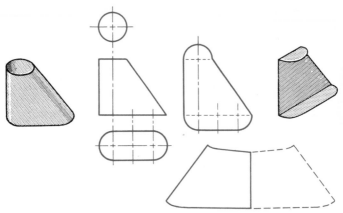

Fig. 19-4. Short method of pattern development for an offcenter oval-to-round fitting.

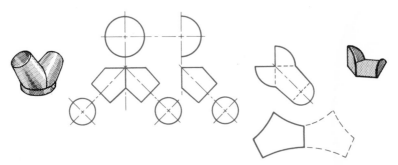

Fig. 19-5. Short method of pattern development for a Y fitting.

forms which lend themselves to the short method of pattern development. The illustrations in Figs. 19-3, 19-4, 19-5, and 19-6 show some representative types of patterns encountered in sheet metal work which may be developed by the short method. They are more complex than the layout for the simple funnel, but apply the same operations previously described.

Making an Adjustable Template Holder

An adjustable template holder, such as the one shown in Fig. 19-6 will save a great deal of time when making templates. A large variety of templates can be attached and changed for a variety of different sizes and shapes. The body is a two-piece slide to provide for different lengths.

For work involving templates up to 12″ in diameter, a good holder is 24″ × 4″ with an 18″ slide. It should be made of at least 24-gage galvanized metal. For templates measuring more than 12″ in diameter, a bigger and heavier holder is recommended.

There are three important points to remember when using an adjustable template holder:

1.   *The templates must be securely in place.* To prevent slipping, holes should be made in the holder and template so

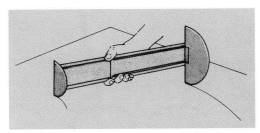

Fig. 19-6. Using an adjustable template holder.

that the templates are held by metal screws.

2. Make sure that the master templates are flat. Slight variations will result in large inaccuracies.

3. The master templates must be at right angles to the holder during the rolling process.

Class Activities

1. *Draw a plan and elevation view of an object that can be made from sheet metal. Exchange your drawing with that of another student in the class. Draw the proper template for the plan and elevation view shown. Then discuss it with the other student to determine if the template is correct.*

2. *Make detailed plans for an adjustable template holder as shown in Fig. 19-7. Assign two class members to make the holder and other members to make templates to use in it.*

3. *Design other methods of making templates and holders using the principles explained in this chapter.*

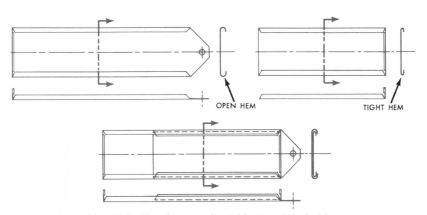

OPEN HEM

TIGHT HEM

Fig. 19-7. Plan for an adjustable template holder.

STUDY GUIDE

1. How much of the final pattern is usually obtained by rolling the template?
2. At what angle are the ends of a template ordinarily bent prior to rolling?
3. How is the template pattern transferred to paper?
4. Why should larger templates be reinforced?

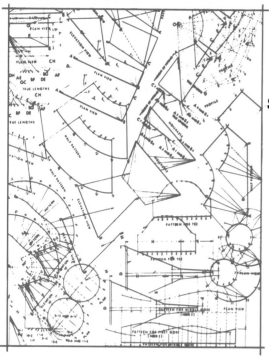

supplementary projects

20

Project 1. Tool Tray

1. The dimensions of the tray can be made to any size desired.
2. Determine the dimensions.
3. On paper, draw a full size end view to the dimensions desired. If the dimensions chosen prove to be of pleasing proportions, turn the drawing in to the instructor for his approval. Suggested dimensions for a standard tray are: Length 16″; Width 8″; Height 4″; and Top 3″.
4. Lay out the end pattern on 16 gage galvanized steel. Mark a second pattern from the first. Cut and notch both pieces.
5. Lay out the pattern for the bottom and sides using 26 gage galvanized steel. Cut out and notch.

6. Bend the 1/4″ edges of the ends. Make the bends in the following order: side, bottom side.
7. Bend the bottom and side pattern. Bend in the following order: Pittsburgh seams, double hems, side bends.
8. Set ends into Pittsburgh seams and knock over the seam edge.
9. Solder the seams of the tool tray on the inside of the tray.
10. Lay out the handle pattern, cut out, punch rivet holes and bend. Bend the long bends on the brake. Bend the short end bends with pliers or on a pan brake.
11. Clamp the handle into position; mark and drill the rivet holes through the ends of the tray.
12. Insert the rivets from the outside and rivet the handle in place.

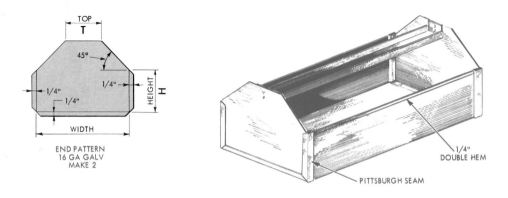

TOP
T

45°

1/4" 1/4" HEIGHT H

1/4"

WIDTH

END PATTERN
16 GA GALV
MAKE 2

1/4"
DOUBLE HEM

PITTSBURGH SEAM

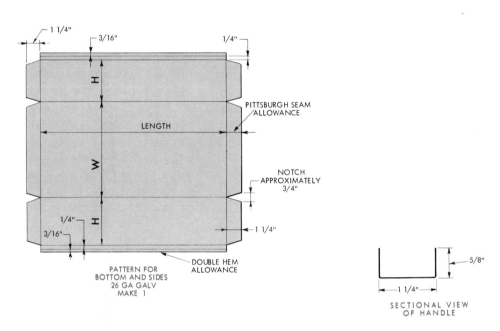

1 1/4"

3/16" 1/4"

H

PITTSBURGH SEAM
ALLOWANCE

LENGTH

W

NOTCH
APPROXIMATELY
3/4"

1/4" H

1 1/4"

3/16"

DOUBLE HEM
ALLOWANCE

PATTERN FOR
BOTTOM AND SIDES
26 GA GALV
MAKE 1

5/8"

1 1/4"

SECTIONAL VIEW
OF HANDLE

NOTES:

1. ENDS OF 16 GAGE GALVANIZED IRON

2. BOTTOM AND SIDES OF 26 GAGE GALVANIZED IRON

3. HANDLE OF 16 GAGE GALVANIZED IRON

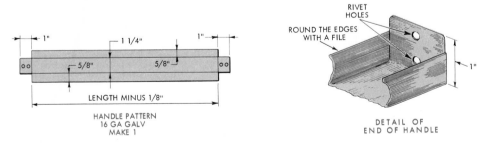

1" 1 1/4" 1"

5/8" 5/8"

LENGTH MINUS 1/8"

HANDLE PATTERN
16 GA GALV
MAKE 1

RIVET
HOLES

ROUND THE EDGES
WITH A FILE

1"

DETAIL OF
END OF HANDLE

Project 1. Making a tool tray.

Project 2. Bucket

1. Lay out the pattern for the bucket bottom. Dimensions must be exact.
2. Cut out the bucket bottom pattern. Cut roughly about 1/2″ away from the line the first time. Then trim on the line. The success of this project depends upon accuracy in patterns and in cutting. Be sure that the distance from *A* to *B* is *exactly* equal to the circumference of a 8-1/4″ circle.
3. Lay out the pattern for the sides. Cut out and notch.
4. Bend 1/4″ edges for the groove seam. Note that though 3/8″ was allowed for the seam only 1/4″ is bent.
5. Form the side on rolls and complete groove seam.
6. Solder groove seam on inside, but leave the last 1/2″ at each end of the seam unsoldered so that the solder does not interfere with the burring machine operation.
7. On burring machine, turn the 3/16″ edge on the bottom of the side pattern. Bend to the outside. *Do not* bend to a complete 90° angle. Bend to about 60°.
8. On the burring machine, bend the 5/32″ edge on the bottom pattern to a 90° angle.
9. Hook the bottom over the bottom edge of the side, as shown in Chapter 9, Fig. 3-32*C*. Clinch the edge over at about 2″ intervals to hold it in place.
10. Turn the bucket over and tap around the edge to make the 3/16″ edge bend to 90°. This will expand the diameter and make the two pieces match tightly.
11. Finish clinching the edge and complete the double seam.
12. On the turning machine turn the edge for the wired edge to 90°. Do not tighten the turning machine wheels any more than necessary or they will stretch the metal.
13. Roll a piece of 1/8″ wire in the grooves of the forming rolls so that it matches the diameter of the top of the bucket.
14. Clamp the wire in place with vise clamps and tap the metal over to hold in place. Finish the wired edge on wiring rolls.
15. Solder the inside seams of the bucket and test for leaks.
16. Make the bail ears and rivet them in place.
17. Roll the 3/16″ wire for the handle. The curve of this handle should match the curve of the top diameter of the bucket.
18. Set the handle in place and bend the wire around the bail ears.

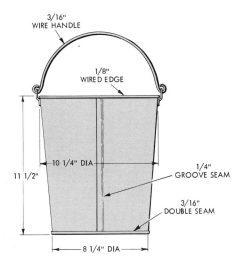

3/16"
WIRE HANDLE

1/8"
WIRED EDGE

11 1/2"

10 1/4" DIA

1/4"
GROOVE SEAM

3/16"
DOUBLE SEAM

8 1/4" DIA

5/16" HOLE

3/4"

1/2"

1/4"

1/2"

1 1/4"

3/16" OFFSET

DETAIL OF
BAIL EARS
MAKE 2

NOTES:

1. BUCKET FROM 26 GAGE GALVANIZED IRON

2. BUCKET BAIL FROM 3/16" DIAMETER WIRE

3. BAIL EARS FROM 16 GAGE GALVANIZED IRON

4. BUCKET BAIL WILL COINCIDE WITH BUCKET RIM
   WHEN LAID DOWN

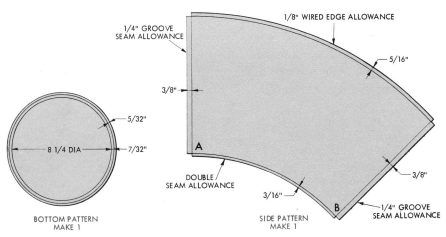

1/8" WIRED EDGE ALLOWANCE

1/4" GROOVE
SEAM ALLOWANCE

5/16"

3/8"

5/32"

7/32"

8 1/4 DIA

A

DOUBLE
SEAM ALLOWANCE

3/16"

3/8"

B

1/4" GROOVE
SEAM ALLOWANCE

BOTTOM PATTERN
MAKE 1

SIDE PATTERN
MAKE 1

Project 2. Making a bucket with a double seam bottom.

Project 3. Funnel

1. Lay out the pattern for the funnel, and cut it out.
2. Turn the 3/16" hems with the burring machine.
3. Turn the 1/4" edges for the groove seam. Note: The 3/8" dimension for the seam in the pattern allows 1/16" for the bend.
4. Roll the funnel as much as possible on the forming rolls, and finish forming on the stakes. Be careful to leave the 1/4" edges straight with no bow or bend.
5. Hook the 1/4" edges and finish the groove seam.
6. Lay out the spout pattern and cut it out.
7. Roll on forming rolls as much as possible and finish forming on stakes. Shape the spout so that the 1/4" laps over tightly and smoothly. It is *not* important to have the spout perfectly round at this time since it will be easy to round up after the 1/4" lap is soldered.
8. Solder the lap of the spout.
9. Round up the spout on the stakes.
10. Set the spout in place and tack solder. Check for straightness and finish soldering.
11. Solder the groove seam on the inside.

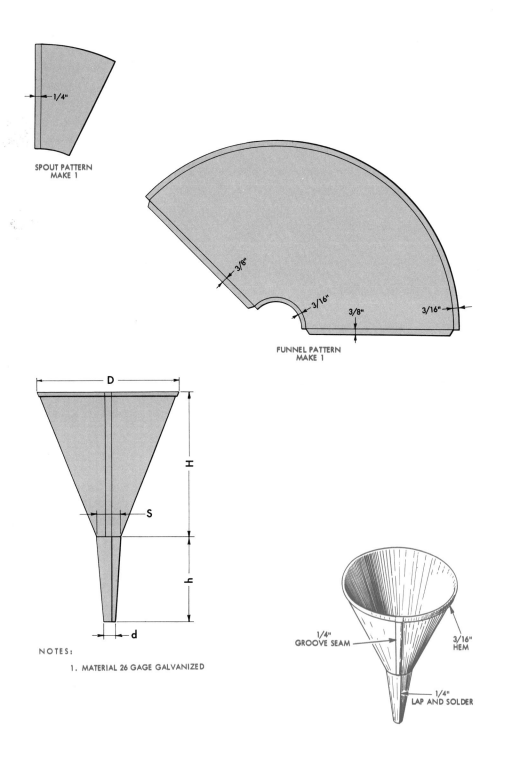

SPOUT PATTERN
MAKE 1

1/4"

3/8"

3/16"

3/8"

3/16"

FUNNEL PATTERN
MAKE 1

D

H

S

h

d

NOTES:

1. MATERIAL 26 GAGE GALVANIZED

1/4"
GROOVE SEAM

3/16"
HEM

1/4"
LAP AND SOLDER

Project 3. Making a galvanized funnel.

Project 4. Waste Basket

1. Lay out the pattern for the sides. Cut out and notch.
2. Bend the Pittsburgh seam.
3. Bend the bottom edges of the side pattern to the inside by pounding over the edge of the brake with a wooden mallet. Bend all the way over as with a hem, but do not smash down tightly.
4. Bend the 1/4″ edge for the Pittsburgh seam.
5. Bend the corners.
6. Bend the edges around the bottom pattern.
7. Make up the Pittsburgh seam, and set the bottom in place.
8. Tack solder the bottom into place. Solder all the seams on the inside.
9. Cut miters on the split pipe. Set in place and tack weld the corners of the pipe. Remove and weld the miters. (A double hem or wired edge may be used if split pipe is not available.)
10. Place the split pipe in place and tack solder underneath.

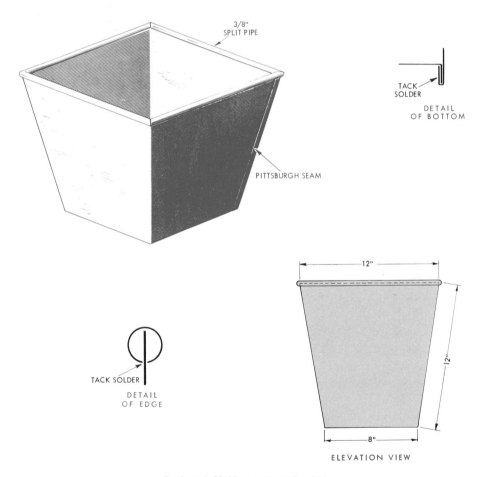

3/8″ SPLIT PIPE

TACK SOLDER

DETAIL OF BOTTOM

PITTSBURGH SEAM

TACK SOLDER

DETAIL OF EDGE

12″

12″

8″

ELEVATION VIEW

Project 4. Making a waste basket.

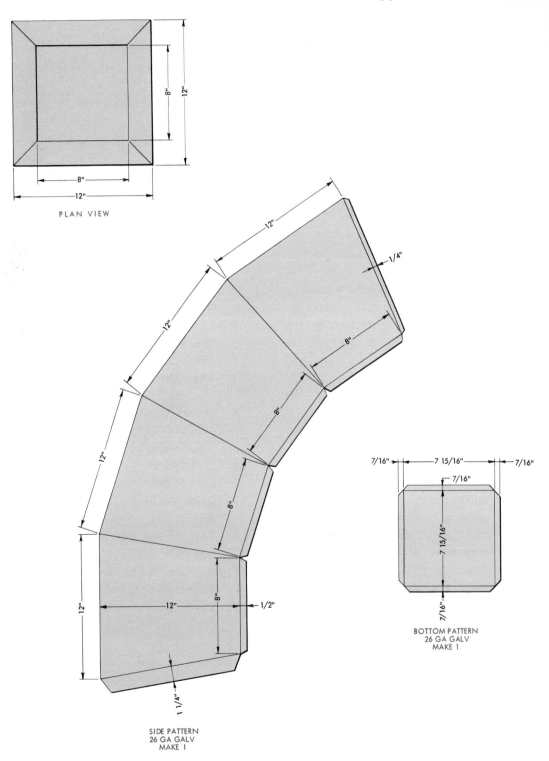

PLAN VIEW

1/4"

8"

8"

8"

8"

12"

12"

12"

12"

12"

12"

8"

1/2"

1 1/4"

SIDE PATTERN
26 GA GALV
MAKE 1

7/16" 7 15/16" 7/16"

7/16"

7 15/16"

7/16"

BOTTOM PATTERN
26 GA GALV
MAKE 1

Project 4. (continued)

Project 5. Free Form Waste Basket

1. Lay out the side pattern by triangulation. Add allowances for seams and edges. Cut out and notch.
2. Lay out the pattern for the bottom.
3. On the side pattern form the Pittsburgh seam.
4. Form the half inch bottom edge by pounding over the edge of the brake. Bend all the way over as with a hem, but do not flatten tight since the edge of the bottom must fit into this hem.
5. Starting with the quarter inch edge for the Pittsburgh seam start bending the corners of the basket. Each bend is to a 45° angle.
6. Insert the quarter inch edge into the Pittsburgh seam and finish the seam.
7. Bend the 7/16″ edges on the bottom pattern to 90°.
8. Insert the bottom into the bottom lock of the side.
9. Solder the bottom in place.
10. Cut 45° miters on the split pipe and fit into place.
11. Tack weld each miter of the split pipe.
12. Remove the split pipe frame and complete welding the miters.
13. Replace the split pipe and tack solder on the under side on the inside of the basket.

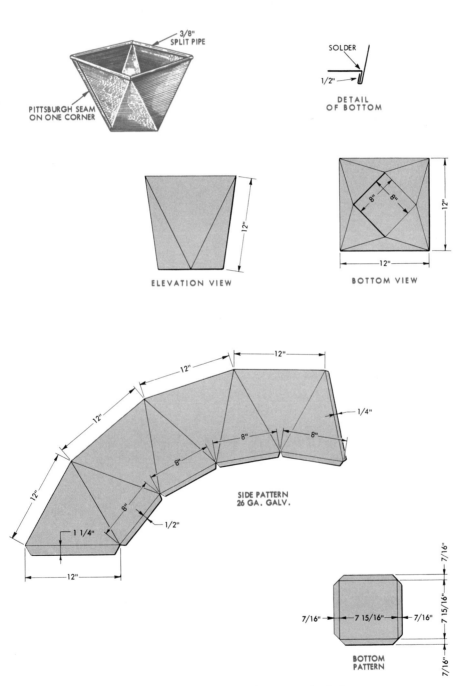

3/8"
SPLIT PIPE

SOLDER

1/2"

DETAIL
OF BOTTOM

PITTSBURGH SEAM
ON ONE CORNER

ELEVATION VIEW

12"

BOTTOM VIEW

8" 8"

12"

12"

12"

12"

12"

12"

12"

8"

8"

8"

8"

1/4"

1/2"

1 1/4"

SIDE PATTERN
26 GA. GALV.

12"

7/16"

7/16"

7/16"

7/16"

7 15/16"

7 15/16"

BOTTOM
PATTERN

Project 5. Making a free form waste basket.

Project 6. Tool Box

1. The dimensions shown for the tool box are suggested only. Dimensions may be made to any size desired. However if different dimensions are used draw a full scale end view of the tool box to see whether the dimensions are in pleasing proportions.
2. Lay out the pattern for the bottom and sides including the rivet holes.
3. Drill the rivet holes with a number 30 drill.
4. Bend the three quarter inch edges on each end of the pattern to a 90° angle.
5. On a pan brake make the quarter bends to complete the bottom and sides of the tool box.
6. Lay out the pattern for the end of the box.
7. Mark a similar pattern from the original end pattern.
8. Clamp the end pattern in place and drill rivet holes matching the ones in the bottom and side pattern.
9. Rivet the end pattern in place.
10. Complete the same operation for the other end of the box.
11. Lay out the pattern for angle stiffener and tool tray rest and mark a second one from the original.
12. Bend the angle stiffener.
13. Clamp the angle stiffener in place 1-1/4 inches below the top of the box side. Mark rivet holes

at two inch centers, drill, and rivet the angle in place.
14. Repeat for the angle on the other side of the box.
15. Lay out the pattern for lid 1 and lid 2.
16. Bend the half inch edges on each end of the pattern to 90°.
17. Bend the corner lines of the lid to a 45° angle.
18. Cut two lengths of piano hinge to fit exactly into the inside of the box.
19. Clamp the piano hinge to the inside of the box. Make sure the hinge works freely. Drill with a number 30 drill on two inch centers, and rivet in place.
20. Fasten the lid to the other side of the piano hinge with two sheet metal screws and test for proper working.
21. Repeat the above operations for the second lid.
22. If both lids work properly, mark out holes on two inch centers, drill with a number 30 drill, and rivet in place.
23. Lay out the patterns for the stiffener for lid 1 and the stiffener for lid 2. Bend as indicated on the drawings.
24. Clamp the stiffeners in place. Lay out and drill rivet holes on 2″ centers as before. Fasten temporarily with sheet metal screws. Test the lid for working operation, and rivet the stiffeners in place.
25. Lay out the patterns for the tool tray and assemble. See the instructions for Project 1 for more detailed instructions.

26. Fasten the suitcase latches and handle in place temporarily with sheet metal screws.

27. If latches and handle are working properly, rivet or bolt into place.

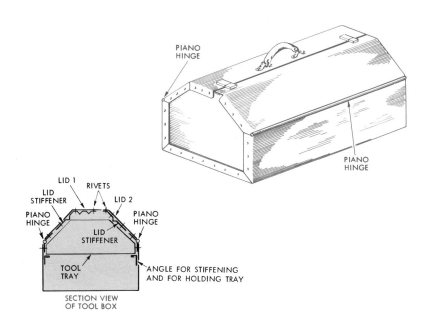

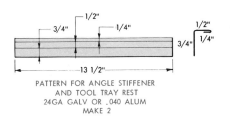

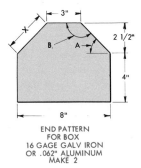

Project 6. Making a tool box.

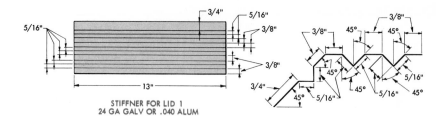

STIFFNER FOR LID 1
24 GA GALV OR .040 ALUM

STIFFENER FOR LID 2
24 GA GALV OR .040 ALUM

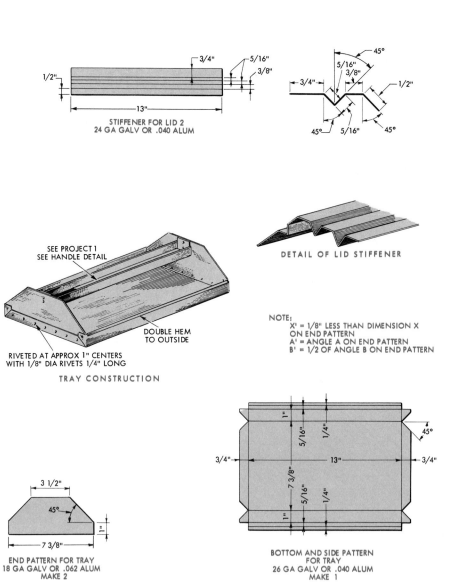

SEE PROJECT 1
SEE HANDLE DETAIL

DETAIL OF LID STIFFENER

DOUBLE HEM
TO OUTSIDE

RIVETED AT APPROX 1" CENTERS
WITH 1/8" DIA RIVETS 1/4" LONG

TRAY CONSTRUCTION

NOTE:
X' = 1/8" LESS THAN DIMENSION X
ON END PATTERN
A' = ANGLE A ON END PATTERN
B' = 1/2 OF ANGLE B ON END PATTERN

END PATTERN FOR TRAY
18 GA GALV OR .062 ALUM
MAKE 2

BOTTOM AND SIDE PATTERN
FOR TRAY
26 GA GALV OR .040 ALUM
MAKE 1

Project 6. (continued)

DETAIL OF RIVET HOLE LOCATION
AT CORNER BEND LINES

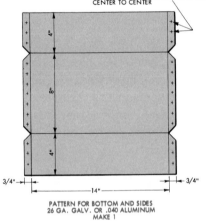

LOCATE RIVET HOLES AT CORNER BENDS
ACCORDING TO DETAIL SHOWN BELOW.
STEP OFF RIVET SPACING FROM THESE
AT EQUAL SPACES, APPROXIMATELY 1"
CENTER TO CENTER

PATTERN FOR BOTTOM AND SIDES
26 GA. GALV. OR .040 ALUMINUM
MAKE 1

NOTE:

1. DIMENSIONS SUGGESTED MAY BE CHANGED
   FOR INDIVIDUAL NEEDS

2. MATERIAL IS 26 GAGE GALVANIZED FOR
   BOTTOM AND SIDES, AND 16 GAGE
   GALVANIZED FOR ENDS. EQUIVALENT
   THICKNESS IN ALUMINUM MAY BE USED.

3. TOOL TRAY SETS INSIDE OF BOX

4. RIVETS—ALUMINUM 1/8" DIA., 1/4" LONG
   BRAZIER HEAD

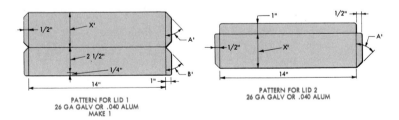

PATTERN FOR LID 1
26 GA GALV OR .040 ALUM
MAKE 1

PATTERN FOR LID 2
26 GA GALV OR .040 ALUM

Project 6. (continued)

Project 7. Pan for Small Jars to Fit between Wall Studs

1. The length of the pan will be approximately 14-1/4 inches. However this dimension must be verified by measurement taken at the spot where the pan will fit. Make the length of the pan 1/4 inch shorter than the actual distance between the studs.
2. Lay out the pattern.
3. Cut and notch the pattern, including prick marking the center holes for punching holes.
4. Punch all holes including the cleanout holes on the bottom.
5. Bend the double hems to the outside.

6. Bend the corner bends. These should be bent so that the double hems are to the outside. Make the two long corner bends first including the bends for the 1/2" flap.
7. If a pan brake is available make the short corner bends on the pan brake. Before the ends are bent up completely open the double hem slightly so that the 1/2" lap will slide underneath the hem as it is bent up.
8. If a pan brake is not available, clamp a board on each side of the metal even with the bend line and tap the metal around with a wooden mallet.
9. Solder the corner laps.

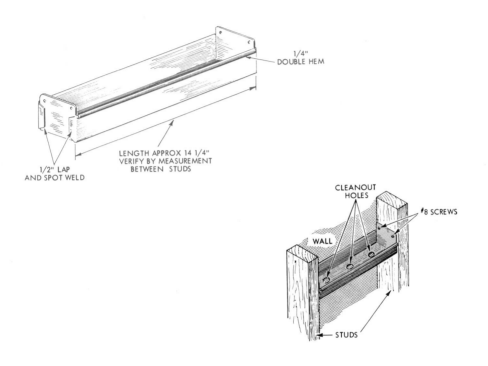

1/4"
DOUBLE HEM

1/2" LAP
AND SPOT WELD

LENGTH APPROX 14 1/4"
VERIFY BY MEASUREMENT
BETWEEN STUDS

CLEANOUT
HOLES

#8 SCREWS

WALL

STUDS

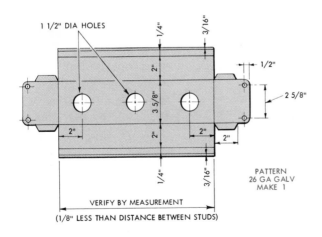

1 1/2" DIA HOLES

1/4"

3/16"

2"

1/2"

2 5/8"

3 5/8"

2"

2"

2"

2"

1/4"

3/16"

PATTERN
26 GA GALV
MAKE 1

VERIFY BY MEASUREMENT
(1/8" LESS THAN DISTANCE BETWEEN STUDS)

Project 7. Making a pan for small jars.

Project 8. Box with a Sliding Top

1. Lay out the pattern for the box. Cut out and notch as shown.
2. Bend the quarter inch hems to the outside.
3. Bend the 3/8″ edges as far over as is possible in the brake. Then insert a steel rule or a strip of 16 gage under the 3/8″ edge and smash in the brake so that a gap is left.
4. Bend both long corner bends so that the 1/2″ lap is bent with the corner bends.
5. On a pan brake bend the short corner bends, making sure that the 1/2″ laps slide in place to the outside.
6. Spot weld the half inch laps.
7. Lay out the pattern for the top. Cut and notch.
8. Bend the quarter inch hems to the outside.
9. Bend the half inch edge on end to the outside to a 90° angle.
10. Bend the 3/8″ edge on one side of the top to the inside.
11. Flatten down in the same manner as the 3/8″ edges on the box.
12. Bend the 1/2″ edge on the same side to the inside to a 90° angle. Leave the 3/8″ edge outside the brake so it is not smashed tight.
13. Repeat the above operation for the other edge of the top, making sure that none of the previously bent edges are smashed in the brake.
14. Slide the top into the lock of the box. If the top and box do not fit properly tap the edges with a hammer to adjust. Putting a small amount of beeswax or candle wax on the slide will make it work much easier.

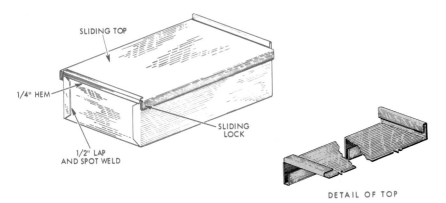

SLIDING TOP

1/4" HEM

1/2" LAP
AND SPOT WELD

SLIDING
LOCK

DETAIL OF TOP

NOTES:

1. MATERIAL 26 OR 28 GAGE GALVANIZED

2. MAKE DIMENSIONS TO SUIT

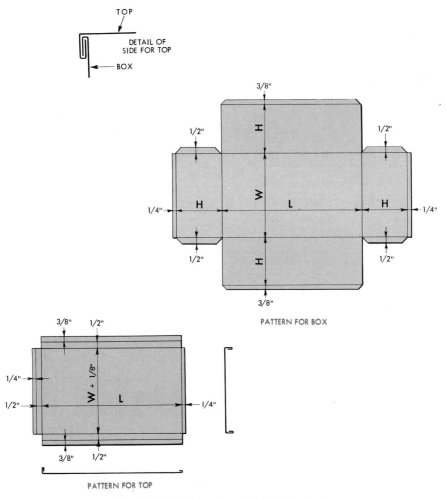

TOP

DETAIL OF
SIDE FOR TOP

BOX

PATTERN FOR BOX

PATTERN FOR TOP

Project 8. Making a box with a sliding top.

Project 9. Copper or Brass Planter with Perforated Metal Jacket

1. The dimensions given on the drawing are suggested and may be altered to suit individual taste. However care must be taken to choose dimensions that are of pleasing proportions.

2. Lay out the pattern for the box. Cut and notch.

3. Bend only the *end* 5/16″ hems to the outside, and smash down tightly in the brake. Do not mar with a hammer.

4. The 5/16″ hems on the long side should be bent over as far as possible in the brake but not smashed down.

5. Bend up the box with the 3/8″ laps on the inside.

6. Solder the box.

7. Rub the outside of the box with fine emery paper in long, straight strokes to give a brushed effect to the outside.

8. Paint or spray the outside with a clear lacquer, clear enamel, or any other clear protective material.

9. Lay out the pattern for the perforated metal sides. Be sure that there are no sharp edges on the ends of the pattern as these will be exposed. It is well to try to cut the perforated metal so that the ends are a complete straight line instead of jagged edges. If this is not possible, file all edges to prevent cutting or snagging.

10. Bend the 3/4″ edge of the metal side to a 90° angle.

11. With masking tape cover part of the 3/4″ bend. A strip about 3/8 of an inch from the metal edge should be covered to allow an unpainted edge for soldering.

12. Spray the perforated metal sides with flat black paint.

13. Slip the perforated metal sides under the open 5/16″ edge of the box being careful not to scratch the lacquered surface of the box. If the 3/4″ edge does not fit flat against the bottom of the box cut a small amount from the top of the perforated metal side.

14. Cover the 5/16″ edge with a rag to prevent scarring the metal and squeeze the 5/16″ edge down flat with tongs. Be very careful not to scar or dent the metal. After this flattening operation the 5/16″ hem may have to be sprayed again with a clear lacquer. If this is necessary lay a piece of metal over the perforated metal sides to protect them from spray. Also spray the inside of the box, especially near the top.

15. After the 5/16″ edges are smashed down turn the box over and tack solder the metal sides to the box. Be sure that the soldering is done at a point where it cannot be seen when the box is upright. Wash off all soldered joints carefully to remove any trace of acid.

16. If desired, four small rubber feet may be attached to the bottom of the planter to prevent scarring a table. An alternative method is to glue felt to the bottom of the box.

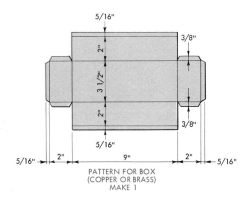

5/16"

3/8"

2"

2"

3 1/2"

2"

3/8"

5/16"

5/16" 2" 9" 2" 5/16"

PATTERN FOR BOX
(COPPER OR BRASS)
MAKE 1

1 7/8"

3/4" 9"

PATTERN FOR
PERFORATED METAL SIDES
MAKE 2
(MAKE OF ANY DESIRED DESIGN)

PERFORATED OR
DECORATIVE METAL
(EXTENDS UNDER HEM)

PLANTER
BOX

TACK SOLDER

DETAIL OF BOX
AND PERFORATED METAL

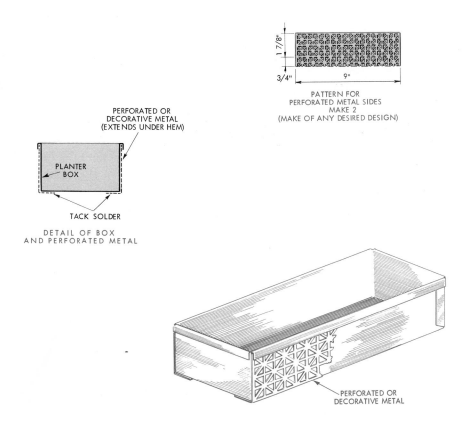

PERFORATED OR
DECORATIVE METAL

Project 9. Making a planter with a perforated metal jacket.

Project 10. Trash Bag Holder for Inside a Kitchen Cabinet Door

1. The dimensions shown are suggested only and these may be altered to fit individual circumstances. Recommended material is 26 gage galvanized steel.
2. Lay out the pattern for the sides including the center marks needed for the tear drop holes. See the detail for the center location on these holes. Cut and notch the pattern; punch the holes and file the edges to make the tear drop holes.
3. Bend the 1-1/4″ edge for a Pittsburgh seam.
4. Bend the 1/4″ edge to the outside to a 90° by pounding over the front edge of the brake with a wooden mallet. Turn the metal over and bend completely over by pounding the edge over the upper leaf of the brake. Put in the brake and smash flat.
5. Bend the 3/8″ edge to the inside. Bend this edge over as far as the brake will allow but do not smash down.
6. Starting with the 1/4″ bend, make all the corner bends to the inside.
7. Make up the Pittsburgh seam.
8. Bend all of the 1/2″ edges on the bottom pattern to 90 degrees.
9. Insert the bottom into the side pattern so that the 1/2″ edge of the bottom is hooked into the 3/8″ edge as shown on the detail.
10. With tongs squeeze down the 3/8″ edge of the side so that it grips the bottom edge tightly.
11. Tack solder the bottom into place from the outside.
12. If desired solder completely around the inside of the bottom and up the side seam. All soldering should be done on the inside where it will not show. Complete soldering on the inside is desirable to prevent any dripping of moisture that may be in the trash.

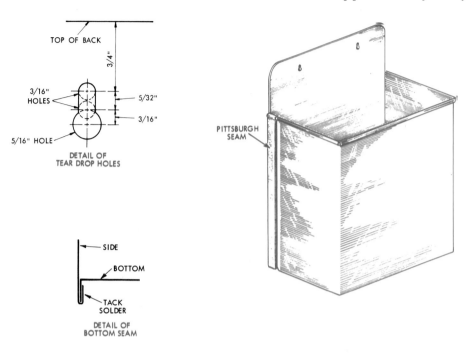

TOP OF BACK

3/4"

3/16" HOLES

5/32"

3/16"

5/16" HOLE

DETAIL OF
TEAR DROP HOLES

PITTSBURGH
SEAM

SIDE

BOTTOM

TACK
SOLDER

DETAIL OF
BOTTOM SEAM

1/2"

6 3/8"

1/2"

10 7/8"

1/2"

1/2"

PATTERN FOR BOTTOM

MATERIAL: 26 GAGE GALVANIZED IRON

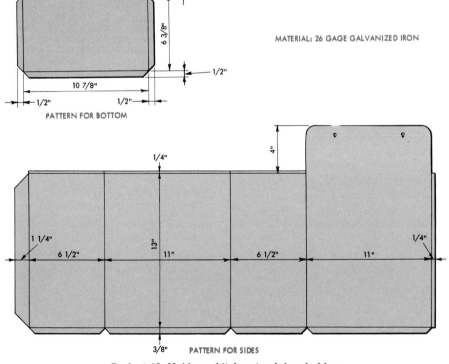

1/4"

4"

1 1/4"

13"

1/4"

6 1/2"

11"

6 1/2"

11"

3/8"   PATTERN FOR SIDES

Project 10. Making a kitchen trash bag holder.

glossary

acute angle: An angle less than 90°.

apprenticeship: An organized on-the-job training procedure through which the beginner can gradually advance to journeyman sheet metal work.

beading: The process of raising a strip of metal around the end of a round pipe.

bench machines: Machines clamped to a bench and operated by turning a crank. Used by the sheet metal worker to turn edges on circles and round pipes.

bench stakes: Steel anvils of various specialized shapes that the sheet metal worker uses to form and seam sheet metal objects.

black iron: Iron and steel sheets covered with an oxidized coating only.

braising: The process of stretching a piece of metal by hitting it with a round head hammer, as in forming a bowl.

brake: A machine that the sheet metal worker uses for bending and folding edges on metal.

burring: The process of turning an edge on a circular piece of metal.

cadmium: A metal used to coat screws and other parts for rust resistance.

circumference: The distance around a circle or pipe.

clips: Special strips of sheet metal bent in a manner to connect two pieces of sheet metal duct.

conductor: A term used to describe any material that allows electric current to flow through.

crimping: The process of corrugating the end of a round pipe to make it smaller so it will fit into the end of another pipe.

cut acid: Zinc chloride, made by putting strips of zinc in hydrochloric acid.

drilling: The process of making holes in sheet metal through the use of a twist drill.

edges: Bends on the edges of sheet metal to eliminate sharp edges and provide stiffening.

50-50 solder: Solder composed of 50% lead and 50% tin by weight.

flux: Chemicals used to clean metal and remove the oxides from the metal surface prior to soldering.

forming: The process of rolling sheet metal into pipe or making bends to form objects.

frustrum of a pyramid: A pyramid with the top cut off.

gage: The system of classifying the thickness in which sheet metal is produced. Also a tool used for measuring and determining the thickness of a metal sheet.

galvanized sheet metal: Soft steel sheets that are coated with zinc.

gore: The section of a round elbow.

ground: When used in conjunction with electricity, such as "electrical ground," it means an ideal path for the electric current to flow into the earth.

hard solder: Solder that has a melting point of 750°F or more.

hem: A folded edge on a sheet metal object.

hexagon: A geometric figure with six equal sides.

Joint Apprenticeship Committee: A committee composed of sheet metal workers and employers that conducts the apprenticeship program.

layout work: The process of developing the pattern for a sheet metal object.

longitudinal seam: A seam running the long length of a pipe.

micrometer: A precision measuring tool used to measure thicknesses and diameters to within .001 of an inch.

miter: The joining of two pieces at an evenly divided angle.

obtuse angle: An angle more than 90°.

octagon: A geometric figure with eight equal sides and angles.

oxides of metal: A chemical formed by a combination of the oxygen in the air with the metal. Iron rust is iron oxide.

parallel line development: A method of pattern drafting employing parallel lines.

pattern: The shape of an object to be made out of sheet metal as it appears when marked out on the flat sheet. Also, the exact size and shape that a piece of sheet metal must be in order to be formed into the object desired.

pentagon: A geometric figure with five equal sides and angles.

pictorial drawings: A drawing of an object in three dimensions as it actually appears after being formed into shape.
pitch: Slant or incline.

plane surface: A surface having two dimensions, length and width, as, for example, a desk top.

press brake: A power machine used by the sheet metal worker to form sheet metal.

punching: The process of making holes in sheet metal by the use of dies.

PVC (polyvinyl chloride): A plastic often used for hoods and tanks that require high corrosion resistance.

pyramid: An object with a square base with all four sides tapering to a point.

radial line development: A method of pattern drafting using lines radiating from a center and using arcs.

raw acid: Hydrochloric acid (HCl).

right angle: A ninety degree angle.

rivets: Fasteners used to join two pieces of sheet metal together. The rivet is inserted in a hole and a head is formed by pounding the rivet with a hammer.

rollation: A trade term that designates a short-cut method of pattern drafting accomplished by rolling a template across the sheet metal and marking it as it is rolled.

seams: Various types of bent and hooked edges used to join two pieces of sheet metal. For lighter sheet metal, mechanical joints are used. In medium and heavy gage metal, a riveted or welded seam is used.

sectional view: A drawing showing how an object appears if it were cut through at a specific place.

sheet metal: Any type of metal sheets that are ⅛" thick or less.

sheet metal screws: Special screws used for joining sheet metal. Also called self-tapping because the screws tap their own threads in the drilled hole.

skimming soldering: The process of soldering by applying solder over the top of the seam—the opposite of sweat soldering.

soft solder: Solder that has a melting point of 750°F or less.

solder: An alloy of tin and lead used in the sheet metal trade to joint two pieces of sheet metal together or to make a tank watertight.

spot welding: A process of joining sheet metal by electrical welding. An electric current through the metal melts the metal in that spot and welds the two sheets together.

square-to-round: The name of a common sheet metal fitting that is square or rectangular on one end and round on the other end.

stainless steel: A special steel containing other types of metals such as chromium, nickel and molybdenum. There are many types of stainless steel sheets. All of them vary in corrosion resistance.

sweat soldering: The process of soldering two pieces of metal together by making the solder "sweat" completely through the seam.

symmetrical: Objects that are the same on both sides of the center line.

tacking: The process of holding a seam in place by small spots of solder.

thermoforming plastics: Plastics shaped by the application of heat. They can be reheated and reformed.

thermosetting plastics: Plastics that set or harden when heated and cannot be reheated and changed to another shape.

tin plate: Iron or steel sheet coated with pure tin.

tinning: Covering an area of metal with molten solder.

titanium: An exotic metal used for its light weight and high heat resistance.

transition piece: A sheet metal fitting that changes size or shape from one end to the other.

triangulation: A method of pattern drafting employing the use of triangles.

turning: The process of turning edges on circles and round objects.

welding: The process of joining metal by melting the joining edges.

index

Note: **Boldface numerals** refer to illustrations.

313